LIVING

TO TELL

ABOUT IT

Young Black
Men in America

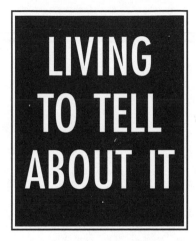

LIVING TO TELL ABOUT IT

Speak Their
Piece

Darrell Dawsey

ANCHOR BOOKS
DOUBLEDAY

New York   London   Toronto   Sydney   Auckland

AN ANCHOR BOOK
PUBLISHED BY DOUBLEDAY

a division of Bantam Doubleday Dell Publishing Group, Inc.
1540 Broadway, New York, New York 10036

ANCHOR BOOKS, DOUBLEDAY, and the portrayal of an anchor
are trademarks of Doubleday, a division of
Bantam Doubleday Dell Publishing Group, Inc.

Book design by Richard Oriolo

Library of Congress Cataloging-in-Publication Data
Dawsey, Darrell.
Living to tell about it : young Black men in America speak
their piece / Darrell Dawsey.
p.   cm.
1. Afro-American men.   I. Title.
E185.86.D395   1995
305.38′896073—dc20   95-7573
                                                      CIP

ISBN 0-385-47313-3

January 1996

1   3   5   7   9   10   8   6   4   2

First Edition

To the memory of my aunts
Kathleen Coleman and Margie Stewart.

To the memories of all the young Black men
who've died violently in America, especially my
partner from way back,
Freddie Beaty (R.I.P.).

To the continuing struggles of
New Afrikan political exiles abroad and POW's
in the U.S., including Sekou Odinga
and Mutulu Shakur.

T hanks first and foremost to God for showering Her blessings on me and mine.

I'd also like to thank my mother, Ruby Jean Gardner. Nobody knows the times we've seen and the love we bear. Thank you, Ma, for your prayers, encouragement and everything else. And through you, I thank all the elders who've preceded me. (And please try to look over the swear words . . .)

I also wish to thank my loving and lovely wife, Kierna Mayo Dawsey. Your passion, devotion and critical eye shepherded me through the bad times and made the good times all the richer. My love and admiration for you defies expression. Thank you, sweet baby.

I'd like to thank everyone involved in the conception and production of this book: my agents Denise Stinson and Charlotte Sheedy; my editor Charlie Conrad, Martha Levin, Jon Furay and everyone else at Doubleday; Patsy Blundell for a superb job of transcribing.

Special thank-yous to all the young Black men who allowed me to build with them in the course of researching our book. I wish that I could've included you all, for each of you is extremely important. I tried, as most of you asked, to keep it real.

And it don't stop . . . One love to all the family and crew scattered throughout Chocolate Cities everywhere.

In Detroit: my bright and beautiful daughter Natasha Coffee; Uncle A. D. Johnson and his family; my grandmother, "Big Mama" Elnora Bowden; uncles Mitchell and Wayne; my big brother Renaldo Dawsey and soon-to-be sister-in-law Charissa; cousin Mary McClendon (your activism has been a beacon for me); my little sister Nellietha Stewart; my soul brothers of other mothers, Kelvin Williams, Derrick Mason (and the entire Mason family), Alvin Williamson, Michael Spight, Stan Black, Roots and Kev Culture; my friend/co-conspirator/confidant Kimberly Trent; my godmother, Dorothy Johnson; Ms. Grace Lee Boggs; Tommy Quarterman (the plots thicken); the Fountain of Truth Missionary Baptist Church; Coplin Street; Mack Avenue; Save Our Sons and Daughters; my friends and colleagues at *The Detroit News*; the brothers and sisters who I struggled with at Wayne State University; the hip-hop underground (Maurice Malone, Proof, Jack Frost, Wes Chill, B-Def, Triplex, Kaos, e'erybody!); Sonya Vann; and Big Up to the east side, ghetto red hot! In Philadelphia: my cousins Jenelle, Tracey and Joy Coleman (my three heartbeats); Troy Coleman; my uncles Aubrey Johnson and John Coleman; Sissy and Erica and Allison. In New York City: my new parents Joseph and Billye Mayo (thank you both for embracing me); my sister Khadijia (holdin' Hampton hostage); dream hampton (my feminine side); Monifa Akinwole and Djbiril Toure (my friends and comrades); Joicelyn Dingle (for the love and patience); the late, great Sophia Joseph; Chi Modu (thanks for the pictures); Oya's Elements; my road dogs Jah Sess and Dynamite and Marco; Michael and Cynthia, "the Robinsons"; Mark "Kamau" Patterson; Heston Hosten; Tiffani Roberts; my partner in thought crime Claude Alcide; Chris Wilder (he's Deion; I'm Rod); Lorena Craighead; the Sega Heads who kept me up late nights, George Davis, Chris Latimer, "Wok." In Ft. Wayne, Indiana: my friend and mentor Justice B. Hill. In Los Angeles: my alter ego, the mad Dr. Thomas "Bumbee" Skinner (Let's keep pushing, Blackman); my big sister Andrea Ford; Joyce Washington; John Lee; my real friends at the *L.A. Times*. In Miami: Professor Tse Tse Wahisi. In D.C.: Earle Eldridge; Angie Terrell; Phil Dixon; James T. Jones, IV; also to all the contemporary Black writers, whose work continues to inspire me.

Contents

Introduction

It was on the F train, I believe, in Manhattan. I was riding alongside another writer I'd just met, our small talk ranging over several topics: hip-hop, racism, colleagues, writing assignments. He
asked why I was in New York. I told him I'd just landed a deal to
write a book about young Black men.

"Of course, a book on Black males," he said with a grin and a
fair dose of sympathy. "What *else* would they let a brother write?"

He wasn't being rude or sarcastic or knocking my project. He
was simply alluding to the stifling impact white folks' mispercep-

tions about Black ability has on the career tracks of Black professionals. And the brother was right.

Nevertheless, I was disturbed, for the comment contained more than a backhanded indictment of racism. Also implicit in the remark was the mistaken notion that Black males have been written about to excess, that our condition is so well-known that to examine the lives mired in these insidious social circumstances would be only an unnecessary repetition of past observations. That it was time for Black writers to journey beyond the comfortable province of Black life, time for us to prove our mettle on more "universal" grounds.

Young Black men, his comment seemed to suggest, were no longer in vogue. Well, I can't think of a time when we were. I also can't think of a better time or reason to grab my pen.

To say what we wish could go without saying: Black males are under an attack that time can only intensify. Of course I refer partially to the bleak math that now places 25 percent of young brothers in the throes of the criminal justice system and much of the rest at the mercy of homicide and AIDS. But I speak just as much of the seminal, and far more insidious, threat of white supremacy—from which all of our other problems spring. As much as at anytime in our stay here, racism is decimating our lives, our hopes, our futures. So what if someone's said this before? As an embodiment of those lives, hopes and futures, am I seriously expected to feel that "before" ought to suffice?

To be sure, we have been the topic of intense debate and discussion in America, by both Blacks and whites. Our humanity has been stripped, restored, attacked, defended, impugned and explained in literature more often than we'd like to recall. We have been hyped and stereotyped, valorized and demonized. As a topic of debate, we've been alighted on by hacks like Patrick Moynihan and Charles Murray, as well as geniuses like James Baldwin and Toni Morrison. In all of this analysis, some truths about us have bubbled up alongside the caricatures, but never can they be enough.

Ergo, a nigga writes.

INTRODUCTION

The idea for this project evolved after I wrote an article in August 1992 for *The Detroit News* that offered vignettes of how various young men around the city coped with violence in their lives. Not long after the publication of the piece, Denise Stinson, a former writer at the *News* and my eventual agent, ran down to me a similar idea she'd had for a book: interview young Black men the country over about a litany of topics and interweave the findings with the author's personal narratives about the issues. She asked if I was interested. I was. By the summer of 1993, I was on the road doing research and gathering interviews.

But how to approach this project? How to begin plumbing the depths of a lode as rich as the subtexts of young Black people's lives? For the sake of focus, I decided to narrow the age group to fifteen to twenty-four. I chose this group largely because it is the group for which homicide is the leading cause of death. But I also picked this age range because it contains an interesting intragenerational cipher. Within this ten-year span young men see themselves go from men-children to outright adults, from high-schoolers to college students to entrepreneurs or employees. Within this ten-year span, worldviews are formed, life paths are often set and that bittersweet, part-public, part-private process of gluing together identity is in full motion. For a people whose identity was already being shattered into a thousand shards on the boat ride over, this process is weighted down with the added burdens that race and gender place on it. Worse, this process is often left unfinished.

But it continues, and is played out on millions of individual stages daily. For six months in 1993, between June and November, I traveled to nine major U.S. cities in search of those stages, running across brothers from all walks of life, talking with them about matters of sexuality and spirituality, about having fathers and being fathers, about living and about dying. I uncovered interview subjects in school cafeterias, high-rise offices, car-rental booths, on playgrounds, in prison. I found no pat answers and bumped into some chilling and challenging questions. Most of all, our discussions underscored time and again the complexity of Black lives in America, the impossibility of fitting those lives into any preset categories of explanation. (Unfortunately, I didn't have enough space in this book to include even half the stories I heard.)

Which isn't to say I resist political assessments of the lives that the interviews laid open to me. In all of my talks, from the most mundane to the most sensational, race, class and gender remained close to the surface and constantly demanded my attention. In some cases, the brothers didn't intend to offer any insights into any broad political realities of young Black men. In some cases, they were merely speaking their piece.

But to be Black in America *is* to be political, whether we acknowledge that or not. Try as some of us might, we simply cannot outrun our collective history, cannot undo our status as racism's victims. I don't even try. Rather, I attempt to marry the interviews with my own sense of ground-level, quotidian Black nationalism. In doing so, I seek to keep my analysis real and true to its moral obligations to Black folks' history and interests. I do not, however, pretend that I have written an "objective" book about Black male life. As a free moral agent, I don't see how this is even possible, let alone desirable.

Some may consider a few of my positions and analyses heavy-handed and/or extreme. That's fine with me, 'cause I realize that to suggest that ideas are extreme doesn't at all invalidate them. Extremism can be appropriate. Where I am an extremist, I am one because, as Black men, I and everyone who looks like me live in an extreme world.

To begin understanding us, you must understand this world. And to understand this world, you must understand our places in it. This is what I set out to do in these pages, toss some attention and, hopefully, a little light on a segment of this nation that remains feared, loathed and obscured.

In doing so, I am searching for myself—for at twenty-seven, I am many of these brothers. To know them, their struggles, their ideas, is for me to know a little more about who I am, why I am and where I need to be.

But in attempting to give voice to the times and troubles of young Black men, by noting the drastic nature of our collective condition, I don't mean to ignore the victories we've enjoyed in both our mass and individual spaces. Young Black men continue to struggle, to resist, to fight to stay alive. We get shot and jailed, yes, but so do we continue to enroll in college, marry and raise productive children. So do we continue to start businesses, respect our elders and clean our yards. We are politicians, lawyers, doctors, architects, child-care workers, pizza deliverymen and artists. Our lives are complex.

And, if any one lesson has come out of the year-plus it has taken me to write this book, it is this: Every brother has a story.

Our challenge is to live to tell about it.

LIVING

TO TELL

ABOUT IT

Prologue

Child's Hood

I'm in a stare-down with the four-year-old Black boy in front of me, and I'm terrified—for both of us.

We're somewhere amid one of the squalid mazes of Washington, D.C., shanties that HUD propagandists would prefer you call housing projects. Outside, in the shadows of boarded buildings, children scramble across the barren, cracked dirt that runs behind a parking lot, climbing jagged hunks of concrete, squealing with a genuine delight not yet tainted by the desolation.

Inside this third-floor unit, the living room is empty save for a coffee table and the battered, ripped, smelly couch where I sit. In what passes for a dining area, two wobbly chairs rest against a wall, beneath a cheesy oil painting of a matador or schooner or something. From the kitchen wafts the smell of cold days-old peas still on the stove. An open can of cooking lard congeals on the counter nearby, not far from half-eaten, grease-heavy pieces of fried chicken. There's no TV out front, no books, no toys, no games, no father.

I'm visiting. Lil' Boy Brown facing me lives here.

Like I said, I'm terrified for both of us. He must grow up with this, absorbing all the blows and lessons and horrors his home has to give. What these will do to him is anyone's guess. Perhaps, like so many Black men before him, he will ride his experiences like a rocket out of this place, to new heights, hopefully bringing along as many of his family and friends as he can fit onto his dreams. Maybe he'll write a book or cure cancer or, best of all, help liberate African peoples worldwide.

Perhaps his young soul will grow calloused and warped in these most unforgiving of environs, feeding not on the love and resilience that abounds here, but on the fear, frustration, anger and powerlessness that fester in the tenement shadows, waiting to infect his innocence.

Perhaps he will die too early.

Perhaps he will kill too often.

Bursts of Black-nationalist love alternately relieve then give way again to my fear. This could be my child. Hell, for all intents and purposes, this is my child. He could also be my killer, or my children's. I'm scared for what our America could make of both of us. I want to snatch this kid, wrap him in my arms and break north—or to the east, Blackwards.

I think back to my own path out of poverty, to the keys that unlocked for me new worlds, new horizons. As I try to retrace the steps, my eyes hold the child. My heart grapples with the fear, the love. Memories explode in rapid-fire flashes . . .

Summertime 1975. I'm sitting on the steps leading to the attic of the small house where me and Moms stay. The 'hood is calling.

Through the kitchen windows, I hear my budding crew shifting childhood fun into top gear. Frozen tag is in effect for a few. Someone else is murmuring about catching bumblebees in a Smucker's jelly jar. In a few minutes, they'll all probably troop across the alley to do flips on the soggy mattresses we stacked a week or so ago.

I'm ready to be out myself. I can't, though. I'm stuck. The new *Weekly Reader* came in the mail the other day, and I have to sit here and read several pages before Moms'll let me out of the house. That's the routine around here. Read first, play later.

"Them kids'll still be outside when you're done," Moms assures me. I don't believe her.

I used to hate these informal sessions. They started when I was about four and have hounded me well into the second grade. I haven't really come to love them, but even at seven years old, I can tabulate their benefits. I'm already reading better than most kids in my class. My teacher, a fiercely supportive, cherubic sister named Miss Johnson, insists I have promise, that one day I might be somebody.

She likes me, in part, I think, because I make her job a little easier. Teaching isn't as hard when you've got a student who not only likes and appreciates you, but stays a pace or two ahead of the workbook. Plus, Moms is one of the few parents who shows up at the parent-teacher conferences. It's always good for teachers to know there's a parent monitoring what a child is being taught; keeps teachers (and kids) alert, even if only to the possibility of being cussed out by a mother who pays enough taxes to know she can't afford to buy that Johnny-can't-read shit from the public-school system.

I'm not sure who Miss Johnson thinks I'll be, but I'm eager to find out.

Fall 1979. They say I'm reading at a twelfth-grade level, even though I'm only in the eighth. I guess that's cool, but I'm not really interested in much of what "they" have to say these days. Reading is still fundamental, but, in school at least, it ain't nearly as fun. So much of the same ol', same ol'. Miss Johnson's a memory now, as are so many of my young aspirations. I've been fucking up in junior high, fighting, disrupting classes with jokes and outbursts, cursing teachers.

The wellspring of my dreams already seems to have dried up. I used to want to be a chemist, till I found out how much I hated math. I used to want to be an anthropologist, till someone told me I'd probably never find any authentic dinosaur bones. Right now, I flirt half-heartedly with alternating visions of myself as petty hoodlum, pro running back and karate-flick celebrity. Still, reading remains a passion—albeit a private one obliged mostly in desperate, solitary respites from the rumpus of adolescence.

My passion has brought me inside this warm fall day, sent me rummaging through yellowing titles Moms keeps stacked in a cabinet near her sewing equipment. My attention settles on a book titled *Swamp Man*. It's the cover art that suckers me in initially, a drawing of a bone-white, green-haired fiend forcefully tearing skin-tight clothes off a reluctant brown honeydip. I flip through with the quickness, hunting desperately for the sex scenes the cover so graphically promises. I find them within the first few pages, taking the next hour or so to indulge quickening hormones. Damn, I didn't know reading—writing—could do this.

"Who is this wild motherfucker?" I ask myself about the author. I flip to the back cover, to a drawing of a lean, mustached brother staring out from behind vacant eyes. His name is Donald Goines, a Detroit addict-cum-author. I comb the cabinets for more of his titles. To my gleeful surprise, I find others, each title more seductively violent than the last: *El Dorado Red, Crime Partners, Death List, Kenyatta's Last Hit*. The plots are muddled, the language often profane, the characters underdeveloped. But throughout Goines's work, I find a Black writer struggling heroically to give voice and dimension to Black underworlds shunned by so much of the "higher" literature my teachers would have me read.

On top of all that, it gets my twelve-year-old dick hard.

"I bet I can do this," I mutter.

And I do. I start penning my own street adventures, my crude scratchings in spiral notebooks and unbound sheafs of paper lifting liberally from Goines's screams into the existential abyss. The prose is wooden, grammatically pathetic and thought through about as well as a grocery list. Still, I revel in every word. For the first time, I find myself truly thankful for the forced lessons taught over *Weekly Readers* and Curious George yarns. After all, it was amid the hot stuffiness of the attic stairway that I became a reader.

Now, in the cool, dim privacy of Moms's basement, I decide to become a writer.

Summertime 1984. Damn, why do Black men die so young? 'Rome, Ron, Ced, Terry, James—all of 'em shot to death between ninth-grade year and now. All of 'em friends from around the way. None of 'em over twenty-five.

My thoughts drift to them even as I glare into the malicious smirk of Bean, this fat, Jheri-Kurled kid my man Steve has introduced me to. All three of us are in my bedroom, them on two folding chairs, me on the edge of my bed. Bean is talking much shit.

"Damn, nigga, you got books everywhere!" he says, laughing and pointing at my shelves as though he's caught me with inflatable girlie dolls. "You got some straight-up bullshit in your room." He stares over at Steve, then points and slips again into paroxysms of laughter, stretching the word *buuulllshit* to lend even more bite to his ridicule. Steve half grins at me, unsure whether the shit is really funny. Bean's derision continues. "Damn, nigga got books and shit. That's what you spend your money on? Buuulllshit like books and shit? Buuulllshit, cuz."

Now, there's not much that separates me from these two, from the dead friends whose specters spook my memories. Steve and I have been doing dirt for a year or so now, executing poorly planned stick-ups near skating rinks and bus stops. We're lucky we're still alive. Most of my partners who've died have perished in equally stupid pursuits: crack dealing, armed robbery, beefs over who looked at whom wrong.

I don't plan to go out like that. Even at a knuckle-headed sixteen years old, I know I'm not into this shit for the long haul. Writing and reading, I've always figured, would be my golden parachutes. I'm still in school. Doing well, too: honor roll, scholarships, college visits. Even with the little bit of work I'm putting in by night, I manage to hit the books.

Still, the teenage urge to be down is a temptation not easily resisted. So when my man Steve came to me last year with visions of other niggas' lambskin coats and patent-leather Adidases dancing in his head, I caught the fever. It wasn't, I didn't think then, that I was trying to prove I was tough. I quite simply wanted, thought I needed, the gear and jewelry. Even a good GPA isn't enough to ward off the pressures of being fresh.

Soon, Steve and I were haunting doorways and unlighted street corners, waiting to see who'd be the next fool we caught slipping in some dope clothes. Shoes, jackets, hats, rings, chains—we're making brothers run it all.

Through it all, I don't compromise by grades. I'm never asked to. Even as we gather on porches and in vacant lots to toss horseshoes or shoot dice or drink 40s or play any thing from chess to tackle football, my boys always have a curious fascination with how school is going for me, what college I plan to attend, what I think about this class or that subject. It's not that I'm special. Around the way, potential is as abundant as it is neglected. I'm one of the few kids, however, whose game plan consists of real deadlines and clearcut options. As a result, I got substantial love. Invariably, my partners' inquiries end with "keep on with that shit, nigga. You doin' the right thang."

So I keep on keepin' on—even as I wonder why some of them won't. Staring at Bean's fat, oily face, I finally understand that it's not that my peoples won't keep on. It's that so many of them figure they can't. We're teenagers mostly, but already ghetto life has begun truncating some of our dreams. Despair and frustration threaten to set in like rigor mortis. We have our spaces, to be sure, the loci we retreat to enjoy our cultural and classical communion— our parties, our impromptu gatherings of crews at the malls, the after-hours joints. But these, like the unending quests for new clothes and chump change, anesthetize our lives as much as they circumscribe the beauty of our Black working-class existences.

We've begun to make a paralyzing peace with the mediocrity of our conditions. We breathe, yes, but in truth, a decaying America has already rendered some of us as moribund as 'Rome, Ron and any other corpse.

Worse, we've chosen to accept our fate rather than master it. The latter we leave to men we never see. We live in an all-Black community, yet in few other places does the myth of white superiority abound as vigorously.

Like I said, there's not much difference between me and Bean— except I've got options. I may be a product of the environment, but I don't figure on being its latest casualty. He's only about a year or so older than me, seventeen, maybe eighteen. Still, Bean has already made peace with the limits America would place on his potential.

I don't plan on going out like that, either.

Facing him, I decide losing my cool would be fruitless. I switch to a no-hard-feelings smile and mutter something I hope conveys my ideas about education affording me options, about books opening up new worlds for me, about how reading has already begun to shape for me a new consciousness and new way of looking at the insidiously narrowed world Black people must travail in.

Bean laughs one more time, harder even than before, as he expands his ridicule to include not only my books but school, my dreams and any illusions I have about education. "Nigga don't need that bullshit. Nigga need to get paid. So while you tryin' to go to school and all that buuuullllshit, I'm gon' get paid."

I haven't yet learned the language to critique that contention. I haven't yet come to draw links and parallels between small-time hustlers and the banks, car dealerships, gun makers and other white-run parasite industries that thrive off the misery and misdirection of the ghetto. I haven't yet come to see how the recklessness of youth, combined with hustlers' newfound access to cash and weaponry, serve to make young Black men the enemies within, unconscious collaborators with those without.

Even if I had the words, though, I'm not so sure they would've been enough to challenge Bean's belief in the power of his hustle. The faith of the desperate is not easily shaken.

Instead, I shut my mouth and strengthen my resolve not to become a casualty. I remember the options that, unconsciously, I have cultivated. I grow more determined than ever to build on them.

Bean's way, alluring as it once was, quickly became the road not taken. By the time I graduate college five years later, Bean has been reduced to a washed-up crack dealer who's now his own best customer. Steve, I learn, has been found hanged and his throat slashed in a crackhouse where he worked. And still, the fast lane remains overcrowded.

Damn, why do Black men die so young . . . ?

As quickly as they detonate, the memories fade. I'm still on the couch in the D.C. shantytown, the four-year-old still eyeballing me. Then, as suddenly as he had walked over to me, he toddles away. He grabs up a misshapen coat hanger, plops down on the dusty hardwood floor and begins banging the hanger against the planks.

"My drums," Boy Brown shouts to me, looking up for only a second as he sends the hanger crashing down on the floor again and again.

I smile, marveling at his energy, at the rhythm of his innocent determination to make the best of the little he's got.

And, as I rise to leave moments later, I pray to God that his beat never stops.

Back in the Days:

Remembrances of Childhood

America has never had the decency simply to eat its Black young. No, ol' Sam gives rousing chase first, hunting us without remorse or mercy, for both profit and sport. His arrows are America's pathologies—its crime and poverty, its highly contagious white supremacist dementia—the government's twisted social policies (three strikes and you're out?) his bow.

The hunting grounds sprawl. The terrain covers places like south-central Los Angeles and north Omaha, Nebraska, where police and gang violence threaten Black boys like twin plagues. It spreads over the flatlands of Detroit and Miami and across the hills of D.C., where drugs crash onto the Black community's shores with riptide force, swallowing many young souls whole. America's hunting grounds extend well into suburban Black communities, too, where, even if comparatively safe from crack and gunplay, Black boys still endure the often-amplified blare of individual bigotry and wrestle with the singular burdens of growing up Black and middle-class, which even in the nineties seems a contradiction in American racial terms.

It's no secret that Sam's chase is proving largely successful. The hunting grounds are littered with the bodies of Black children, dying as we are at eleven, twelve, fourteen and sixteen years young, of overdoses and self-inflicted gunshot wounds, in crossfires and mis-fires.

Of course, plenty of Black boys make it through, most with memories of growing up that can be as pleasurable as others can be painful. Sometimes we find escape routes through hobbies like collecting comics, doing somersaults on musty mattresses or firing basketballs through milk crates, imagining we're in the Palace or Madison Square Garden. Sometimes our upbringing, that Herculean task that is rearing African-American boys, generates enough power to bear us over the pitfalls of youth. Sometimes, though, we become the hunted in our own homes as well, the security that should be a child's birthright rotted away by the ills of alcohol or crack or child abuse. So we often wind up saving ourselves—finding amid our anguish the smarts, determined courage and foresight to stay alive, even if it means aging beyond our years.

Yeah, plenty of us move through childhood with our bodies intact. Few of us, however, make it out with our souls unscathed.

HANNIBAL H., 15: TIGHTROPES AND TURNING POINTS

OMAHA, NEBRASKA—If you're Hannibal, you negotiate adolescence as though it were a tightrope. Stay balanced. Keep stepping. And by all means, hold your head up—'cause if you slip, you're done for.

At various points, Hannibal's approach toward adulthood has been tense: thrilling sometimes, dangerous others. En route, he's endured a broken home, the lure of gangs, disciplinary problems, racist teachers, arrest. But not unlike many Black boys around his age, Hannibal has survived, battling through the singular woes of growing up Black and male in urban America with a combination of fists and family, persistence and penitence.

The journey's far from over, and Hannibal is steeled to finish in high fashion. He's mostly nonchalant about his struggles to date. Life, he calls them. Still, occasionally, Hannibal's fifteen-year-old soul takes time to look back and wonder how he got over.

We sit at his mother's kitchen table in their cramped, neat apartment in north Omaha, a working-class community of tiny clapboard homes, three-story "high-rises" and deceptively quiet streets. His face is cherubic, smooth and nearly as subdued in countenance as his puberty-wracked voice is in tone. Dressed in a blue T-shirt and jeans, he sits ramrod straight at the table, smiling, flattered that someone seems to care what a fifteen-year-old Black child in Nebraska has to cope with. He's a sweet kid, I realize, yet another innocent whose social climate has made aging an actual challenge.

When I ask him about the biggest problem he's faced in life, he tells me, simply and without a sliver of irony, that it's been "growing up."

"I grew up fighting," says Hannibal. "That's what my brothers taught me mainly. It was just to keep myself protected. I didn't fight just to fight, but when it came time to and I had to, I would fight."

And it seemed as though he had to all the time. Hannibal says that by the time he was in junior high school, he'd grown accustomed to scraping with rivals on school buses and in classrooms and the streets around his home. Jumping enemies—and getting jumped—were routine.

"The worst time was when three dudes jumped me once on the

way home from school," says Hannibal, who tells me they attacked him after he'd argued with one of their girlfriends days before. "It was a Friday, a day before my birthday. We was getting off the bus, and I was the last one off. Everyone was telling me, 'Don't get off the bus.' I wasn't going to. I just told the bus driver to close the door and take me somewhere else. But he wouldn't. The dudes came up on the bus and the bus driver just let them! He didn't even try to stop them. I ran out the back door, and they caught me at school trying to go in the front door. One of them grabbed me by my hood and pulled me down. The rest of them just started kicking me, kicking me."

He was barely thirteen but had already come close to having his brains stomped out. Fights like these, says Hannibal, hardened his attitude. Compassion, warmth, trust—they had no place in the heart of a little boy who had to trade blows to make it home from school.

Hannibal says he also developed a bad temper, one that went off in school as regularly as the third-period bell. He got expelled more times than he cares to count.

"I had some disciplinary problems at some schools," he tells me. "There was one school I got kicked out of mainly because of my attitude toward the teachers. Some of the teachers there was racist. They didn't put no effort into trying to help me at all. Wasn't no use in me trying to put no effort into work. The main two classes I got kicked out of was my math class and my science class. I got kicked out for fights and for cursing out teachers. One time, we were in the classroom, and I had fell asleep. The teacher came over and hit me in the head with a ruler. I jumped up and cussed him out."

Hannibal says the other times were because teachers had walked up and tried "to put their hands on you." Even then, at twelve and thirteen, Hannibal and his classmates sensed that the teachers tended to target Black students the most.

"Most of the Black boys got picked on," he says. "Most of them just didn't get kicked out. Either they couldn't hold their temper or they could hold their temper. I couldn't. My temper wouldn't hold for that. The teacher just wanted to pick on you in front of students. My attitude just went sky high and blew up."

Hannibal says he could feel himself falling deeper into a pattern he figured might only compound his problems. He started hanging with what he calls "the wrong crowd."

"Changing schools you lose friends and start to meet new people," he says. "You get to the point where you hang out with different people and you ain't known them good enough. So then when you get to know someone, you probably don't want to quit hanging with them. When I started hanging with them things just got worse and worse."

It's too simplistic to believe that Hannibal was drawn to his friends solely because he wanted to be thought of as "cool" or "tough." He says the camaraderie was real, founded on a genuine easiness he felt in their presence.

"We always used to sit at the same table, and we just started to get to know each other," he says. "At lunchtime we didn't eat lunch. We would just sit there and talk all day, talk through lunch."

Hannibal says lunch led to being invited to parties. At the parties, he discovered a taste for alcohol. He started drinking heavily. Hannibal was barely a teen, but he was already coming home pissy drunk. But after spending much of fourteen puking up Old English 800 and Tanqueray, he decided that drinking wasn't as fun as he'd thought only a year earlier. He quit.

"But my problems got worse," he says. "My friends started stealing cars, and they got me doing it. I wasn't the one stealing them. I was just in them."

Hannibal says the turning point came one night when he and his friends decided they needed a ride to a party. They broke into a car and started off. Within minutes, though, a police car was on their tail. The boys were arrested, their parents notified.

Hannibal says the prospect of jail time frightened him. He admits that, to stay out of trouble, he told on his friends who'd actually broken into the car and driven it away. He says he got a light punishment but heavy criticism from his crew. Branding him a snitch, most of Hannibal's old crowd shunned him.

He likes it this way.

"I turned in the people 'cause I wasn't about to suffer, and they did," he says. "They got mad 'cause I snitched, but it made me feel better that I ain't with them now. I don't got to worry about being chased by the police. That ain't a good feeling."

He feels he made the right move. Some of his friends have gotten into worse trouble, joining gangs or selling dope. He sees them now, on their porches and street corners. In them, he also sees himself, what he might've become. He passes them by as though stepping over a banana peeling on the tightrope.

After the arrest, Hannibal opted for another route. He began paying more attention to his school work and cultivating closer ties with his family. Hannibal's father, long since separated from his mother, stepped in and began counseling his son on the dangers of waywardness. This helped his turnaround, too.

"I learned to control my temper better than I did mainly through my dad," he says. "He helped me a lot by talking to me and helping me out, by keeping me out of the streets. He said I'm growing up faster than I should be. I thought about that in the streets a lot of times, but it just never dawned on me until then."

He also decided that he wanted to be more of a role model for his eight-year-old brother, who he often refers to when he talks of finishing school and helping his family.

To this end, Hannibal says, he wants to make his teen years more productive than they started. His goals are simple and two-fold: finish high school; steer clear of trouble.

Hannibal understands that the objectives seem modest, but he also recognizes the enormity of the tasks. Only one relative he's close to, a cousin, has graduated high school. And staying alive and out of trouble's way in a community with more than three thousand gang members is no small feat.

"I've been recruited by both the gangs, the Crips and the Bloods," says Hannibal. "They would talk to me about joining and I would be like, 'No.' One of my old associates tried to get me in. One day we was all sitting on this porch. It was him and all his relatives and his homeboys. We were sitting there and he was like,

'Man, you should be a Blood. You know everything about them.' I was like, 'No, man, I ain't going to get down like that. I have little brother to take care of, and I have to watch out for my family.' He understood. Only reason he became a gang member is 'cause his brother got shot and killed, and he wanted just to get back at other people.

"And I got two relatives that're Crips. I turned them down, too. I won't join so I won't get in trouble with the law. I got a record as it is from getting caught stealing that car."

He chooses instead to concern himself more with his academic record. His grades are picking up, and he's thinking about going to college. Hannibal's pleased, but not surprised, at his progress. He's not a problem child—just a typical child with some problems.

"People around here who know me don't say that I'm a bad kid," he says. "They look at me like I'm just someone who got into more trouble than he should have."

Hannibal made childish mistakes. Nothing unusual there, particularly for a child. Problem is, they could've just as easily landed him in jail or the graveyard as in another classroom. Black children often aren't allowed the mistakes of youth, the sort of errors Hannibal waded through fairly unscathed.

Up there, on the tightrope, there can be little margin for error.

JAMAL TERRELL, 19: GRANDCHILD OF THE DREAM

COLUMBIA, MARYLAND—Yes, there are plenty of Black boys who've grown up without poverty or violence or crack cocaine assaulting their lives. There are plenty who grew up without keeping a body count of dead homeys or gunfire rocking them to sleep, with enough food to go around and both parents nestled under the same roof.

They've come of age in a range of backdrops, from the white-collar enclaves in America's Chocolate Cities to the promised lands of its Swirl Suburbs. They are grandchildren of King's dream, sons of the Black America that parlayed hard work, ingenuity and civil rights gains into those tenuous, laudable spaces we take collectively as the Black middle-class.

Jamal is one of them. The son of an entrepreneur father and journalist mother, he's split his childhood between Atlanta, Philadelphia and rural Maryland. Wherever he's gone, he says, he's enjoyed the benefits of good schooling, a loving home and a stable community.

They are luxuries that his contemporaries view skeptically at times. For a generation of New Jacks prone to measuring a brother's authenticity by his proximity to hardship, the temptation may be to cast Jamal's upbringing as "soft," somehow less than real.

Not one given to manufactured equations of poverty and nobility, Jamal considers his childhood a blessing.

We're outside, atop a log perch rising in the wooded expanse that stretches scenically behind the tract of cozy homes that includes his parents'. Thin and short, Jamal sports a fresh baldie, a crisp T-shirt and baggy shorts that seem even baggier as they flutter about his legs. He's warm, funny, his smile framed within the stubble of a hastily trimmed goatee. As we talk, he leans forward atop the perch he sits on and his hand sweeps the woods.

"I don't pray a whole lot, but I pray—because I'm thankful," he says. "Look where I live, it's beautiful. I could be stuck in the ghetto somewhere. My dad could be shot or in jail. My mom could be out of work. My sister could be knocked up; my brothers could be dead. I went to a good school. I'm going to college. I'm happy 'cause of my family. I have good friends. I don't do drugs. I'm not doing anything negative."

From the start, Jamal says, his parents worked tirelessly to keep him and his two older brothers on track. His mother and father drove home compelling life lessons, lessons about race and struggle, inspirational lessons drawn from their own triumphs. His parents were sharp, educated and success-driven despite sober, candid outlooks on the particular burdens of being Black in the U.S.

They had withstood the stings of racism and wanted to fortify their children as well. *Consciousness* became a watchword during

Jamal's upbringing, one transmitted in his parents' practice as well as the cultural standards, on matters great and small, of the world around him.

"My mom being an African-American woman journalist, she was the one who really brought me into an understanding about Blackness," he says. "She always had the books. She used to be a part of this African film society down in Atlanta. And my dad always worked with Black companies. It was all about just Black. Then where I lived in Atlanta, if you didn't know 'Lift Every Voice and Sing,' you were a poor excuse. People would look at you like you should be ashamed of yourself.

"As I got older certain things came of interest and I started reading the paper. I said, Wait a minute. Why is this and why is that? Another key to me was hip-hop. Hip-hop did a great deal to educate me. That is why I'm so much of a hip-hop junkie. Public Enemy and stuff like that."

His race consciousness didn't develop in all-Black surroundings. Though Columbia, with a Black population approaching about 35 percent, is the most integrated setting Jamal grew up in, he spent time with whites and Blacks throughout much of his childhood. In an America that remains as segregated as in its Jim Crow heyday, Jamal nonetheless got to know whites as friends, neighbors and, conversely enough, minorities in his communities.

"When I was in Atlanta, I had next-door neighbors that were white and were cool," says Jamal. "That was the only white people I saw. They're like family. They were white guys my age. We just found interests. We used to play baseball together, ride our bikes and stuff. When you are born you don't develop a sense of racism. It is taught to you. Say you have a white neighbor, you play together 'cause you like playing together. It's no more than that. That is why a lot of kids now don't start thinking about 'nigger this' until they get a little bit older and their parents teach them.

"My friends' parents were the coolest parents I ever seen. They didn't really look at color as an issue or they would have moved out of there. My next-door neighbor's father had a pool, and it used to be a neighborhood pool. And since the neighborhood was predominantly black—in fact, all black except for them—he'd let them in. Everybody was equal."

But life ain't a swimming pool. To the world outside, color counted, as had been forewarned in Jamal's house. In urging him to be smarter, more ambitious, Jamal's parents had always taught him race matters. Not long into adolescence, he got some practical lessons that buttressed their words.

One experience in particular has stayed with him.

"I was about twelve or thirteen," he says, "and my friend Craig and I were just chilling in a record store at the Columbia Mall. We were looking at the records, and he picked up one that was already opened. I saw it and he showed me—and before you knew it the [clerk] was already standing there. He said, 'You opened that record' and pointed the finger at Craig—just because Craig had it in his hand. But why are you checking on us? There were other people in the store. We left."

Jamal says the experience was his first hint that, to the America outside his neighbor's pool, Black males inspire fear at most any age.

"You can't let something like that pass without reacting," he maintains. "I'm not saying you go off and just beat up white people. But you just react differently, you start not trusting them. I'm thirteen years old. What harm can I do to anybody? I'm thirteen years old and here is a white man who has to be thirty-five or forty years old. What am I going to do to him unless you suspect that I have a gun or something like that?"

Jamal understands that these are the sort of experiences that have tied him inextricably to the brothers whose conditions he pities, that have made him understand Blackness as a badge of honor, point of unity and target.

"I was just realizing that it is me more than anything," he says, dismissing notions that brothers are marked because of their wardrobe or background rather than complexion. "If I was walking down the street today and there is a white person, some just feel threatened 'cause I have a bald head now. Like that movie, I'm a Menace II Society."

Not because he engages in gun talk or swaggers or holds down a street corner. His childhood, he says, ensured that he wouldn't have to be about these things. He's not hard or a ghetto bastard or straight outta any hood to speak of—nor does he wish to be. Jamal just wants it understood that a childhood marked by good schools, integrated blocks and attentive parents doesn't necessarily blind a brother to the world awaiting Black men.

In fact, they sometimes sharpen his vision.

DA GHETTO COMMUNICATOR, 23: LITTLE CHILD RUNNIN' WILD

NEW YORK—Ghetto and I slip onto a bench near the periphery of Washington Square Park, and his eyes cast wearily about, in search of the closest hint of trouble, danger. He exchanges brief glances with a bored patrolman strolling a few yards away, but then dismisses him as Kindergarten Cop looks over at me with my tape recorder and sober stare framed by wire-rim glasses and keeps stepping, presumably in search of Black men who better fit the description. With another sweep of his deep-set eyes, Ghetto sizes up the slew of homeless men, NYU students, joggers, hustlers and vendors slaloming in and along the edges of the park. They too pass his quick, furtive inspections.

Then he turns his gaze to me.

"Yo, how I know you ain't a cop?" he asks, his words molasses-slow, his New York accent thick with Bed-Stuy.

I stare back for a second, exasperated, anxious that his suspicion may cost me what I figure to be a gem of an interview. I've been trying to catch up with this brother for the past few weeks. I've wanted to interview Ghetto since I read a piece he wrote for *The Source* on homelessness—his homelessness. Written with passion and a defiant dignity, Ghetto's first-person account detailed not only an impoverished b-boy's struggle to scrape up a hot meal and dry bed each day here in the land of milk and money, but leveled a powerful indictment at a nineties America grown cold and callous in its regard for its increasingly obsolete labor pool.

The piece goes a lil' something like this:

As soon as someone hears about my unfortunate state, the first thing they suggest is, "go to one of them homeless shelters and they'll help you get on welfare." Fuck welfare—I want a job. Besides, the shelters for the homeless men in New York City are unfit for human habitat. They're overcrowded, very unsanitary, subhuman armories where homeless victims and veterans alike meditate on broken dreams . . .

I know as I'm writin' this right now, the average rude boy will ask, "why the fuck won't that bum ass niguh get a job?" You can't get any legal work without the proper ID, and you can't get ID without money. Off the books jobs are temporary and hard to find. I used to hustle on the down low until I seen how real shit is. I ain't tryin' to get locked down and lost inside the penal system (who am I gonna call?). Yo, even if I got J-O-B today, I would have to worry about being able to go to work looking presentable—minus the wrinkles, the funky ass and the gun for gossip. And I hope that the employer don't riff about my kinky locks, but bald heads get fired too. So I know, as hard as jobs are to come by in the '90s, the homeless population is virtually locked out of the job market. I don't sell drugs, I don't sell sex and I roll with hardrocks that fiend for hip-hop—so how should I get plugged in?

I'm asking myself the same thing as we stare from opposite ends of the park bench, me conjuring ways to puncture his disbelief, him holding grudgingly to his mistrust. I explain to him again how I'm interested only in what he chooses to tell me about his world, his life, about the particulars of how yet another talented Black man wound up fighting for food co-op scraps and bedding down for the night on subway cars.

As feeble as I think my explanation sounds, I know it's the truth. I just hope it's enough to penetrate the suspicions of a brother who's on a first-name basis with the consequences of Americans' slavish devotion to the profit motive and its custom-built, trans-generational cruelty toward Black people. I ain't a cop and, even if I were, Ghetto ain't a crook.

Nope, he's only young, Black, male and struggling to find steady shelter. What better reasons to fear and loathe five-o?

Still, I see him thinking, a good sign. A second later, Ghetto accedes.

As he recounts his sojourn through homeless shelters to the pages of the major music magazines, where, since his *Source* piece, his work has begun to surface regularly, he makes it clear that his tragedy indeed began at the beginning. The streets became his refuge, Ghetto explains, because they were, in many ways, a lot kinder than home.

"I grew up in Brooklyn," he says, "but I was a chronic runaway so I was raised all up on the streets of New York. If you check my police record, it will have fifty-some-odd cases of runaways. Coming home like two, three weeks later. I started running away about the age of eight, 'cause there was mad drugs and shit in the crib, child abuse, all that type of shit. And to be honest, I wanted to see what the world really was 'cause my Moms used to always keep me in the crib.

"I just rebelled totally. Everytime the cops would bring me home, I would take the ass whippin'. Next time I'd get, I'd jet out again, youknowwhatI'msaying? Throughout my experiences as a youth, I did all sorts of wild shit. How could I put it in words? I'd say, as a child, I experienced all aspects of the hip-hop culture inside and out."

Ghetto says he first ran away because he was too scared to go home. His mother had sent him to the store, but somewhere along the way the money must've fallen from his pocket. He retraced his steps, searched long and hard, but the loot never turned up.

His worry over the money, however, quickly gave way to another concern: the inevitable punishment that awaited him when he told his mother what'd happened. His Moms—young, new to child rearing and fearful of her son getting away from her—wasn't one to spare the rod, Ghetto says. In fact, she sometimes turned to it in excess. I ask Ghetto whether he viewed his punishments as abuse even then.

He pauses for the longest. He's thinking again. I wonder if he thinks I'm asking him to dis his Moms. I'm not. Black mothers do the best they can raising their boys. Sometimes, though, their best still isn't enough. Even so, his Moms was there, was the only one there. (Ghetto tells me later he didn't meet his pops until he was eighteen.) So no matter what, Moms remains above disrespect, even in the face of frank recollection about child abuse.

When his pause ends, Ghetto says slowly, "To be honest, subconsciously, yeah. But I realize it wasn't done conscious. She didn't do it intentionally."

Intentionally or not, though, she'd stricken a numbing fear into her son's heart.

"I knew she was going to kick my ass 'cause it was the last money in the house," continues Ghetto. "I couldn't go back home so I said, 'Damn, what can I do?' I just got on the train. Jumped the turnstile and I started riding the train. I ended up in Coney Island, and from there it was history."

Ghetto stayed gone for four days, before the police finally picked him up.

"I fell asleep on the train," he says. "I was sleeping and the cops seen me, this little kid sleeping on the train. They woke me up and started asking me questions: 'Where you live at?' 'Where your parents at?' This, that and the other. They figured I was a runaway and just bagged me up, brought me home."

Ghetto says his mother was relieved when her son first came through the door. The happy glow of the reunion, however, vanished soon enough.

"The same thing happened again like two weeks later," he says. "She had just whipped my ass for something else I did stupid—I lost some money again—so I was like, yo, I ain't going home. I went back to Coney Island.

"After a while it just became like a cycle. Any little thing would happen and I would just jet, because I felt confident in my survival skills on the street."

Coney Island provided the backdrop for many of those street lessons, he says. And his teachers weren't too much older than him. Ghetto wound up banding with other young men—some runaways, some not—and together the clique of urban urchins sharpened hustles that kept them alive and outdoors.

"I started fucking around in the arcades and shit like that," he says. "I got with this other kid. He was about ten. He taught me how to pickpocket, and from there, I just became a mad thief, livin' like a gypsy. At first it was me and Jose, but after a while there was a little posse of, like, six of us all together. My man Jose, he wasn't a runaway, but his moms was never home. His house became like a club house. He lived in the projects."

In his budding crew, Ghetto says, the child who had been mistreated and felt unloved so often had finally "found somebody who was like me, in a similar situation, same age group. We all was into comic books and shit like that."

Further reflection, though, forces revisions on his sentimentality. Ghetto says his crew probably imagined more common ground than they actually strode. "What did we have in common now that I think about it, besides being little bad bastards? We had nothing in common but just being mischievous."

I ask him about some of the mischief.

"Somebody taught me how to steal diamonds from old ladies, like wedding rings and so forth," he says. "I was coming out to the city, Columbus Circle and Fifty-ninth Street, snatching wedding rings. I was taking them to the fence, and the fence was robbing me, hitting me off two hundred, three hundred dollars for diamonds. Now, I'm a little kid. I'm thinking that's a lot of money, knowwhatI'msayin'? So I was surviving out here, but by the same token, I was getting mad jerked."

Beyond the work of his hustle, Ghetto says, he enjoyed plenty of play on the streets of New York. Even as he was coming of age, so was his first real love: hip-hop, our generation's tributary to the inexorable flow of Black culture.

LIVING TO TELL ABOUT IT

Before it was a billion-dollar-a-year industry, before it jump-started the stars of no-talents like Vanilla Ice, before it became marketing fodder for Pillsbury and Reebok and MTV, hip-hop meant a mic, two turntables and a city park where scores of overburdened Black and Latino boys like Da Ghetto Communicator first learned to free their minds and put their boogie down.

"Straight up and down, the first time I found hip-hop it was the summer of seventy-eight," recalls Ghetto. "That was my third time running away from home, and me and my man Jose, we went to this jam in Coney Island. It was pumping out there, yo! I seen people jam in the park, but I never really been in the midst of the people jamming and shit. So I'm just checking it out. I'm listening to the DJ getting busy, scratching it up. The MC is on time. There's graffiti on the wall. Everybody just bobbing this way. Everything is just all point. It was like the perfect jam—and I was like, 'Damn! I got to get up in here.'

"And then, they just started shooting."

The party broke up, but Ghetto's passion had already been kindled. A b-boy was in the making. In the postadolescence that followed, Ghetto found himself becoming more entrenched in hip-hop culture. He became a graffiti artist first, then he developed skills on the microphone as well, rhyming for classmates at the schools he still managed to sporadically attend. Eventually, his poetry would give way to the prose he now cranks out for the likes of *Vibe* and *The Source*, to the singular and enthusiastic insider's views he gives to a subculture that mainstream America would still ignore, dismantle.

Don't be misled. Hip-hop never rescued Ghetto from the abusive home, the bouts with homelessness that worsened when, at sixteen, he finally left his mother's house for good. No, brother struggled on his own—sleeping in shelters and on trains, cobbling together an education from various public schools, Job Corps, Covenant House and, of course, the streets. He has only recently found steady shelter.

But like the gospel hymns that buoyed generations before him, hip-hop kept Ghetto sane, focused, informed even as the world around him grew stingier with its helping hands. The music was both soundtrack and outlet for a child who could've easily suffered his indignities in silence and creative morass.

Now he has the luxury of slowing his pace—albeit perhaps only a fraction. He doesn't fully trust it, as his suspicious glances at the world around him still suggests. Still, slowing down is a luxury Da Ghetto Communicator can appreciate nonetheless, especially after a childhood spent on the run.

TIMOTHY WASHINGTON, 23: WATTS UP

LOS ANGELES—Tim admits that, in some ways, he was "kind of like the peculiar kid on the block" as he was growing up in Watts.

When other kids were making their way through gang turf to get to the local schools, Tim was climbing on a bus headed for private school. When his neighborhood friends were throwing on their Levis and khakis and T-shirts to beat the morning bell, Tim was stepping out in a uniform, complete with jacket and tie.

He believes the differences—which were less about class than about the lifestyle his mother dreamed of for her babies—paid off. He graduated from Morehouse University in '91, with a business degree. He landed a job with corporate giant Kraft Foods. And, in time, he saw enough value in his talent to leave the company and make a run at his own business.

That, however, is now. Back then, Tim says, those same differences earned him little more than contempt.

"It was kind of like, 'You think you are Goody Two-shoes. Your mom send you to Catholic school, private school or whatever . . .' And I'm not even Catholic—but that's the thing that I dealt with. So my childhood was rough, man. I don't know how many times I've been held up, robbed. I got jumped once or twice because I was in uniform on the bus coming home. I had guns pulled on me. I had my money taken."

He pauses ever so briefly. He doesn't want to exaggerate the downside of growing up in Watts, doesn't want to throw fire on the pyre of American stereotypes about Black youth or the ghetto. He doesn't see his bullies in too different a light than the schoolyard bullies that haunt every child's playground and route home. He knows guns shouldn't be part of the mix, neither should gang violence. But that's what it means to grow up poor in urban America. This is the legacy white supremacy and economic and political disfranchisement have bequeathed our young people.

Taken in this light, Tim says, very little about the downside to his experiences seems "peculiar."

"If you tell those stories to a kid growing up in the ghetto right now, it won't phase him. Because, I mean, that's not a big deal; everybody goes through that. That's not a big deal because you had a rough childhood. It's like, 'So what?'" Tim laughs. "'Everybody had a rough childhood.' So for me to speak about my childhood growing up in Watts is kind of like a comic thing, too. Someone who grew up in any inner city or ghetto, wherever it is in the United States, Chicago or wherever it is, knows that every ghetto is pretty much the same. The ills that exist for the ghetto are going to be the same. No matter where they are, it's going to be a variation thereof."

But home was another matter. At home, Tim reveled in the love of a close-knit family, growing up with four other siblings. They didn't dwell on the fact that his father had left when Tim was young. They didn't obsess over the poverty surrounding them. They went to church. They went to school and work. They lived and they loved. For Tim, that made all the difference in the world.

"I was all about doing better, man," he explains. "Not necessarily interested in 'getting out,' but just exploring. I was real curious as a kid. I was like, 'There's gotta be something more than this. This can't be it; this can't be it.' So I made it a point to explore every opportunity that came my way, you know. Whatever it was, I looked at it, I read it . . .

"And if I had to say that that came from anywhere, I'd have to say it came from my mother. That's how she raised me and taught me. She wanted me to learn to think and see for myself."

In a sense, Tim is right about Watts. Much about it is indeed similar to conditions, for better and worse, found in working-class Black communities from coast to coast. But too, it has its differences. For decades, not merely years, gang violence has turned Black and Brown communities here into war zones. Some gangs boast two, sometimes three generations of Crips and Bloods. Outside of Chicago, no other major city has suffered so many intractable gang conflicts.

To a large degree, Tim saw his childhood shaped by these conflicts, both in terms of what he did and did not want to become.

"For example, where I went to school was in a different gang territory. It was basically a Blood neighborhood. I grew up in a Crip neighborhood, for the most part. I had to come through there. When I got off the bus, I got off the bus in a Blood neighborhood. And when I walked home, I would cross into a Crip neighborhood. So the Bloods would basically meet me at the bus on any given day and pull out their knife, pull out their gat, take my lunch money, probably psyche me out. We'd get into a fight if I didn't have nothing.

"Sometimes, they thought I was in a gang. Whether I'd joined or not has nothing to do with what happens to me when I go into a different neighborhood and they ask me where I live. I'm automatically put into that gang because that's where I live. 'Where do you live? Well, okay, I know where you are from.' So it's automatically on."

I try to picture a young Tim, suited up, tie flapping in the breeze, books under arm, staring down a crew of Bloods. The odds don't seem inviting. Why not simply lie? I ask.

"You can't lie," he tells me. "I mean, you can, but then brothers get beat down anyway. Plus, then it becomes an issue of your manhood: 'Why I got to lie to you about where I live? And no, I'm not a part of that gang.' But they don't believe that. It's probably, I guess, not so much about being a man even. After a while you be like, 'Fuck it, I'm going to tell you where I live, and what's gonna happen is gonna happen. I'm not goin' be lyin' to you about where I live.' It's just something that exists, man. And it's just . . . it's sad, but it's true. So wherever I went, I was automatically affiliated with the gang in my neighborhood because that's the way it is.

"I lived in the territory of a gang called Homestreet Watts. And right across the way was Bounty Hunters, The Bloods, The Pirus. But, man, you just learn to accept that after awhile because as a youth, you don't have no money to go buy no house and move. So you just adjust, and you deal with it."

Some young brothers "deal with it" by involving themselves in the gangs, the operating logic, of course, being "if you can't beat 'em, join 'em." Tim admits that he thought about letting gang bangers jump him in, a ritual in which several potential gang comrades pound on a candidate for several minutes to test his mettle.

He came close, but stopped just short.

"I didn't avoid joining, but not getting in was a choice that I made. I can't say that I never did try to run around with them. As a youth, your mind is very impressionable, and because of the types of pressure you get—it's like you live in this neighborhood, right?— either you are going to be part of this gang to get protection or you are going to be harassed by the gang. So that was the thing that I dealt with growing up.

"I had to be part of the gang. When I was in the neighborhood, I had to be down. I grew up saying *cuz*, which is what Crips call each other. It was just part of my vocabulary. Every other word, *cuz*, because if I was outside at play, I heard it so much in the neighborhood that you can't help but become a part of it. The older brothers called you *whatever cuz*, and that was your name. 'What's up, Tim Cuz,' you know? It was just thrust upon you daily, and so out of force of habit you just started saying it."

Tim says he never joined because his mother and older brother kept a close eye out for any signs that he might be moving in that direction. They tried to make sure he was preoccupied, though obviously they couldn't keep tabs on him all day long. After a while, though, Tim came to respect their efforts. And he helped.

"It wasn't like that, because I never really channeled my effort toward actually becoming a member and wanting 'to put in work,' as they call it. It just wasn't in my heart. That wasn't the way I was taught. It wasn't the way I was brought up by my Moms. All the ass whippings I got kept me from running around with them too long. I mean, I did a little dirt. I got into little spats with whatever, did a couple of little things, man. But it was never really anything significant. And I was able to know that what I really wanted was far beyond what was going on around me."

LARRY ABRAMS, 24: ON GROWING UP GAY

NEW YORK—Some fifty yards east and two flights up from the shoulders of Manhattan's West Side Highway, Larry Abrams sits cross-legged, balancing my tape recorder on his knee. He looks to be at ease. Dark-skinned with only the faintest trace of stubble atop his scalp, Larry wears black jeans, black Nikes and a black T-shirt. Two hoop earrings are affixed to either lobe. Another hoop punctures a nostril. He's reclined, smiling as he twists to and fro in his swivel chair and, like I said, balancing.

As he shifts and gestures throughout our conversation, I glance occasionally at the recorder, hoping it doesn't fall. It never does. Doesn't even so much as teeter. Obviously, Larry's good at balancing acts.

He's been performing them most of his life, he explains. Balancing the demands of being both a brother from Harlem and the Bronx and a Yale Ph.D. candidate. Of being a counselor as well as a young man still groping for his own way.

Of being gay and Black in an America that values neither.

It is from this office that Larry shares secrets of his balancing act with others. At the Hetrick-Martin Institute, Larry helps thousands of gay and lesbian teenagers—most of them Black or Hispanic—sift through feelings of guilt, inadequacy and fear and to come to grips with their sexuality. Negotiating the emotional outback of depression, confusion and suicidal tendencies, he encourages his charges to make peace with themselves, to recognize normalcy in the homosexuality many believe an abomination.

As Larry explains the pain that often accompanies this trek into self-realization, I try hard not to stare, even as I fumble with projecting earnest concern. A straight Black man very much fettered by traditional notions of African-American masculinity, I'm slightly nervous as Larry and I begin to talk. Beyond listening to lurid rumors about how gay brothers around the way got "turned out" as kids, I've never felt compelled to examine the childhood development of gay Black men. Despite the fearlessness brothers like me often think ghetto living imparts to them, I've always been somewhat afraid of homosexuals and lightning quick to dodge 'em. Don't ask why. Perhaps it's paranoia, the unthinkable fear that they might try to push up. Perhaps it's the deep-seated tenents of my long-abandoned Black Baptist upbringing telling me they're "unnatural."

But whatever. Brothers like me gotta get over it before we go under. After all, there's no denying that gay men are very much a part of the Black community. They lead church choirs (and sit in plenty of pulpits as well); they teach; they run civil-rights groups and produce music and broadcast news.

They're also equally as much victims of white supremacy as heterosexuals, racism being no respecter of sexual orientation. To merely look at Larry is to know that he'll catch hell before catching a cab on Broadway, too, that he gets odd glances from white women in elevators also, that the police are just as willing to stop his car and kick his ass as they are Rodney King's.

So, even as I ask the brother to tell me when he first knew that he was gay, I manage to chill. Then listen . . .

"I've always known that I was different to some degree, in terms of my attractions toward people, how I oriented myself toward people and what I find attractive. And what people in my age group did, I didn't necessarily feel was the appropriate thing for me. Just the way your friends are around talking about other women within your peer group and how they oriented themselves toward them and what I perceived them as feeling about women—that wasn't necessarily what I wanted or where my desire lies in terms of my primary orientation sexually.

"I've always known. Since, my earliest memory, when I was six, I've always known. There were always people around, in my age group, that I was attracted to in different ways. The feelings weren't necessarily acted upon, but the feelings were there. And I was introverted so I didn't really talk about it.

"I dealt with a lot of things that I don't think a child should deal with, so it wasn't so much one moment as it was a strand. There's a strand going through the fabric of my childhood that really shouldn't have been there. We had domestic violence. The police got called a few times. I was dealing with issues of alcoholism within my family, of growing up with a grandmother who was alcoholic and what that meant about my development, what that meant about my relationship to her. She was my primary caretaker because my grandfather, who was in the house, was legally blind. How my grandmother dealt with that situation is she linked a part of me to take care of her. So that set up a dynamic that wasn't the most healthy thing for a child to be dealing with, [when he] should be running through the trees or outside playing basketball with his friends or just hanging out being seven, eight, nine, ten, eleven.

"That type of relationship was something that I would not have liked to have been there, but at the same time it's easy to say that, looking back, I would not be the person I am now if I had not had that experience.

"I lived with my grandmother until I was twelve. I moved from that household to live with my mother, my stepfather and what would become one of my half-sisters 'cause my mother was pregnant at the time. We moved from working class, urban Harlem to Riverdale up in the Bronx, an upper-middle-class Jewish community. Also living in that building at the time was my father, my stepmother and my two half-sisters from that union. Also living in that building at the time was my father's sisters and their respective families: one is married with two children; the other one has a child. So I had four different households. It was also a big class difference. I went from being in a whole Black/Latino environment into being in an all-white, Jewish environment. And because I was 'smart, gifted, special,' the junior high school that I went to placed me in more advanced classes, where I was the only Black kid in my class. My peer group was 'tracked' into regular vocational kind of sort of stuff.

"I also lost my 'virginity'—for lack of a better word—when I was twelve years old, with someone who I was growing up with at the time. To this day, if I thought about it, I don't know how it happened. He was two or three years older than me, and we became very close, in terms of hanging out and stuff. Then our relationship, for whatever reason, began to take on a sexual nature. It lasted four years, till I was sixteen and he moved away.

"It was, you know . . . it was very interesting. I knew at that time I was attracted toward people of the same sex. I didn't necessarily call it gay, bisexual etc., etc. I knew what the terms were, but they weren't necessarily labels or identities that I adopted for myself. It was something that he and I did as part of our relationship. We never talked about it, but it was always the assumption that it would happen.

"It wasn't about hiding as much as about something we had to be private about 'cause somebody else wouldn't necessarily understand. And so we would go out, hang out, bullshit with our friends, go in the park, play ball, play football, play Frisbee, whatever we did. But our time—you know, when we would go off and do our thing and be intimate—was always separate from that. And that was just how it was. That's how it functioned, and no one was any of the wiser. To my knowledge.

"Even though I lived in a predominantly white neighborhood, the building I was in was all middle-class people of color, Black and Latino mostly. So my peer group was a bunch of guys who were Black and Latino and they really did [engage in gay-baiting]. I mean, part of the cult of masculinity is 'faggot this, faggot that.' As I grew older and I began to struggle with these issues more, it became very scary, the whole notion of being found out as being something 'negative.'

"I don't recall taking part in it, but if I said no, I think that would be an oversimplification. I must have 'cause that was part of being a part of the group. That's what you did. And it's automatic.

As much as it's about using 'faggot this, faggot that' as a form of deprecating somebody unlike yourself, it doesn't necessarily always take on the connotation of being about gay people. It's not necessarily about gay people; it's just another tool that I used to put somebody else down, like calling somebody a spic, a nigger . . . it falls in that line. So even though I was beginning to make the connection [to gays], I don't think that when 'faggot' was used, people always made the connection.

"I was always like a square peg in a round hole. I lived in this building with all these relatives and everybody got along—so that alone made me unique. Then I was in more advanced classes than my friends—and that made me unique. I don't think I was a nerd, but people perceived me as such because I was smart. So I was 'Brainiac.' And because I tended to speak proper English, people automatically assumed I was trying to be white. So, you know, I was always . . . That stuff made me 'other than.' That was a very awkward place to be 'cause I didn't fit in. And then dealing with the homosexuality piece, I really didn't feel like I fit in.

"And I was very introverted and very thoughtful. So I think a lot of my adolescence I went through in silence."

EDWARD WOODS, 23: STREET SMARTS 101

WASHINGTON, D.C.—Ed seems proud enough of his academic accomplishments: graduated Hampton '91, finished Howard Law in '94, 3.6 cumulative GPA in undergrad. Still, the Queens, New York, native tries to keep his formal education in tight perspective, careful not to overvalue it—certainly not next to what he considers at least as equally an important intellectual asset: street sense. Having grown up a bright but consummately mischievous shorty in urban Black America—draining 40's of Old Gold by age thirteen, driving a New York gypsy cab at sixteen and, in the inbetween time, as likely to be hitting skins or hip-hop clubs as he would his advance-course textbooks—Ed figures that good grades may get a young Black man into law school, but street smarts are more likely to keep him alive long enough to collect the sheepskin.

As we talk, the early afternoon sun glares at us from the spotless sky above Washington, D.C. We sit in a wooden gazebo atop a knoll just yards from the parking lot of Howard Law. Ed is kicked back to my left, a chunky brother framed by black, plastic-rimmed glasses and a cream baseball cap. He wears a black *Source* magazine T-shirt and blue jeans that are puddling over the top of white shell-toe Adidases.

Running down his ideas about street schooling, the Hollis, Queens, native explains that his parents—a rough-hewn cab-stand owner father and registered nurse mother—taught him best. He recalls basking in that wonderful knack working-class Black parents have for scuffling for their paychecks, rearing their kids right and still enjoying raucous good times.

"I grew up in an environment where my Pops used to gamble, so we had a card game that used to take place at the house," Ed says. "And every Friday, Moms cooked chicken [for gathering friends]. So it was that type of environment. I didn't grow up in no household where we had a lot of money. It was just day-to-day shit that was coming in; we took care of it like that."

When Ed got old enough to work, his father's lessons on life were often doled out at the cab stand, over the blare of car horns and the crackle of two-way radios.

"First job I had was delivering papers," Ed says. "I did that just to spite my father, who wanted me to come work for him. I was like, I'm not working in no cab stand! I was twelve years old. I was delivering papers in the morning, and I was getting a lot of flack from my Pops because he was like, you know . . . he wasn't really with that bullshit. I wasn't making no money, bringing twenty-three dollars home a week, if that, and a lot of problems collecting.

"So I quit that and I went to work for my Pops. But he wouldn't give me a decent job. I was cleaning toilet bowls! He had one toilet in there that was real nasty."

Ed digresses briefly to make ground-level distinctions between his family's business and, say, the local Yellow Cab garage.

BACK IN THE DAYS: REMEMBRANCES OF CHILDHOOD

"In Queens, cab stands are totally different," he says. "They're gypsy cab services, so you had a lot of motherfuckers working for him, a lot of immigrants coming in the country [without] the right type of papers. They'd do anything, so they ride gypsy cabs in the neighborhood.

"When I was about fifteen years old, I started dispatching at the cab stand—and anybody who knows anything about dispatching in a Black neighborhood for a gypsy cab service [knows the job] is some wild shit: getting cussed out, dealing with people, fighting, different customers coming in. We had various incidents that would go on. People come in there wielding guns, shooting up the place. We got robbed six or seven times.

"The cab stand was right on the corner of Farmer's Boulevard, which was a major drug hole way back. I saw a lot of shit growing up. I think my Pops wanted to keep me aware of it 'cause he was like, 'Just because someone does something that you might not agree with, you don't put him down or say you can't be a part of it. You just got to learn how to deal with people so they'll feel comfortable around you. But you just got to know when to say you're not with that.'"

At the stand, Ed was introduced to the vital art of sizing up situations, characters and hunches, learning as he listened to the cabbies' tales of danger. There were tales like the one of a cabbie who was robbed on the toilet—"they rolled up and stuck a gun to his dick." And the time Ed's own father was nearly vic'ed—"they called a cab and told him to meet them at a certain corner to pick up somebody; when he got there, the kid stuck a shotgun through the window."

When he turned sixteen, Ed started driving for his father's service and found his own wits being tested.

"One time I drove these kids to Brooklyn, and I picked them up off a corner," he recalls. "Anybody that knows anything about driving cabs knows you don't pick anybody up from where you can't go back and identify a house. If I went to a house and didn't actually see a customer walk out the door, I was supposed to pull off and leave him.

"But, you know, Brooklyn trips was like twenty, twenty-five dollars, so I wasn't passing on the loot. So we went to Brooklyn, and they tried mad slick shit to get me in the alleys like [saying,] 'I don't know where the spot is'; 'I think it's down this block'; 'Turn here, turn there.' But I played the shit off kind of good. What I did was, I hit the gas and went down a spot where there was mad brothers on the corner. My idea was to make them feel like I knew motherfuckers in the area!

"I pulled up in the spot where motherfuckers was standing at the light, started honking the horn and"—Ed smiles and thrusts up a fist as though acknowledging a friend from a distance—"throwing my hand up at the motherfuckers like, 'Yo! What up?'"

The shady passengers wound up paying and exiting the cab quietly.

Ed's lessons didn't come only at work. Between the cab stand and his schoolbooks, Ed was also developing a growing fondness for corners along Farmer Boulevard, as well as other local hangout spots. On the avenue, he moved into advanced courses in hanging out, learning how to posture and roll with the fellas, run head games on honeys and, in what has become an often destructive staple among urban Black men, to guzzle 40's with frightening regularity.

"I was hanging out with older brothers and shit," says Ed. "I started drinking when I was about thirteen. We started off drinking one 40. We shared between five motherfuckers, and it would get us drunk.

"It started from looking up to other brothers around the way. We was kind of rebellious, and that was the thing they were doing. They were nineteen, twenty, twenty-one; here we are, thirteen years old and shit. That was just the thing to do. I mean, it was just the only thing we saw. This is what's in front of you so this is what you're supposed to do, start drinking at this age. It wasn't a fantasy to drink to me. Some kids would just do it as a fantasy. I used to like to get drunk.

"And I could go in at thirteen and buy a beer with no problem. We had these stores around my way, stores on each corner that serve beer. There was liquor stores every couple of blocks. In my neighborhood, right now, a kid ten years old could walk into the store and buy a six-pack of beer. Nobody's going to question it. They might assume it's for his parents or whatever, but nobody was going to question it."

Ed says he began drinking regularly with his friends, sometimes to excess. His mother, concerned about her son being drunk in the streets, stepped in and made an unusually liberal offer.

"When I was around sixteen, my Moms said, 'You're going to drink regardless [of what I do]. So from now on you bring your friends to the house. You all can drink in the house because either you going to drink here or you going to drink on the corner.' So my house became the spot to drink beer at."

After a while, Ed says, he grew tired of malt liquor and, more than a little concerned about the brew's effect on his body, stopped drinking it. He credits his parents' lenience with compelling him to be more responsible, to think for himself about the consequences of certain actions and freedoms.

"My mother knew it was some shit that you got to go through and grow out of," he says. "A lot of parents try to shelter their children at a certain age. I think you should shelter them when they're like six and seven. You know, I wasn't able to cross the street when I was six, had a curfew, certain rules. But after I was about fourteen, fifteen, that shit changed."

He went through other shit, too, as he honed his instinct for survival. Growing up, Ed would get jumped over girls, lose friends to gunshots and nearly take a bullet himself.

"When I was thirteen years old, I was at a big carnival they used to have in Queens and one brother started arguing with another brother," says Ed of this last incident. "An old man came over with a stick and hit him with the stick and ran him off. I was standing right next to the old man, who was a security guard, but I didn't know he was a security guard at the time. He was undercover. So I'm standing right next to him and I thought to myself I'd better step aside. I learned that from cab driving, I picked up on perception. I said, 'Yo, step to the side for a minute.' And I'm not lying, I swear to God, it was no less than five seconds after I said 'step to the side' that the same kid who'd left the carnival came back in and shot money up. I was standing in front of [the wounded guard]. That kid shot six other people that day, all in the ass and everything. But something just told me, 'Yo, let's step to the side.' I just didn't feel right standing. There was no reason to move. It was just that [feeling]."

Still, as much as he learned in sink-or-swim firefights on the streets, Ed's basic street knowledge was formed under the protective, long-suffering guidance of his rollin' stone of a father.

"Even though my father only went past eighth grade, I learned more from him than the majority of professors that I had," Ed says, "just in the fact that he was able to sit me down and say, 'Listen, there's certain ways to get to certain points. Just because you're going to law school doesn't make you no better than me.' In a way, I spited my father for getting me out there driving cabs, but I think that's one of the best experiences I ever had 'cause I learned to deal with people.

"It goes beyond what I picked up in school. I can walk you through Howard's law school right now, introduce you to motherfuckers that got the top grades in the school but won't last a day on the street 'cause they can't hustle. They don't know that there's a sense to hustling and that experience is the most valuable thing you can have."

ASINIA TYEHIMBA, 17: NEW AFRIKAN PANTHER

ATLANTA—Asinia has been raised to be a soldier in a war that many young brothers would deny even exists: a war to be free.

Certainly most anyone will give a knit-browed nod to the high-profile casualties—the Rodney Kings of the world—as testament that "America still has a long way to go." But refracted as it often is through the narrow, rose-colored lens of American propaganda, the war—the stark political, economic and social terrorism that America inflicts on its Black subjects—tends to assume more palatable euphemisms: history, the slave trade, the Black problem, justifiable homicide, an "isolated incident" of flagrant police misconduct.

Anything but war.

Not so for Asinia. He chooses not to peer through that lens, thank you. He knows better. He was raised better. His parents are among the architects of the present-day Black liberation movement, key figures in the New Afrikan Peoples Organization, a Black independence movement that evolved out of the famed Republic of New Afrika of the 1960s.

New Afrikan, they call Black people in America. We're not born in the Motherland. The West has had undeniable influence in shaping us. Neither, though, are we American. "Just 'cause a cat has kittens in an oven," Malcolm once illumed, "that don't make 'em biscuits." But it certainly makes 'em different than a cat born in an alleyway. African in some ways. Of the West, reluctantly, in others. New Afrikan. A people with a shared history, shared cultures, shared fate. A nation.

But a nation ain't free without land, and land is what NAPO seeks. To be exact, the group aims to one day collect five states—Mississippi, Louisiana, Georgia, Alabama and South Carolina—on which to build a progressive, independent Black nation-state. Won't happen tomorrow, they'll tell you frankly. Not in their lifetimes. Or their children's. It's a protracted struggle—but one for a debt long overdue. Reparations, some call it, compensation for the Black men and women on whose backs America was built. Damages for the horrors of a war we never provoked, never saw coming and, even now, only a fraction of us still actively fight.

At seventeen, Asinia has been taught to stand among those soldiers.

"My childhood is unlike a lot of young black males' growing up," he tells me, sitting on his father's porch in Decatur, an Atlanta suburb. "I grew up in south-central L.A., right across the street from a crack house with heavy gang warfare. I grew up in all that, but my parents were heavily involved with what is now the New Afrikan Independence Movement. I went to an all-black private school called Marcus Garvey."

On this day, little about Asinia's appearance—a baseball hat with 2Pac's logo stitched in the crown, a T-shirt, light blue jeans, no shoes, no socks—says anything about either his politics or the old neighborhood. Reclining on the porch steps, he looks more like a country kid at rest than anything else.

In truth, though, he's more. He's a student of peoples' politics, a legacy of sorts in a movement that envisions an end to the conditions that have rendered Black Americans the wretched of Uncle Sam's little plot of Earth. He's also a survivor of those conditions.

"We used to have to walk blocks away to school, so I'm walking through different gang territories," he says. "I saw a lot growing up and learned a lot from the streets. I also learned a lot about my people and myself. On weekends when my friends would hang out on the avenue, I used to go to programs. Nation-building forums and stuff. There is a program for youth called New Afrikan Scouts. I used to be there every weekend. My father started a martial arts fighting system called *kupiguynamgubie,* and we used to have to go to classes there. My weekends were booked, and I used to get home from school at five and all my friends were inside. So my childhood was basically dedicated to the movement."

As a child, he grew up idolizing not merely baseball players and singers, but activists and orators, men such as Malcolm X and jailed revolutionary Mutulu Shakur. And always there were the Scouts. The New Afrikan Scouts gave Asinia an alternative to south-central's gang-life subculture, whose bloody cross-currents had long since begun to take young Black men under.

"The New Afrikan Scouts is the opposite of the Boy Scouts," says Asinia. "Instead of teaching about pledging allegiance to the white flag, we talked about teaching Blacks love for self, about African heritage. We also learned survival skills. We went camping and did drills, learned basic skills and an alternative to the gangs and drugs and stuff."

His family suffered its share of tolls for its commitment to revolutionary change. Asinia's father was jailed in the 1980s in connection with the jailbreak of freedom fighter Assata Shakur, was held for eighteen months with no charges being filed and, says Asinia, no evidence against him. He was later charged and convicted. His children watched him led away in cuffs.

"That was a sad day," says Asinia. "I was told all along that [the American justice system] wasn't built for me. That just proved my point. It was a slap right in the face." Eventually, his father was freed, but the point was driven home to Asinia: There's a war going on, brother. His devotion to the movement intensified.

Though he cherishes the Scout experiences now, Asinia admits that, as a kid, he sometimes resented having to hurry off to this meeting or that conference or some other call to action or another. He was twelve, thirteen. His friends were off playing somewhere, or perhaps with their families celebrating some national holiday or another, ones Asinia had always been raised to eschew. The young nationalist in him recognized the importance of those meetings, knew the pernicious cultural implications of those holidays. The adolescent in him missed his neighborhood homies.

"It's okay now, but I used to be really feeling salty," he confesses, smiling and shaking his head. "I didn't get to see my friends. We didn't get white holidays like the Fourth of July. We would get Kwanzaa off, and that used to run into Christmas so I could kick it with them then, but I just felt like I was robbed: 'I'm dedicating my life so young. I can't see this now.' Even though I was dedicating my life to all this, I couldn't conceptualize land and independence and stuff. I wasn't thinking about that so young."

Asinia says most of his friends outside the Scouts didn't know much about his political affiliations.

"The people who were in the scouts were people whose parents were in the same organization as my parents, so we all stuck together like that," he says. "We didn't really recruit that much from off the street. We would have wanted to, but it just didn't fall in like that. My friends used to see me in the uniform, and they used to laugh. It used to get to me—but when the rest of the Scouts came around, it would be like, 'This is the move right here.'

"In the Scouts, we were like a big family. We used to complain about the same things, so we could all relate. We would talk about what we would be doing if we weren't at this meeting," he says with a laugh.

Participating in the Scouts didn't shield Asinia from the tragedies and dangers of LA's streets. He lost three childhood buddies to gun shots. He avoided being a victim of violence himself, but sometimes only barely.

"The first time I got shot at was probably the worst moment of my childhood," he says. "I was at a party in LA, at my cousin's, and we were on the porch. My father had told me not to be kicking it outside because of the drive-bys. So I was outside with this girl when these Crips came in the house. I didn't think they were going to do anything. The next thing I know, they started shooting inside the house and they come running outside shooting while I'm on the porch! So I'm hopping over the fence and the guy they were shooting at was running right behind me. I'm looking back like, 'Damn, are they shooting at him or me?' The girl and I ducked and dodged, and I could hear the bullets flying right past me. They eventually shot the guy behind me."

At first, he says, he was scared. Then angry. In the years since, he's grown compassionate for the young Black men whose childhoods he's seen scarred, snuffed out even, with bullets and blades. This, too, has reinforced his commitment to the struggle, a struggle he was born to wage. It's even in his name: "My father says my name means 'stern' or 'stubborn.' They named me that 'cause when I was born the doctor slapped me on the butt and I just looked at him crazy. I don't believe him, but that's what they say happened.

"My full name is Asinia Adigun Otheano Tyehimba. Asinia means 'stern.' Adigun means 'righteous.' Otheano, 'born at night.' My last name, Tyehimba, means 'We stand as a nation.' "

VIONDI COPELAND, 20: PROJECT-BORN

HOUSING PROJECTS have always seemed particular and rich subcultures unto themselves. To accompany the ills we hear broadcast weekly about life in the projects—to go along with sensational reports about gangs and gunplay—there has always been about the PJ's a sense of closed community, of a shared fate and, thus, solidarity. Certainly much of it stems from a strange sort of social snobbery among the children of working-class Black communities that often relegated kids from the projects to a station even lower than the rest.

We always used to crack jokes on the project kids. Talked about their cribs. About their obvious reliance on federal aid. About the crushing poverty that seemed always to define their material conditions.

But, too, we were envious. The project kids stuck together. And, man, were they tough. In many ways, their lot seemed the most severe manifestation of the concentration-camp mentality with which America approaches Black people. But they were survivors. America had confined them to some of the most wretched conditions it could muster outside of the penal system. Cabrini-Green. The Robert Taylor Homes. The Jeffries and the Brewsters. The Polo Grounds. The Jordan Downs. Desire. But the projects glowed nonetheless with a sort of scrappy pride.

Viondi hails from the Perry Homes, a housing project in southwest Atlanta. He was a toddler when his family moved into the complex, just another of the working-class households harboring dreams of a better life. A week after he enrolled at Morehouse, his mother and stepfather fled the units for Washington state.

Growing up in Perry, Viondi witnessed a saddening evolution of life in the projects, one that went from everyone knowing and caring for each other to one in which neighbors eyed each other with suspicion and fear. As the years passed, the streets where he'd played were invaded by drug dealers and crackheads. Squeals of children at play stopped echoing into the night. Gunshots replaced them. The sense of collective fate wasn't so shared anymore. Families began moving. The solidarity unraveled. Life became more unglued. Viondi watched, too, as the glee he once brought to life in the complex turned into a gnawing desire to "make it out."

"When we first moved into this community, the first six or seven years, it was a real close-knit thing," he says. "Everybody knew everybody. If I did something and if the lady next door saw me, I would get in trouble. If my mother couldn't go to the PTA meeting, I would go along with the other families.

"As time progressed, those people began to move out to other communities. The new people moving in weren't as family-like. The first people were older. The new people were young. I was in the eighth or ninth grade when I noticed things changing. It was a constant change. All of a sudden problems started and I was having run-ins with the new people in the community. It was a big thing and that is what prompted my mother to say it is time to move out of here.

"Drugs got worse. It started to move into our front yard, compared to when the other people were there. Those ladies I knew growing up were fighting to keep the neighborhood clean. 'If you are going to do drugs,' they'd say, 'take it somewhere else.' Then it started moving into our front yard. Couldn't go outside or sit on the porch, had to be in at a certain time. Things began to change so my mother was like, it is time to leave. As soon as I finished school and enrolled in college she gave me a week to get settled—and they were gone."

CARLOS WILLIAMS, 22: THE LAST BOY SCOUT

ATLANTA—In discussing the limits of nonviolent protests during the heyday of the Civil Rights Movement, historian Howard Zinn once called Albany, Georgia, "the first dramatic evidence of a phenomenon which now has been seen often enough to be believed:

that there is a part of the South impermeable by the ordinary activities of nonviolent direct action, a monolithic South completely controlled by politicans, police, dogs, and prod sticks."

Before arriving at the Morehouse School of Medicine in 1993, Carlos Williams had spent his entire life in this same Albany, Georgia. He grew up hearing the stories of the racist attacks on Blacks, of how white political bosses kept the people terrorized and downtrodden, how even Martin Luther King couldn't march through his city.

Such are the nightmares that inspired his parents to push him, he explains. Get an education, they told him. Create your own opportunities, they stressed. Follow God, follow your heart, do what's correct. They emphasized convictions and community service, taught him the necessity of giving back and being involved, of respecting others and, above all, himself.

In the meantime, they protected their son, sheltered him from the racism that continues to pollute Black life in the South. They didn't hide the obvious—that Albany, not unlike Birmingham, Atlanta or, for that matter, Boston or Seattle, remains a bastion of white supremacy—but they tried hard to spare him the scars Blacks in Albany had borne for so many decades.

In short, they were, to Carlos, glowing examples of how to raise your boy right.

Even today, Carlos carries those lessons like so much currency. He remains the devout Christian he was brought up to be: doing unto others as he would have them do unto him, loving everyone (or trying to at least), ever mindful that, as a Black person, he is and must continue to be the moral vanguard for a nation that despises him. He remains committed to his dreams of helping Black folks when and where he can. And like so many young Black men whose achievements and sterling character are shunted aside amid the sensationalized hubbub about "urban pathology" and "endangered species," this small-town boy remains, simply, a good kid:

"Most of my life was in Albany. As a matter of fact, all my life was in Albany. Albany is a medium-sized city, about a hundred thousand people. It is in southwest Georgia. A lot of people think

Albany was a racist place—and the history of Albany does have some racist about it. It's the only place that Martin Luther King went that he couldn't break during his freedom march. He came to Albany in the sixties. He said he had never seen no place like it.

"Lo and behold, I didn't experience blatant racism until I was in college. Small kids may say words and you know that they are not supposed to say it and it would hurt. But I didn't see blatant racism until I was in college. That's interesting because people think, You live in Albany all this time; you are just not seeing it. I love Albany. My heart is at home in Albany. I want to go back and give to my school, Albany State, a historically Black college. That's where I was an undergrad. I want to give back to my community regardless of the downfalls. Anything that you are from, then you are also a part of. Since it is a part of you, you should give your all to it.

"My dad is a retired schoolteacher. My mom is an assistant principal in the high school. I lived the sheltered life of a kid. The older I got the more responsibility they gave me. That gradual responsibility made me appreciate life a whole lot more. Appreciate my family. I had some things that happened in my life that made me change, but growing up in Albany and never being exposed to racism is something I could never know why, to this day. I think it is because my parents had a big role to do with where I went, how I looked and what I did, and people look at all that.

"One thing I can say that Albany gave me was a sense of pride, a sense of respect and sense of knowing that this is my home. No matter how far away I go in the world I will always know where I came from. I see a lot of people, they go places and they are ashamed of coming from small places or big places. If they are from New York, they may have a bad attitude about it. I can say Albany gave me a sense of knowing that you have a place here.

"Now, there is racism in Albany, no doubt about that. I am not saying I appreciate the racism—but Albany to me is my home, my family. My family is in Albany and my roots are there. You should always give back to the community that made you what you are and who you are. I have no desire to live in a city that's huge because, to me, if I go to a large city, I'm just a little fish in a huge pond and nobody will ever know me. But living in Albany, people recognize the achievement that I made in school, the achievement I made in the community, and every person knew me. It was nothing for me to know the mayor of Albany. The position that I was in was fine. On the news, everyone knew you. One hundred thousand people may be a lot of people, but the setting of Albany was like a country town. Therefore, we gained a lot more because people appreciated you for who you are. Either they liked you or they didn't—but you knew who liked you and who didn't.

"Growing up, I wasn't the type of person who wanted to prove to myself that I can do this or that. So I didn't get involved in every activity, but the ones I was in were important to me. In high school, I got involved in Boy Scouts. That was one of the most significant things about my childhood. Not a lot of Blacks are members of Boy Scouts. I'm an Eagle Scout, which is the highest-ranking scout. Obviously, even fewer Blacks are Eagle Scouts. One in every hundred even make it—that's Blacks and whites—so you can imagine the ratio. I got in the Scouts, me and my brother both made it. We were the first Blacks to make it in the southwest Georgia region. I excelled in that, and I was proud of that.

"Scouting instilled in me a sense of self-pride. It gave me a chance to lead where I couldn't before. Every Black kid didn't stay in scouting, because of peer pressure. People think if you are in scouting either you are a nerd or you are a sissy. I had friends, and I was well-respected when I was in school. For me, to be in scouting still would be respectable. It was something that people had to look at me like, 'He is out here in this uniform in a parade but yet he's still one of the boys.' I gained that respect, and I wasn't ashamed to put on my uniform and do this or that, because the stuff I gained in scouting, I can utilize years and years to come. It taught me leadership skills that I couldn't learn anywhere else. We had one of the best black troops in the southwest Georgia region—an all-Black troop. It taught me leadership. It instilled in me how to be a man.

"In addition, my father was always home. He taught me about being a man, too, but sometimes you can't learn everything at home. My parents taught me how to make decisions and take responsibility. Helped me get in contact with myself. They let me enjoy myself and have peace of mind.

"I started believing in myself. I took this lifeguard course and it was demanding. I got in it and I excelled. My parents always instilled in me that you can do anything in the world you want to do if you set your mind to it. That's why I believed it. I got in martial arts and I excelled in that 'cause I believed that I could and I did. In high school, people knew me for who I was. I was just plain old Carlos around campus and I had my friends and that was that. I never thought I could do some of the things that I have done in life.

"As a result of doing these things, I know that there are a whole lot more important things in life than just being a doctor or a lawyer, making more money than anybody else. You got to have peace of mind. If you don't have peace of mind then life is not worth living in the first place.

"So growing up in Albany was a good thing. Like I said, I never really had to deal with the blatant racism there. I didn't have to handle that until I got to college. I remember it: It was one day after classes had started and I went to the store right across from the college. It was a white-owned store. I went into the store, and I was talking to him. It was no big deal to me; I talk to everybody. Anyway, I had my dad's gas card. I went up, and I signed the gas card and he threw the pen at me and threw the receipt at me. And he called me a boy . . .

"For one split second, I could not move or say a word 'cause it hurt me. There is a white man across the counter from me with a gun on his side. He called me a boy first of all and then he threw something at me—but yet I'm buying something from him. I couldn't handle that. I never had anybody show blatant racism like that. This person was like forty or fifty years old, so you think of people [of] age, regardless of what color they are, as your elders. That is how I was brought up. You say, 'yes, ma'am,' 'yes, sir'— regardless of the color that people are. That's just giving people respect. Respect is something you got to give in life to get anywhere. For me buying something from his store, I didn't understand how to take that. For that one split second I didn't say anything 'cause I didn't know what was going on.

"I had already pumped the gas so there wasn't much I could do about that. But again, I'd been taught leadership and how to handle situations that weren't pleasant. That's one of the skills I was talking about. I want to respect everyone, but you have to respect me, too. I was a kid, but I was still a man. And as a man, I have to expect that.

"What I did was I wrote a letter to the owner of the organization. I took actions that were deeper than just cursing the man out. I took actions that were worthy of what he did to me. When I went in there the next time, the man wasn't there. They'd fired him."

The Mother's

2

Load

W̲e have a common enemy. We have this in common: We have
a common oppressor, a common exploiter . . . But once we
all realize that we have a common enemy, then we unite—on the
basis of what we have in common. And what we have foremost in
common is that enemy—the white man . . ."

As Malcolm X's harsh indictments of white American imperial-
ism bubbled over from my stereo system and filled my basement
bedroom, I could sense my mother upstairs listening to me listen
to him. And I knew that, as was increasingly becoming the case

when I surrendered my ears to Malcolm's speeches, she was worrying.

"If violence is wrong in America, violence is wrong abroad. If it is wrong to be violent defending Black women and Black children and Black babies and Black men, then it is wrong for America to draft us and make us violent abroad in defense of her. And if it is right for America to teach us how to be violent in defense of her, then it is right for you and me to do whatever is necessary to defend our people right here in this country . . ."

It wasn't so much Malcolm's words that disturbed her. As much as the recorded speeches I'd blast seemed to sometimes shock her senses, my Alabama-bred mother also knew what conditions Malcolm was talking about. Though, like many Black Americans, she often opted to couch her pain in quieter terms, my mother's bouts with racism left me with little doubt that she knew the observations that gave bite to Malcolm's calumnies were deathly real.

It was, I think, Malcolm's unbridled rage—the burning, righteous fury that informed his talks—that stirred Moms's concerns. To her mind, Malcolm X's moral indignation amounted to nothing short of sheer race hatred, to a blind and blanket loathing of whites that her Christian heart refused to embrace. She feared that one day I would adopt that anger as my own, that I too would come to "hate every white person you see."

When the phonograph needle lifted, I trudged to the foot of the basement stairs and gulped down two deep breaths. Quietly steeling myself for the debate I knew awaited me in the kitchen where she sat, I found myself grinning in anticipation. As heated as our debates could get, I loved talking to Moms—no matter the topic or the fact that our positions on it would invariably be polar opposites. My mother had long ago turned our home into a marketplace of ideas, stoking intellectual discourse about everything from the nightly news to the gossip of the ghetto grapevine.

Ever since I had begun college two years back, race had swiftly eclipsed everything else as our central point of exchange.

Once upstairs, I pushed open the door and walked past Moms to the kitchen sink. Her hands busied themselves with the crinkly, beige paper of her dress pattern. Her eyes on a bolt of cloth draped over the table in front of her, she wasted little time trying to measure just what crazy ideas Malcolm had filled me with this time.

"Darrell, why d'you listen to that stuff?" she asked. She was smiling, too, though her knitted brow told me it was as much a sign of anxious parental curiosity as of her own love for our talks.

"'Cause it's the truth, Ma," I responded, knowing full well so absolute an answer would set it off—and fast. "Malcolm spoke the truth. People were just afraid to hear it. And they still are."

"Malcolm hated, Darrell. He was angry, and he was bitter. That's no way to get anything done."

"Malcolm wasn't anti-white, Ma. He was pro-Black. He loved Black people—and was as critical of our behavior, our inaction and gullibility, as of anyone's. If he was bitter, well, he had good reason to be. Look at what white people have done to us. . . ."

On and on it went: Moms arguing passionately against what she saw as Malcolm's needless anger and hatred, me parrying her arguments with my own condemnations of white supremacism.

Through it all, my love for Malcolm's wisdom remained undiminished, and I believe my mother's disdain for him ebbed the better acquainted she became with his ever-expanding ideas. Still, I never understood her fears of Malcolm's rage, why she worried so about it sparking the anger of my own young soul.

Years later, I think I have some idea. Hers, I believe, was the abiding dread of most Black mothers: She feared for her child's life.

America, after all, has little use for "angry" Black men. Understand, I don't mean angry in any gangsta sense of the word, wherein outrage is defined in dead-end attacks on our own through drive-bys and drug deals. Neither do I mean angry as in frustrated accommodationism, in which our struggle becomes protests for better wages, senior partnerships or more black cops in the hood.

No, I mean angry the way Malcolm was angry, the way Fred Hampton was angry, the way Mark Essex and Nat Turner and Zayd Shakur were angry. Angry enough to love, live and labor for the whole of Black people. And if need be, angry enough to die for Black people.

For men such as these, America holds only contempt, jail and, perhaps, a shallow grave or two.

It was this sort of rage I admired. Understand, I had not yet grown into a full appreciation of the keen intellect and overpowering love for Black humanity that informed this anger. I was still young, caught up in romantic notions about revolution, not yet a respecter of the labor and pain and sacrifice that lifelong struggle demands. But I knew the rage was justified, and I honored it, let it run its course. It was this sort of rage that inflamed my mother's concerns.

Don't get confused, now. Moms hasn't made it to forty-*ahem* by being anybody's coward. She's been known to dress down everybody from the rowdiest fellas around the way to the snottiest of the rich white men who've lorded over the various bank offices where she's worked. She and my late great aunt Kat were also tough enough teenagers to help raise two knuckleheaded little brothers after their mother died and their father collapsed under the weight of alcoholism.

No, her fear for me wasn't about faintness of heart; it was about her unwillingness to allow unchecked rage to claim her baby. And what mother—for that matter, what Black man, woman or child—isn't scared, given the trauma America, Inc. has inflicted on us in the name of profit and race superiority and a few kicks. Still, hers was a fear I felt Black people could no longer afford.

Moms's fear didn't operate at the surface of her awareness. I doubt if she realized how frightened she seemed whenever our talks turned to the outrage that accompanied my burgeoning Black consciousness. For her, the terror went by softer names: tact, diplomacy, moderation, discretion.

And fairness, of course, was the ideal that justified these euphemisms. Time and again, her arguments transformed into moral appeals, as Moms urged that Black people "not do to white people what they've done to us."

I tried to convince her that mine was not reactionary rage, but the fury that demanded action, activism. I tried to tell her that, in matters of race, there was no room for diplomatic silence, that Black people's reluctance to give honest voice to our trauma only made us quiet collaborators in our own oppression. And with all my heart, I tried to explain that, even if we wanted to, Black people could never do to whites what they've done to us.

"Ma, we're not oppressed because of anything we've done," I would argue. "We're not poor or miseducated or despairing because we asked to be. Shoot, we didn't even ask to be in this country. It's not like being angry and speaking the truth will make matters any worse."

Deep down, I felt as though I was repeating what she already knew, what she chose to forget—or, at least, to ignore. Perhaps she thought this the genuinely right thing to do. Perhaps she simply believed it the safest thing to do.

Either way, my Moms was wrong, dangerously wrong.

Moreover, she wasn't alone. Too many Black parents refuse to equip their children with the tools to navigate the turbulence of American racial waters, largely because they themselves are poorly prepared. They make us believe things are getting better, when in truth they're worsening. They make themselves believe they are shielding us, when in fact they're leaving us vulnerable and unarmed.

They mean well, I know. They mean to buoy us, to give us confidence and a head start on survival. And in this, ofttimes, our parents do confer on us the potential to grow into an honest understanding of our lot, of a mastery of the tools needed to improve it.

Ultimately, though, in refusing to speak honestly to the stark intractability of racism in America, too many of our elders only extend our lease on confusion for yet another generation.

"I've done all I can," Moms once told me as we debated various Black liberation ideologies. "I've done my part. I've raised a healthy, intelligent son who's not dead, on drugs or in jail. What else do you want me to do? That's enough, isn't it?"

Ma, as much as I laud and appreciate your work—more than doing "your part," you've been mother, father and friend—no, it's not enough. Sadly, no one person's is.

As long as the conditions surrounding your son threaten to undo that work, as long as death, drugs and jail remain real options for Black men and women, it can never be enough.

In fact, it's just the beginning.

Heavy is the womb that bears Black boys.

It is, after all, the mother lode, crucible to men and mankind alike. Humanity drew its first breaths there, and civilization found its origins. Our mothers have given the world rulers and revolutionaries, scholars and soldiers. Black mothers have given the world life.

In America, hardship and struggle have been their recompense. Here, our mothers saw themselves pimped in service of chattel slavery, their wombs opened for the business of brutality. Their children were born to serve, to be sold or, if not, to be slain.

Still, they endured.

They held families together with determination, courage, grit. They survived both labor pains and the pains of slavery's labor. For freedom, they fought, killed, died. And, as always, Black mothers kept right on giving life.

Today, the struggles continue, and thus, so do the triumphs. Our mothers rear genius in an America that scoffs at Black intellect. They conjure pride in children ashamed of simply being. And, in their hands, minimum wage jobs become like lead to an alchemist.

As always, death shadows them, their seed. They used to see their boys auctioned off to unknown plantations; now, they weep as damn-near a generation of us are carted away to maximum-security netherworlds. They used to see us lynched; now, they cradle our corpses in blood-soaked streets.

Through it all, their love remains transcendent, unconditional. They love us when we're right, when we're wrong. They love in spite of all we think we are, all we'll ever—and never—be. No doubt, some of our mothers fear us, for reasons real and imagined, but they embrace us nevertheless. We're their sons.

And just as their sons have been demonized, so have they. The Black mother has been reincarnated as the worst sort of social parasite, from crack 'ho to welfare queen. She's the bug-eyed, bullying matriarch on that "new" sitcom, the cold-hearted careerist bitch on the talk shows.

Still, Mama endures.

Which isn't to suggest our mothers are perfect. They aren't. Sometimes, their pressures—sexism, racism, mounting debts, fears that, one day, Junior might not make it home—become too intense, too heavy. Sometimes, they're just not prepared for the obligations of motherhood. Sometimes, fissures riddle their armor, and they go under, to drugs or to liquor or to a wholesale psychological shutdown. They hurt us. They use us. They leave us.

Who in America, however, can stand in judgment of Black mothers? Who can really know their burdens, their pains? Who can really know the fears and expectations and hopes of women whose sons, it often seems, are born only to die?

Black men may love our mothers, cherish and respect them. We may be as familiar with them as well as anyone.

But who, besides our mothers themselves, truly understands how heavy is the womb that bears Black boys?

SEKOU O., 17: THE INVISIBLE HAND

CHICAGO—Even before he was born, Sekou says, his mother was nurturing his intellect. A teacher at an African-centered school in Chicago, she often read textbooks to the baby boy bulging in her stomach.

"I learned a lot while in the womb," he says. "I came out and started reading at a very early age—almost like a prodigy. I was surprising everybody. I used to pick up the newspaper, look at it and my mother'd think I was just looking at it. But I started talking and I was reading. My brother used to bet his classmates that I could read better than them—and win. I didn't get no money out of it, though."

Nevertheless, the reading has paid off. At a time when more and more young brothers are catching bullets, court cases and jail terms with frightening frequency, Sekou is in his freshman year at Illinois Institute of Technology. He's a metallurgical engineering major and on scholarship. So far, says the one-time high-school salutatorian, college has been a breeze.

But more than any grades or awards, Sekou credits his mother—the woman who read him phonics and Black history and primers even when he was a fetus—with getting him here. His Moms placed a premium on education, giving learning a priority Sekou saw most clearly reflected in the family's meager budget.

"She didn't spoil her children," says Sekou, who has an older sister and brother. "We never had much money. We were always some of the poorest kids on the block. But we always went to private school. She always provided."

Identity, though, carried as high a value as intellect in Sekou's household. His mother surrounded her children with information about African and African-American history and heritage. And she tried as well to teach by example, her practice transmitting lessons her child still hasn't forgotten.

"African culture was very much emphasized," says Sekou. "I used to speak Swahili when I was little. I used to go to the Shule Yawa Toto school. They shut it down now, but I used to go to that school and speak Swahili. My mother is very pro-Black. My godparents are pro-Black. My cousins are Muslims, so that was another pro-Black influence in my house. We had Halloween, and I used to go dressed in African garb. My mother is the type of person that everything has to be Black."

The baby boy, Sekou was doted on, and guarded, the most. Both his mother and sister kept him sheltered and in line.

"I was like a nerdy type of kid who read a lot of books," says Sekou. "I can't remember me going out much. I stayed in the house. My sister, I don't know if she cared for me more or not, but she looked out for me. She kept me from wild things that my brother was doing. She snitched on me or hit me when I was trying to do what my brother was doing. She kept me back and kept me in place."

THE MOTHER'S LOAD

An adage says that Black parents "raise their daughters and love their sons," giving the boys a latitude girl-children can only envy. While he insists that his mother attempted to guide all of the children with equal firmness, Sekou hints that his sister may have been asked to shoulder responsibilities the boys never took on. He talks often about his mother keeping his sister home to work while his brother, who's a year older than Sekou, hung out with friends. His sister, he says, was reared to be responsible, nurturing. His brother ran wild.

"My brother got into the wrong crowd, 'cause he normally finds the wrong crowd wherever he goes," says Sekou. "He can't be in one place very long. He has to be out roaming around."

Sekou believes that his older brother's troubles—arrest, drug dealing, theft, a possible homicide—compelled his mother to tighten the reins on her youngest child. She wasn't prepared to compete with the streets for another son. She made sure Sekou was loved and raised.

For the most part, his mother's firm hand did indeed steer Sekou away from many of the problems his brother encountered. As expected, the teacher's precocious child excelled in school.

"If my mother would have let me get the double promotions that I was offered, I probably would be a senior in college right now," says Sekou unassumingly. "I could have skipped first grade, second grade, all that, 'cause when I was two and three, my mother couldn't afford a baby-sitter so I had to go to school with her. I was sitting in class learning while she was teaching the older kids. By the time I was ready to go and start school, I was already on a higher level, and they couldn't place me, really."

For all his academic accomplishments, though, Sekou still felt the urge to be down, to prove his solidarity with the fellas. Occasionally, he confesses, peer pressure drove him to petty crimes, mostly small-time thefts meant to impress friends and, more important, his brother.

"My brother started doing such and such and he got me into it and I started doing it," Sekou says. "When I was fifteen, we robbed

Cadillacs off car lots, broke into stores. My brother is so influential. He influenced my boys into doing bad things. He asked me, and I'd be like, 'No, I ain't going to do it.' I know what kind of person he is, but they were saying, 'Cool, whatever.' He influenced them and after a while you get that peer pressure from your brother and your friends."

Sekou says that, despite all her teaching and guidance, his mother probably could never have stopped her sons from getting into some sort of trouble. The pull of the environment often was just too strong.

"My mother is one of the best mothers in the world, to me," he says. "I can't see no mother being better than her but even she couldn't stop me from doing what I felt I had to do. There are just some experiences I had to have."

But ultimately, his mother's influence triumphed. Try as he might, Sekou couldn't stray too far from her admonitions about right and wrong choices, about the bright future she'd equipped him to carve out for himself.

Further, Sekou didn't want to break his mother's heart the way he says his brother has. He's watched on plenty of nights as she shed tears for the older son she was afraid she was losing.

"I could tell she worried about him all the time," he says. "She used to cry about him, pray for him. I remember he told her that he shot and killed somebody. He had gotten into gang banging, selling drugs. Somebody tried to rob him for his jacket, and he shot the guy. He told my mother about that and she started crying on the phone. I just sat there. Later, she gave me a lecture about not getting into the things that he was doing."

But Sekou had already made up his own mind that he'd choose another path. The least he could do, he figured, was give his mother one less son to fret over.

These days, Sekou hopes that since he's away at college his mother will begin to enjoy the life she sacrificed so much of for her children. She's shepherded him safely to adulthood. Now, he wants her to live a little.

"She always has boyfriends but they never last that long," he says. "I never asked why. We let her do her own thing. I understand she's a woman and she needs sex or whatever. I ain't no little kid. I can understand that. When she has a boyfriend, that's her life. She has to be happy, too. Two months ago, she was asking me how I'd feel if she got married. I said I don't care. She should do what she wants to do."

After all, he notes, she's spent the last seventeen years of his life doing what she's had to do.

JAMAL D., 23: WHEN MAMA BREAKS DOWN

MIAMI—Sometimes, the loads grow too heavy, the strains too intense. Sometimes, the pressures and demands of parenting, of being —the same ones that often bear testimony to the resilience of many Black mothers—are simply too much. There are moments when our mothers stumble, and their minds give way—to drugs or alcohol or the murky chaos of an emotional breakdown.

It was this last form of collapse that would scar Jamal's upbringing.

He remembers clearly the day his mother surrendered, the day her own mind vanished down insanity's abyss. She just lost it one day. "Flipped," he says. A nervous breakdown right there in the middle of the house. There was a phone call, then a brief pause. Then sobbing. Then shrill, hysterical laughter.

She would spend the next month or two in a mental institution.

Jamal couldn't see it coming back then. Hell, he was only thirteen the day the house filled with that eerie laugh. How could he have known the weight she carried? How could he have known then that that weight was leaving stress fractures in Mommy's consciousness?

Today, he doesn't know how he didn't see it coming. The omens abounded. So did the pressures.

She was forever searching, his mother. Forever trying to find a fulfillment, a serenity, that seemed just as intent on remaining hidden from her. She'd sought it in romance, but the men seemed to leave almost as soon as she got comfortable with them. She'd sought it in friendships, but they'd often fizzled. She'd sought it in her children, but they too drained her.

Most of all, she'd sought it in God. She bounced her and her children from faith to faith, temple to temple, looking desperately for a peace she feared she'd never have. Through his mother, Jamal says, he was introduced to a panorama of religions: a version of Yoruba, Christianity, Jehovah's Witness. But nothing worked for her. Nothing seemed to confer the satisfaction, the peace his mother sought. Her spiritual trek turned into a treadmill.

Meanwhile, the burdens were mounting, her focus splintering. She had four boys to care for, to raise and steer through the asphalt free-fire zones that were fast replacing what Blacks in Jamal's native Boston used to call neighborhoods. One of her sons, Jamal's older brother, was already getting away from her: He was stealing from her, taking money to buy drugs. The others weren't as attracted to the streets, but neither did they seem to care for her.

Not even Jamal, her introverted second-oldest, the one with the penchant for computers, the one she'd pinned many of her hopes to even as she saw another child wasting his potential. Even Jamal didn't like her.

It wasn't like she hadn't tried to win them over. Hadn't she given them the latitude to speak their minds in the house, to vent and to engage her in discourse? Hadn't she tried to send them to good schools and ensure they received top-quality educations, even though there was barely enough money coming in to keep the lights on, even though their fathers hadn't lifted a finger to help out? Hadn't she tried to expose them to various cultures, various ways of seeing the world?

She had. Yet it all seemed to have failed her. The children. The men. The gods. So here she was: young, black, smart, no husband, four boys—the youngest about a year old—little money and only the faintest traces of a college education. Her older children seemed either alienated or at risk. The babies had different sets of needs, though the diaper changing and feeding times were no less demanding.

She'd had dreams, too, you know. Didn't want to live out life on welfare the way others in her family had. Wanted to be something, a doctor maybe. But the hopes all seemed so far off now. Her life had continued without them, had left them behind, had jumped out to a start before she'd even had a chance to get set. There was no starting over now. It all seemed so much, so soon . . .

Then the phone rang.

"She was chilling out on the phone, then she was like 'Whaaaat?!' And she just freaked. She started screaming, laughing and crying and going nuts. I was like, 'Damn.' "

It would be years later before Jamal would learn about the call, that it was from a friend informing his mother about the death of an old acquaintance. An acquaintance who, when his mother was younger, had raped her.

The stress fractures opened into gaping maws.

For the next three or four weeks, she tried to live as though she hadn't gotten the call, as though all was well and normal. Her mind refused to cooperate.

"She was flipped for a while. One of the things that told me was when we went to the park. She had her purse with her. This guy came and took the purse and ran. She just sat there. She was saying, 'It doesn't matter. It will solve itself. There will be no problem.' I wasn't understanding that she was technically insane. Maybe she needed to be committed. She wasn't getting any help."

She found help a brief time later, though, leaving the children to be cared for by an uncle. The kids didn't know much, just that Mommy was sick, that she had to leave to take a rest for a while. She had just gone to the hospital for a little while. Jamal sensed that something was wrong, but he was so terrified by the sight of his mother's breakdown on the phone that he just withdrew further into his shell, turning more than ever to his computers.

When she returned home, though, she returned whole, Jamal says, having confronted for the first time the trauma of a rape she'd tried to deny for years. She returned whole, inspired and, for the first time in a long time, at peace.

No, the problems didn't vanish. But where she couldn't before, Jamal's mother found the will to handle them. Her oldest son still ran wild, but she was able to draw closer to him nonetheless. She and Jamal, meanwhile, became the best of friends. She's currently working toward a master's degree.

Jamal speaks frankly of her trials and triumphs out of pride, yes, but also out of a disturbed recognition that his family isn't alone in its experience. Mental illness has long abounded in Black America, the consequence of centuries of enduring the punishing malevolence of white supremacism, poverty, degradation. He hears the hushed tones in which we speak of so-and-so's nervous breakdown and how whatchamacallit's father or brother just "lost it the other day."

Sure, we may act as if it's okay, as though therapy is some sort of anathema. We may pretend that we can ignore it all, the psychic scars, the collective nightmares, the cold detachment from ourselves and our realities. But all too often, our wounds are eating us alive and driving us crazy.

"It took my mother years of exploration. It took the phone call, that was what triggered everything. She was coming to understand that she had been duped since day one, like all of us have in this society. We're trained to believe that we are not worth anything. Trained to believe that we are supposed to submit to our man— which is crap. Trained to think that we are supposed to push things under the rug. That is what the women's liberation movement is about. She came to understand that the whole traumatic experience was something that she had to learn from. Now, she's hooking up with the right people. She is really connected with the world and the universe."

THE MOTHER'S LOAD

RAYMOND ROYCE,* 18: A CYCLE OF ABUSE

DETROIT—The social worker has already run down for me the file on Raymond: bright, sincere, hot-headed, emotionally disturbed. "He's basically a good kid, man, but he comes from some serious abuse in the home," he explains in the near-vacant conference room here at the Detroit boys' home where Raymond lives. "His family's fucked up, mostly because of his Old Girl, his Moms. His mother used to get mad and just beat his ass. She was crazy, straight up. Still is. One time—and you're not going to believe this—but one time, when he was a baby, his Moms threw him, I mean threw him, across the room and into a wall. They had to take that boy to the hospital."

Moments later, I'm still trying to catch my breath from this last revelation as we walk downstairs into the social worker's office to meet Raymond. As he and I shake hands, I search Raymond's face, his posture, for signs of stress and abuse. Instead, all I see is a fidgety Black teenager, hair cut in a low fade, small gap between his front teeth, short, compact. He sits forward in his straight-backed chair. Then sits back. Then forward again. He wrings thick hands over each other, then straightens and knifes his fingers into his waistband as he tucks his T-shirt into his khakis.

He's polite to a fault, repeatedly calling me "sir" despite my assurances that I'm still too young to fit the title.

He could be nervous, I think at first. Then, remembering the social worker's horror stories, I realize that nerves have little to do with it. It hits me that I'm watching Raymond struggle to muster the courage necessary to recount his story once again, to resurrect memories of the home life that ultimately landed him in this boys' home. Not until he begins do I realize how much of that courage he must need.

"My mama said I got the blood of my father," he says. "She

* Not his real name.

always called me crazy. Mama was always egging me on, aggravating me.

"See, my father was a real mean and feisty person, fought all the time, committed murders as well. He did some crazy stuff, sold drugs back in the seventies. In seventy-two, he killed a man, went to jail for about a year and a half but got out 'cause a friend took the fall for him, said he had done it. I knew my father did it. My mama didn't let me in on why. It's probably over some drugs or some man owing my daddy. My daddy was crazy. He was a wild man. They called him Evil Eye. He was real crazy all around.

"And mama said I was going to be like my father—crazy."

I think about the social worker's concerns for Raymond's temper, the fear he has that "one day, this lil' brother is going to get mad and kill somebody if he doesn't watch out." I ask Raymond whether he'd ever bought into his mother's calumnies, whether he truly believed his temper some sort of genetic heirloom. He never did, he says. He knows from whence his anger stems. He picked it up at home, he tells me, a home perpetually filled with rancor, despair and the clamor and screams of domestic violence.

"My stepdad is an alcoholic," he says. "Every time he'd go off drinking he'd come back home slapping on mama. It was like he was crazy. He'd slap my mama in the face; Mama slapped on me . . . That's part of the reason I'm not comfortable around a lot of people, I'm not very friendly at times. People always tell me I'm mean, I'm a stone-hearted person, I don't care too much. Sometimes I do, sometimes I don't. Depends on my mood swing."

Raymond says his stepfather beat his mother without mercy or relent, often sending her to the hospital with cuts and contusions. The children feared he'd kill her one day. He certainly seemed to be trying hard enough.

"I seen him straight-up slap her, knock her down, knock her out," says Raymond. "I seen him push my mama into the door, dislocate her arm and, on top of that, hit her up. She stabbed him with a butterfly knife once, and he came in the house trying to stab her with one of them machete. My mother would have been dead. I was crazy over that."

THE MOTHER'S LOAD

The most frightening incident, Raymond says, came one evening when his mother confronted her husband about his chronic infidelity:

"One time my man came back drunk. Mama asked him, 'What you doin' all night; why you ain't come home?' My man kept telling her, 'I was working. I was working.' He was smelling like whiskey. He was at the door, staggering in. My older brother was there then. Mama said, 'Why you didn't come home last night, George?' I went to get something to eat, got his belly full. Mama kept asking, 'Why didn't you come back home? Why didn't you come back home and check on us?' Then he started saying, 'I was working late.' Mama said, 'Yeah, you was sleeping with somebody else! I know you was!' And George said, 'Baby, I told you—I was working and all that shit.' Mama said, 'Don't cuss at me.' My brother Mark spoke up to George, said, 'You know you was, you know you wrong, George. You know what you were doing last night. The girl was preaching to me about what you did.' George really got fired up then 'cause he knew the truth was that my brother Mark knows everybody. That girl even described George. She described that man. So he started to tell my brother to shut the fuck up. Then Mama, she started getting outrageous, too. George like, 'Shut the fuck up, wife, shut the fuck up.' He started going off the wall. Mama started saying, 'George you gonna hear it; George, you gonna hear it.' And George says, 'Shut up, bitch!' And Mama says, 'Fuck you, nigga. Get the fuck out of my house.' George says, 'Well, then, bitch, I will.' As soon as he step out of that door, he looks at her and he got in a big fit, big fit.

"He just looked at her and—*bam!*—hit my mama so hard she hit the door, hit the wall. *Boom!* When she hit the wall, she ricocheted off and hit the floor. She just fainted. After that he just looked at her."

As with most of the beatings his stepfather inflicted on his mother, Raymond and his brother broke it up. As with most of the beatings, little in the household changed. His mother stayed with the man. The children grew ever more frightened, resentful of the adults raising them. And the violence that their mother was unable to return to her husband, she unleashed on her sons and daughters.

He'd slap my mama in the face; Mama slapped on me.

In some ways, Raymond tells me, he has come to see the beatings he suffered as "family tradition."

"We're from the South, and parents from the South whip their kids with anything they can get their hands on," says Raymond, who was born in Mississippi and moved to Michigan as a toddler. "I don't care if it's an extension cord or a knife or a skillet. It's in them. Family tradition. She whipped me with switches, hit me with broomsticks . . . Maybe she tried to raise me the way my grandmama raised her, about all the whippings and stuff."

In some ways, Raymond's "family tradition" assessment may be correct. Many Black parents do whip their children frequently, a tradition that has roots in our peoples' history as white folks' chattel and, later, their sharecroppers and servants. Parental beatings were administered to keep Black children quiet and passive, to teach them the common sense and safety of subservience in an era wherein brashness in Black kids often raised a murderous ire in slaveholders and overseers. An outspoken child could easily be lynched for speaking out of turn or acting in the brazen, daring manner that young children often do. Parents beat their children to keep them alive.

Plenty of Black parents have abandoned physical punishment as a form of discipline, unconvinced of its effectiveness in communicating long-lasting lessons. But in at least as many other quarters of Black America, the tradition has held (primarily because of the same antebellum fear that, unless broken, the defiant spirits of Black children still invite death). To this day, many of us tend to look askance at child-abuse activists who wag disapproving fingers every time Moms or Pops snatches a belt from around their waistline.

Still, we figure we know the difference between whippings and outright torture. No matter the community's division around the efficacy of corporal punishment, few would argue that what Raymond Royce endured at his mother's hand was anything short of raw, mean-spirited abuse.

THE MOTHER'S LOAD

As bad as the beatings were, though, Raymond says the verbal abuse he and his siblings faced may somehow have been worse. When she was drunk, his mother often taunted her five children, attacking them and the three men who fathered them. His mother's soul ached, like her battered body, tormented from years of being impregnated and abandoned, beaten and degraded.

"Mama would get drunk and she would start preaching," Raymond tells me, "talking about all the husbands she had, talking stupid. Then she'd start talking about my father. She'd go all out on my father: 'Out of all the husbands I've been with, he's the worst, that crazy nigger's daddy.' She'd talk about me in front of everybody. I'd just sit there and listen. [She'd] point at me: 'Yeah, you, nigga! Your daddy put scars on my face, beat on me and all this, your daddy put me through hell.' So after about a half hour of this, I'd say, 'That's why you dog me, 'cause of what my daddy did to you. My daddy left you a long time ago, before I was born. Then, when I was born, nigga didn't buy me nothing. What do you think he did to me?' "

Raymond says the abuse wasn't contained to his home. He says his mother also humiliated in public.

"I remember one time when I was in this store," he says. "You know kids, they want toys. I was little, and I saw this toy I wanted. Remember the Stretch Monsters? They have gum in the middle of them. I wanted one so bad 'cause my brother would always get stuff. So Mama went shopping and I pointed out what I wanted, and she wouldn't get it, claimed she had no money. So I started crying real bad, and she hit me in the head. In front of everybody. Started calling me all kinds of names and everything. I was little."

Through it all, though, Raymond says he's begun to scour away the stain of resentment his mother's abuse left on his spirit. He says he doesn't hate her. In fact, he takes time to detail much of what he loves about his mother—the garden she'd grow to feed her kids, her generosity to neighbors.

And despite his mother's steadfast refusal to visit Raymond at the youth center, one of many where he's lived off and on since he was fourteen, Raymond makes clear that he still values the relationship with his mother. He just hopes he can forgive her one day.

Their relationship is "not over—but I just can't be the son," asserts Raymond. "You have to be the son [biologically], but you can't be running back to Mama. You know you ain't going to have no good memories about it."

QUINCY HALL, 16, AND ROBERT SOMERVILLE, 15: HARD HEADS

OMAHA, NEBRASKA—Sometimes, Mama can't catch you before you near the precipice. Sometimes, she isn't strong enough or fast enough or alert enough to stop you from skirting the edge. Sometimes, the roar of the TV, of the videos and movies and parties, are too loud for you to hear her. So you sprint for the edge, deciding somewhere along the way that you can do without all the cautionary tales about gang banging and drug dealing, without all this talk about staying in school and out of trouble.

You're not a bad boy. Nobody'll attest to that quicker than Mama. But the streets present a lure you cannot resist. You don't understand the insidious danger that Mama warns of. If you're Robert, you're a lanky, quick-witted fifteen-year-old whose only real solace seems to be in your status as a member of north Omaha's Jaynes Street Gangstas, a Crip set you hooked up with in junior high. If you're Quincy, you're an amiable but hot-headed part of a local Bloods crew, down to die for your red bandanna since you were twelve.

You know Mama's worried about you, but you're not totally sure why. Okay, so you've seen some homeys fall in drive-bys and gang fights. That's not going to happen to you, is it? And even if it does, you can handle it, right? And if you can't, well, everybody's got to go sometime, huh? So you keep moving toward the precipice.

Mama can try to stop you. She can take the belt to that ass. She can lock you in your room or snatch your TV privileges or cuss you out like a sailor. But you keep moving. You're fifteen, sixteen, but you feel much older. You tell yourself lies like "I need to learn for myself" or "She don't know how it is out here," not knowing that Mama's forgotten more about how it is out here than you'll probably ever remember. To you, it's all in what little bit of fun you can scare up around the way. Mama knows it's much more, and she tries to stop you before you, too, learn—the hard way. Deep down, though, she knows she can't stop you. She knows that she can only pray that you learn enough to stop yourself.

You know this, too. Brash in this knowledge, you inch close to the edge. She can't stop you.

But something way down tells you Mama's right. You know it. You just don't show it. She's that little voice that keeps telling you you don't need to be on this corner or in this dope spot. She's the one that tells you to quit the gang, to hit the books. Someone turns up the stereo a mite louder. Still, you hear her behind you, calling, warning, helpless. There are times, like this one, sitting on some old bleachers at a park near Forty-second Street and Ames in the heart of the north Omaha ghetto, when you acknowledge her desperate efforts to turn you around. And even as you creep ever closer to the precipice, you take a moment to look back . . .

QH: What happened when my mother found out I joined a gang? My mom at first was mad 'cause she saw me wearing all red. She used to get all my red clothes and put them in a bag. She felt that I'd gotten away from her. But what could she do about it? She couldn't stop me. She didn't say nothing about it. She knows everybody around here and everybody knows me.

She thinks about moving to Indiana. She got the control right now. If I go there I can start over again and do something different.

She still punishes me, too. I haven't got no whippings since I don't know when—a long time—but she still puts me on punishment. No TV or whatever. My mom tries to be strict, but then she lets me do some things, too, that I wanted to do. If there is a problem that she sees that I got, she'll talk to me about it. She does not say nothing like other moms who can't talk to their sons—'cause that's when you get in trouble, when you don't have no guidance. So she tells me to stay in school and all that. I'm not going to drop out, either. She wants me to graduate, and I think I should graduate, too, because then if I graduate I can look back and say that I done something. And my mom didn't graduate—that's why she wants me to do something.

RS: That is how my mom is, too. I told myself when I was about twelve, if I don't do nothing else with my life I am going to graduate from high school. I am going to at least have one piece of paper that said I did do something. Even if it ain't an award from police academy or mayor or councilman. At least I will graduate from high school.

QH: But about the gang, nah, she can't stop me. She still tells me that she is still worried about me. I know why. It's bad out here and me, I'm out here and anything can happen. I just can't say that I know that I'm not going to get shot. I could just be walking somewhere and somebody is shooting at somebody else and a bullet might hit me.

So I know this, but she knows I'm serious about it. I think she's figured out that I wanted to do it. That's just the way it is.

RS: How does my Moms feel about me being in a gang? Well, she knows and she stressed about it a lot and that is why she worries about me not coming home every once in a while—because she feels like I might have gone to jail or got shot. I know it makes her worry, but there ain't too much she can say about it. If I could change, I wouldn't even be in no gang. If I could just turn back and just be like, "Forget it, I ain't in no gang," I would do it. It won't do no good now. If I do, everybody would still think "he is still in the gang." I would probably still get shot and that would just make me mad.

Okay, I could not be a gang member but people are still going to be shooting people. The same people who had a grudge against you when you were in a gang are still going to have a grudge against you. My mom doesn't understand this when she talks about getting out.

THE MOTHER'S LOAD

She thinks I can just quit and there won't be any more problems. I try to tell her it's not like that, but she doesn't want to hear it.

ANDREW KIRKLAND, 19: IT TAKES A VILLAGE . . .

CHICAGO—There persists in this country a belief that women cannot teach their sons to be men. More than the obvious wisdom central to the maxim that "a boy needs his father," this particularly sexist strain of parental convention argues that, without a father present, the boys will grow up adrift, unsure of themselves and their manhood, denuded of the tools to survive and succeed.

Clearly, convention doesn't know the Kirklands.

Andrew grew up in Harlem in a parental crucible that was four sisters deep: his mother, his sister, his grandmother and his godmother. Each played a role in shaping him, in making an ambitious and bright young man of a boy whose father, an infrequent visitor to Andrew's life, never seemed to hang around for extended stays. There were other men around, an uncle, his mom's boyfriend, but like Andrew's dad, their influence was always secondary to that of the women who collectively reared him.

To be sure, Andrew's quartet of caregivers must've harbored their own private concerns of what the streets held for one more Black boy bereft of a quotidian male role model. But what were they to do? Wait around until some brother decided to show up and raise their child/lil' brother/grandbaby/godson? Instead, sexist convention once again got shot to hell.

"Four women," says Andrew, savoring the memories of growing up everybody's "little man." "They are the most important people in my life."

And it is a life whose promise is a testimony to their influence. At present, Andrew attends the Art Institute of Chicago, where he is specializing in three-dimensional animation. "You know," he explains, "like what they did in *Jurassic Park.*" He plans to finish by

1996, then hopes to develop a career in film and interactive video games.

There's nothing really lofty about his goal. Black boys dream big dreams all the time. But far too few of us have the road maps to make our fantasies real. Mom and Co. pressed Andrew's into his hands early.

"To be honest," he announces upon reconsideration, "they *are* my life. Period. Without any one of them, things would be different. I don't know how different or whatever—but different. More drastic with one missing than the other maybe, but there would be a change in my life if it wasn't for them. Those are the four people I give the most respect to."

They sustained Andrew like the elements, grounding him, driving him, stoking his intellectual curiosity as well as his Black consciousness. Mother Juanita was water, the source of life, the woman who nourished her younger child intellectually and morally.

"She made sure I was a pretty straight kid," says Andrew. "I didn't get into too much trouble. If I did do anything, I never got caught. I was pretty straight. Always pretty much good in school. My biggest thing was, even now, I can't let my Moms down. Really, my Moms had to be both; she had to be Moms and Pops. Even though Bill, her boyfriend, was there, she had to be both still."

His grandmother, he says, is his wind, a force that inspires and drives him to ever-higher pinnacles of aspiration. Knowing her life, her unquenchable zest for it, Andrew says, has made him realize that he could be so much more than even he sometimes dares to think. Most of all, she pushes him, lifts the sails of his own young soul whenever he feels too flat to keep moving. After all, Arlene Mooney, he tells me, is nothing if not a survivor.

"Nobody has ever asked me this, but my grandmother, her aura is just so positive and strong. It is like, 'How did you survive?' She grew up poor as hell. She's in her late fifties, sixty. She had six kids, one died, got shot. She was abused as a wife. Poor as hell and on welfare all the time. Never had a childhood. She has been through about fifteen operations, and she is still kicking. She is hardheaded as hell. She don't need to be doing this or that, but she's like, 'Fuck that.' She is trying to have fun in her life. You never know when you could die. The old saying, you only live once, so I guess that is what she has been living by. She still takes precautions 'cause she could have been gone a long time ago, but God must want her to live. She always prays that she lives long enough to see us become big and shit. She could have been gone a long time ago but I guess God blessed her with that last wish. There have been times when we thought she was going and sure enough she would pull right on through. I guess I ain't really looking for her to go no time soon. I am prepared if she does."

A factor in his life since he was a toddler, Andrew's godmother has been, in many ways, his earth, the footing a boy requires when scaling the slippery slopes of young manhood. Dale Thompson has kept Andrew sane at times, has imparted to her "adopted" son a calm and reassuring wisdom.

"A lot of people got godmothers that are just that in name," he says. "But this isn't about a title. She is like . . . well, we call her Mom. That is exactly what she is. I am fortunate to have two mothers. She just is there all the time for advice, financial help, whatever."

His sister, Rachel, meanwhile, has been his fire, stoking Andrew's social passions and kindling his political and cultural interests. She taught him, he says, what it means to be young and Black in America, what it means to challenge and resist and fight back. A graduate of Northwestern University, she also schooled her sibling in the power of aggressiveness, of showing no relent in the pursuit of his goals. At twenty-two, she is only three years his senior, but she's invested a lifetime of learning in her younger brother.

"She was a big inspiration growing up," says Andrew. "I sort of wanted to follow in her footsteps. My sister is real Afrocentric. I happen to be Afrocentric myself. I am not as militant as she is, but I'm definitely pro-Black. I'm ready to go to drastic measures, too, but she is more of an activist. She does more than I do. She is just like, 'I am going to go do this,' and then she'll turn around and do it. She's like a teacher almost. Not on a corny, be-all-you-can-be level. She's like, 'Straight up! Do this shit, stop bull shitting, get this done.'

"Another thing: Sometimes I try to be cautious. I don't like to offend people straight up in their face. But she doesn't give a fuck. Even so, she is kind of in better control. She is the one that got me into the struggle. I am a follower behind that. My sister is a crazy big inspiration in my life. If it wasn't for her I might not be doing as good as I am, either."

Four women. Four indomitable souls. Just the sort of village it takes to raise a child.

"It's their spirits," says Andrew. "They're all different, but all of their spirits are just incredible."

RAS BARAKA, 24: MOTHER'S WIT

NEWARK, NEW JERSEY—Political consciousness can be, at times, a double-edged sword. On one hand, it can urge you onward in struggle, keeping your mind clear and your spirit stout. You know what you face and you arm yourself accordingly.

But for a parent, such awareness can also exact a high toll. For to know the evils of racism, to know what oppression can do to your family, your children, is a daunting realization indeed. Sure, you prepare yourself, steel your children. Sometimes, though, your worst nightmares come true anyway. Sometimes, despite your best efforts, America eats your young.

Ras has seen the price his mom has paid in the course of raising her sons. He has watched her suffer through seeing one son shot and another jailed. And while she has had plenty of cause to rejoice —even in the heat of urban woe child-rearing remains a treasured endeavor—Ras explains that she has also shed innummerable tears. But more than simply for her own family, Amina Baraka, he says, has shed tears for children she doesn't even know, for the countless

THE MOTHER'S LOAD

black men shot down in this nation's streets daily, for the tens of thousands caged in America's jails.

She understands why they sit there, in the graveyards and in the prisons. She knows the desperate measures racism and capitalism have driven them to. A writer and activist, she fights to change these conditions. She organizes and reaches out and teaches and lectures. But each life lost, each Black future cut short by bars or bullets, is just one more measure of the success of her foes, one more tiny piece of her heart cut out.

You fight her fight long enough and you come to know the possibility, the likelihood, of losing. So it's not that Ras's mom doesn't recognize that our communities will suffer setbacks and defeats. But losing, whether that loss is defined by her own children's troubles or the devastation of other black lives, hurts all the same.

And it costs.

"My mother is a nervous wreck, man," Ras says. "My mother smokes and she drinks and she never did that when she was younger. She was one of those health people when she was younger, very nutritious, never ate this and that.

"My little brother got shot in the head two or three years ago. He is the youngest one in the family. He got shot in the head with a .357. He lived but my mother . . . My oldest brother is in jail. He is locked up and has been locked up all together maybe two or three years, back and forth.

"My mother is always nervous about what is happening because our community is in such disarray. You got to be careful when you walk in the streets, and you got to watch out for the police 'cause they might do something to you. You might be hit by a stolen car, or this one got into a fight and they shot him. My mother is scared. Most Black mothers are afraid for their own children.

"Once, my brother was having a fight in front of the house. The guy pulled out a gun. My mother ran to the guy with the gun and grabbed him and held the gun. She was talking to him, holding the gun in his hand and saying, 'I can't let you shoot my son.' This is what she was saying: 'Don't make me make a choice between you and him.' She was talking him out of fighting. She said, 'When the police come they are going to lock everybody up. They don't care.' While she was out there, more guys had come around the corner from Eleventh Street. My little brother ran and got more people. By this time, all of us were out there, all types of people. It really could have got wild—but my mother squashed the whole thing. I have seen her do that on a lot of occasions. But she's nervous.

"Another time, my brothers went to a basketball tournament in what we call The Hole. The Hole is on Prince Street in the projects. My mother thinks about you down there on Prince Street and is like, 'You all shouldn't be down there playing basketball.' My little brothers would be like, 'Oh, God'—but I understand. It's not that she don't want them down there 'cause of anything she thinks about the people. She is afraid for their lives! She knows that things are rougher down there because making a living is rougher. You got to make ends meet, and when people live like that they go all out. Police are all over the place down there. You could be mistaken for this one and that one, plus the fact that you are Amiri and Amina Baraka's son.

"My mother is always fearful—but she deals with it. She writes and tries to allow all of the friends to come in the house. She tries to organize us, politicize us, make us see what is happening and what is going on. She lets people come in her house and stay. That's how she deals with what is happening in the community, and she tries to change it in some way that she can."

When he was younger, Ras says, she schooled him less through conversation than by example. He watched her pull political groups together, saw her challenge daily the contradiction of American racism and capitalism. And though his father, the poet and playwright Amiri Baraka, was better known, Ras says his mother exercised a sweeping influence over his life that often affected him far deeper than any of his father's famed works.

Ras: "My mother has a very great influence on what I think emotionally and what I believe. My passion for my father, the ideas and stuff, is there, and a lot of that formulation, looking up to him and what he thinks, had an effect—but you don't make a choice about your family. You can grow up in a family full of Jehovah's Witnesses, strict religious family, and you can come out an atheist, so it really doesn't make a difference 'cause you make your own choice once you have the ability to.

"My mother is really the one who allowed me to make the choice to become involved in activist struggle, not because she sat down and told me to. My mother and father never sat down with us and said, 'This is this, the white man, capitalism, such and such.' Never did that. It is just watching my mother struggle and the passion that she has. My mother will cry over somebody she don't even know. You tell her that somebody got hurt in the community —that will hurt her. She has a relationship to that. She thinks that could be her son. That's what she thinks. She really has a passion for this. She grew up in a working-class family, and it was hard for her most of her life. She wanted to be an actress and a singer. Gave that up to have my father's children, as well as be politically active, and so what she feels and how she says it has made me know that what I'm doing has got to be correct. Because if my mother likes it, then it's got to be right.

"I think I've got a close relationship with my mother. I think it is becoming closer as I get older because, now that I have my own ideas, my mother and I have discussions and we talk. Now, she finds me. We talk and I come and show her stuff or say, 'Guess what happened to me today?' more so than I do my father. We think alike, a whole lot alike. My passion for struggle has developed a lot just by watching and observing her.

"When I was younger, we weren't as close. My family traveled a lot, and my mother was always involved in a lot of stuff and my sisters usually baby-sat us a lot. My mother did a lot for us and tried to be active at the same time. It was difficult because she was teaching African pre-school, and she took care of a lot of people's children. I guess in some way that affects your relationship with her. Plus, as a younger guy you're too busy trying to be too hard to have decent conversation with your mother or to act toward your mother in some affectionate way—other than wanting to fight people 'cause they talked about her. That had a lot to do with it. My respect for my mother is just getting greater as I get older because I am able to see more.

"She made her mistakes. I think everybody makes mistakes. A lot of mistakes that my mother made had to do with the situation that she was in. Trying to be active. Trying to be the wife of Amiri Baraka and a mother to these children at the same time. And there were differences my mother and father had. Some of them were class differences that caused arguments and fights. That and a lot of the tension and stuff might have been misdirected to us when we were younger. But my mother would go all out for us. We knew that when we were little. She would come to school and rant and rave if she had to—barefoot. It's hard for me to say she made a mistake 'cause she did the best job that she could under the given circumstances. That's all you ask of most people. That is what you get respect for. Some people think less of them 'cause they didn't do what you thought they should do—but they did the best damn job they could do under the given circumstances. Given circumstances might be very little money, no help in the house, no man, got to work two jobs, got a drinking problem at the same time. Given the circumstances a lot of women do a hell of a job. I think we tend to be harsher because of sexism about what women did and the things that they didn't do as opposed to the men."

Ras recalls the sacrifices his mother made during his childhood, the burdens she bore trying to mother a family in the midst of the turmoil of grassroots political action. He doesn't think her burdens all that unique in some ways. Other black women must know what it means to fear for their children, must know what it means to see their sons and husband walk out the door and not know if they'll return breathing, must know what it means for the children's fathers to be away for any significant period of time, be it on business or bullshit. He figures that most black mothers, political or not, endure some level of strain that men often don't see. He's irked by the stigmas that often compound their loads.

"My father wasn't in the home a lot, so in some ways she was a single mother. And this stereotype about the single mother, it bothers me all the time. One time I was talking to my mother about it and she drove it home more: The bourgeois idea says that the single-headed household is the reason why the family is messed up and the man is messed up.

"No, the reason why the man is messed up is because we live under white supremacy and capitalism. That's why society is messed up. The single-headed household, these women have been raising children by themselves since the beginning of time. Even when the man is there, the women raise the children anyway. There are women who have had fifteen, sixteen children and have to raise them all and the men, too. It is a phenomenal task to be a mother. I think that this is putting the blame on the single mother. 'You can't do it by yourself, you need a man there'—like we have just discovered that we need men in families. You need a man in the family because he belongs there. He made the family so he ought to be there to help raise the family. But don't attack the mothers. Because the man is not there does not mean that the family is dysfunctional. I know. Sometimes, my mother was the only one there. And she raised me right."

Man's

Child

You leave me messages that I don't return. You await phone calls I don't make. You look for visits, cards, letters, some sign, any sign that I know you're out there somewhere thinking about me. You don't get them, so you think I'm mean, bitter, that I don't understand you.

You think I don't understand, but I do.

You think I don't know how you must've felt, why you were so compelled to run. You think I can't understand that you were a young man, twenty-four years old, a cab driver, in and out of jail, already father of one child from another relationship. And, now, oh, great, here I come, yet another bundle of obligations and sacrifices.

It was Detroit, 1967. Black America was in the throes of racial tumult, targets of a government that branded us enemies of the state because we dared to dream freedom. Likewise, you were dreaming, too. Wanted to be an R&B singer, I heard. You moved east, said you'd send for us. You didn't.

Some five years later, I see you for the first time I can recall. I'm next door, at Ms. Dickey's eating a ham sandwich. My mother calls me home. I bounce up the steps into the living room, where you're standing, tall, dark, gaunt. Even then I could see the resemblance, see my reflection shimmering on the surface of your gene pool.

Most vividly, though, I remember your first words to me, right after Moms introduced us rather unceremoniously. You looked at the Wonder Bread sticking to my fingertips and asked what I was eating. I told you a ham sandwich from next door. You snatched it, tossed off a no-nonsense frown and, like a good Muslim should, began explaining loudly and sternly why pork would kill my kinder-gartner ass. And damn if you didn't wag your finger.

My five-year-old skin crawled, and I could feel myself being vis-ited by that sense of tense discomfort that would become a fixture in any room we occupied at the same time. I made up my mind right then: I didn't like you.

Images of that first exchange have endured not merely as some personal milestone. They've meant more. Over the years since, I've come to see that first meeting as, in many ways, a prophetic sum-mary of this hazy acquaintance neither of us can seriously bring himself to call a "relationship." After that first meeting, that's the way all of the intermittent run-ins we had went—not that there were many of them. But whatever those occasional summer visits to your house were, whatever your cameo appearances at mine, they definitely had a pattern. Like in the living room that day, it would be my mother hastily trying to push us together, because she felt a boy needed a father, because she felt a man needed to own up to his responsibilities, because she refused to understand how I just couldn't like you if we'd never spent much time together. It would be me not knowing, and barely caring to know, this stranger staring back at me with my face. It would be you looking to domineer, trying to bully me into obedience, thinking that the half-articulate criticisms you shouted into my face constituted even part-time parenting. It would be me and you sniping, arguing, ripping to tatters whatever vague notions about bonding we thought ourselves entertaining. In the end, it'd be us both receding once more to the distant poles of our very separate lives, bitter and hard pressed to recall why we'd even bothered with this father-son sham in the first place.

How deep does the discomfort run? How abject is the lack of familiarity? Consider that I have never, ever, in all my years addressed you as anything. Not "Father." Not "Dad." Not "Pops." Not your name. When we're in a room together and I need your attention, I say whatever I have to say and hope you answer. If someone else responds, I'll tell them, "I was talking to my father." But never, man, have I, or do I plan to, address you as "Dad."

It's not just about being mad, either. Obviously, you've never done much to merit the title "father," but I don't avoid calling you anything directly because of your failure as a parent. Bitterness hasn't prevented me from finding some suitable designation for you. Instead, it's that nothing fits; nothing seems right. I don't know you. I don't have a name for you because, strange as it seems, the part of me responsible for that has never really acknowledged you, what or who you are. You have no name because, in some quarters of my soul, you simply do not exist.

My heart hasn't killed you. You just never took life there.

Perhaps all this makes you believe that I don't understand, that I can't see, as you've feebly tried explaining before, that you were scared of a second kid, anxious over the life's dreams that seemed to be shrinking with each day farther from the grasp of your potential. "How could I take care of a child when I couldn't even take care of myself?" you say your thinking went.

I understand, man. I understand that you probably really did believe you were coming back for me and Moms. I understand the pangs of selfish desire and ambition that kept you away. You had a life of your own to live, and you wanted to do it unencumbered. You didn't want your paycheck going to feed another mouth; your time wasted at PTA meetings and over sickbeds; your energy squandered scuffling to pay for diapers and jars of mashed peas. You wanted to travel, to own nice cars, to have a decent home. Damn it, it wasn't fair to ask you to be bound to a woman you didn't want or to support a child you weren't prepared for.

So you left it up to Moms to handle the shit alone. And she did, 'cause she's Moms. You wanted out. I understand.

But I haven't always understood (and, I guess, don't understand everything now). There've been times when, yes, I've outright, blindly hated you. I remember how you used to berate me whenever I visited you, how you'd yell and boss me for the two weeks I'd spend at your house, contemptuously hinting that I was a mama's boy who needed you to toughen him up. I remember how we nearly fought when you'd taken me home after one particularly upsetting visit, how I said I wasn't going to let you push me around in front of Moms. I remember how we didn't talk from that day until I was nearly out of college. I remember how I pulled my rifle on you the day after my college graduation, when you came by the house and started trying to bully and threaten me again. (I'd have shot you, too, if Moms hadn't stepped in front of me, but I'm glad she did.)

My mother scolded me, explained to me how I ought to love you more than that. But you never put anything into my heart. Don't expect to get anything out. It's not harsh, just a realistic tallying of love's ledger. I understand why you did what you did. I know now why you left me to other men—to the preachers you were so quick to condemn, to my uncles, to those decent if sometimes misguided older brothers on my block, to my homeys—to raise. You couldn't hang. I understand, though understanding doesn't always accompany forgiveness. I cannot respect your choices, but I recognize their motivations.

The years have passed now, not just the five between the day I was born and the day we first met, but a full lifetime. We've made our stabs at forging a relationship. They've all failed. I accept this failure, mostly because I'm tired of trying. I'm tired of playing the role of the angry ghetto bastard, of bitching about how sorry and no good and selfish my "father" is. I'm tired of cutting through the thickets of my own emotional underbrush to get to this appreciation for you that you and Moms and everyone else seems to think I'll develop one day.

See, in my understanding, I realize that you'll never give me much reason to think it's worth the trouble.

TIMOTHY WASHINGTON, 23: FORGIVING AND FORGING FORWARD

LOS ANGELES—Tim doesn't have time for the bitterness, the pain that often corrodes father-son bonds when the Old Man leaves. He has grounds to be angry, you understand, to be vindictive. He was only a year into this world when his daddy left Moms and the five kids he'd helped her bring here, so Tim never knew the man back then. Still, he's heard the stories of their fights, of his father's sometimes violent bouts with alcoholism. He recalls his father's visits to the family's Watts home, the chronic absences, the absence of interactions great and small that fill the mundane cracks of boyhood: He had no one to play catch with, no man to hug or hide behind or to teach him all those things older brothers insist our mothers cannot school us around. For a lot of his childhood, Tim missed his father, and his father missed out on him. For this, Tim could've just turned his back on his Pops, could've let him keep walking.

But those things all seem petty now, and Tim Washington doesn't have time for pettiness when it comes to his father. His daddy is dying. "He's got a bleeding brain tumor," Tim tells me. "He's got not even less than a year to live."

Tim's too busy playing catch-up to dwell on what's past. He's living for the present with his father, drawing strength, guidance for his future. When his father's gone, Tim'll be all the man he has left. No, son has too much to learn from father, too much to teach, to allow his heart to harden.

Tim: "What I try to do, man, is I try to make the best of the time that we have now, try to make up for lost time and really try to gain a solid understanding. And I know I'm a lot like my dad, so what I try to do is pick his brain on certain things, because he's my genetic fiber. He is where I come from. So if I can see his thought process on stuff and the way he reacted to stuff, I can almost, in a sense, see myself. And I can find out what bad traits I got from my dad and what positive traits I got from my dad, dispel the bad and get on with the good.

"It's a trip. I live with my Moms and sometimes just in passing, she'll be like, 'That's just like your father.' And I'm thinking about it and I'm like, 'Damn, you're right!' as much as I might hate to admit it because of the relationship that we had. So, in essence, if I can get into my dad's brain, get into him while he is still here, learn about him, I can learn about me because he is where I come from."

In the past several years, Tim and his father have grown much closer than they were when he was younger, when the Old Man would stop by just to drop off a few dollars to the kids, or invite one or another of them to his house, just to make sure they knew he was still around and kicking. Still, Tim only knew *about* his father back then. Nowadays, he can safely say he knows the man. With that knowledge has come a profound understanding, appreciation even, for the man he missed out on growing up.

Tim: "The relationship I had with my Pops has been probably one of the best things that could have happened to me because I was fortunate enough to be able to step out of a situation and look at it from an aerial view and get a basic understanding of why things were the way they were. The situation was my dad divorced my mom when I was one year and left her with five kids.

"But the thing is, my dad ran track in high school, and he's still got track records at the high school he attended to this day. He went to Jordan. He got my mom pregnant while they were still in high school, forfeited all of his scholarships and all that because he had to work and get a job to support his family because that was the way he was taught. You know, his parents made him do that. And I look at myself. If I was still in high school, had I taken the same route he had taken . . . I mean, his dad didn't teach him nothing about being a father, you know. His dad didn't teach him nothing about being responsible, about being a man, basically. So, if he wasn't equipped for that situation, of course it was going to come out like that. And due to all the pressure, you know, it led to drinking. He became an alcoholic and now that I'm a man and I can understand that, based on the choices that I made, had I made some other choices, I probably would have been on the same path."

Tim didn't. He stayed in school, graduated Morehouse with a business degree. He's an entrepreneur now, repping for a black-owned rapid-transit company looking to build high-speed trains in big cities around the country. His life is working out, in part, he says, because he can see where his father's didn't.

"I guess I feel sorry for him in a sense, man, because he didn't have the mother that I had and I didn't have the father that he had. He was a father to me in an economic sense because he was able to go on and work that corporate job. He was making a little bit of money, bought him a nice house out in the white area, and I would go out there on the weekends. And it was a nice area, the Pomona area. He had a little chunk of change—but now my dad is flat broke. And he's got that brain tumor. So, I feel sorry for my dad because he didn't have the exposure that I have. He didn't have the opportunities that I now have. And I talk to my dad now, man, it's almost like I'm educating him, telling him why I understand. He's amazed: He's like, 'Man, how can you have so much insight?' "

Tim admits that it took a while to develop his understanding, his willingness to open up to his father, to let himself into his life, to allow his dad into his. To his father's credit, Dad never let Tim go long without seeing him. He'd left the house, but Tim's father never wholly abandoned his kids. And so, even when Tim couldn't really know as much about the man who'd fathered him as he'd have liked, he knew some. And even then, what he knew he admired.

"He was there, not as a father, as in teaching me what I needed to know about life, not as in manhood, but more as a provider. And even then, not to the extent that it should have been. But every now and then, he would drop some bucks to Moms or help me out with this and help me out with that. And I always saw my dad as someone who was always very successful. He had a little bit of money and I wanted to strive towards that. Because no one else in his family was. All his brothers were basically alcoholics and that was just the way it was. My dad was the only one who was 'successful,' who really made it, so to speak. I looked to him for the business knowledge. Only recently I have been able to talk to him as a man. We didn't have that open-door policy of communication. Whenever my dad called, it was routine: 'How you doing? How's your grades? How's school? What do you need?' He was never there on those father-son outings, so to speak, so I missed all of that, but I think I have enough depth within my character to where I can look above that and move beyond that. And when I do have a son, I know exactly what to do. Because I have seen what not to do all my life."

Tim hates, though, that he's had to learn at his father's expense, at his family's expense. He hates that his house was wracked with domestic violence and excessive drinking, that his father had to leave to salvage the family he and Tim's mother had built. Most of all, Tim hates that he'll never get back all those years of pain, will never get a chance to replace them with a relationship he'd love to cultivate for years to come.

His father is dying. He has accepted this fate, just as he has accepted the past that has brought the two of them, the father and the son, to this place.

"How do I deal with it? It's a trip, man, because I didn't have that close attachment to my father, I can deal with it really, really easy. I go by to see my dad, man. I talk to him. He's in good spirits, you know. I'm in good spirits. It's just something that exists. There is nothing that I can do within my realm of power to change his condition. It's inevitable that he's going to die because of his condition. I mean, I looked at the situation for what it was. I mean, I said my dad has a brain tumor and it's bleeding. And he's having seizures. Past situations like this have resulted in death fairly quickly so I look at what I'm dealing with, factually, and look at what I can do. And sad but true, there is nothing I can do to change his condition.

"So where do I go from there? Take advantage of the time that exists. Talk to him, ask him about all those things that you wanted to ask him about. 'Hey, Dad, why did you beat Mom? What was within you?' You know. And personally, man, I think that when a man beats a woman—and this may seem kind of far-fetched—but it's an expression of love almost. It's almost an expression of love in a really weird form because you have to care a great deal about somebody to act upon them in that fashion. It may be displaced anger and what you are doing may be wrong, but I just can't fathom that attachment isn't there. If someone could do something to you that would make you angry to that degree, you must really care about that person. Because the people that are closest to you hurt you the most.

That's one thing that I am dealing with right now, trying to weed through: 'Why did you beat Mom? Why were you always out?' So I talked to my dad about those kinds of things, man, and, it's kind of hard for him to express it now because he can't really talk as good. But I could see his expression and I can see the hurt in his eyes and his expression like it was all wrong.

And my dad is still in love with my mother to this day, man, you know. If he could change everything, he would go back and do it all over again. I know he would. But it has a lot to do with his background and what he was taught, and what his father was taught; he didn't have nothing to pass on to him. So he was basically winging it, you know, and he's confused because he knows that he doesn't know what to do and it becomes displaced anger. And that's why things happen like that, the beating, and the drinking and the being with other women—it's about being a man. He wasn't taught how to be a man, that when you make a decision you stick with it, when you pledge your life to this woman, you give your life to this woman, good times and bad times. He wasn't taught that so how could he know? He didn't have an example of that. My grandfather beat my grandmother, you know. Lucky for me, I took advantage, you know, and was able to see through all of that. I'm never going to beat my wife. And I can sit here and say that, you know. And once I do get married, if I decide to get married, I'm not going to cheat on my wife because I hold marriage as sacred. Because I know how much further along I could be had my parents stayed together, and had I had a father there. I had a mother who was playing dual roles so I couldn't have got all the benefits of a mother and all the benefits of a father. I got a portion thereof. But what can I do now? That's ex post facto. It's already done."

MARCUS FRANKLIN, 22: TWICE LOST

IT WAS bad enough for Marcus to watch one father destroy himself with drugs. It was bad enough that his biological father, who left right after Marcus was born, was living his life out of the hypodermic needle, bad enough that he poisoned his veins daily with heroin.

But bad as it was, it got worse.

To compound the tragedy, Marcus and his family had to suffer through his stepfather's drug addiction as well. Marcus never did find out what it was his stepfather used to shoot in his arms. He says he never cared enough to ask. He's calloused, he says. Has been for years now.

Calloused and confused. Recounting the story, Marcus can only shake his head and search fruitlessly for a reason. These men, they were supposed to be his protectors, his compasses. They should've been able to foster love, discipline, manhood. But they were fiends, man. Both of them. A crackhead and a junkie hooked on something Marcus still can't name. They didn't even have enough love for themselves, let alone the children they should've been raising. So instead of direction, they sowed confusion; instead of love, they sowed anguish.

In return, Marcus says, they reaped from his spirit a resentment that bordered on outright hatred.

Then they both died.

Marcus wishes they'd taken his resentment with him. To hear him, though, is to be painfully aware that it is still his to bear.

"Oh, man. Okay. My old girl's going to kill me. I ain't going to let her read the book but, ahh, check it out:

"My mother and father broke up, separated, not long after I was born. My father was a drug addict; he was addicted to heroin. He's dead now because of that in part, I guess. Ultimately because of that.

"My stepfather, my mother's husband, he's addicted to some shit. He was an IV drug user. I never really knew what it was because he never did it in front of us. I give him that much credit. But I remember him doing it, locked up in the bathroom for hours and shit. I got to pee and this motherfucker is locked up in the bathroom for hours at a time.

"But anyway, one particular Christmas I remember my mother, her old girl and him had just finished going shopping for me and my brother. My sister wasn't born yet. That nigga just took everything that we were supposed to get for Christmas! That Christmas sticks out. I wasn't in high school yet so it must have been sometime between the early to mid-eighties. But yeah, he took everything, man. That was a fucked-up Christmas. We didn't have anything that Christmas. We had plenty of food. My mother still cooked and food was there—but we didn't have shit. No toys. He took everything from cars and trucks and shit to underwear and clothes and shit like that. We weren't dirt poor, but we were, you know, pretty poor, I guess. But we ate every day and during Christmas and shit, my mother did what she could. I mean we got shit. We got our fair and shit on Christmas. But this particular year this motherfucker tripped out and took everything!

"We learned about it before Christmas. It happened maybe four or five days before Christmas and my mother and him, they were arguing and shit about it. I just remember them fussing and arguing about it. I was like, 'Damn.' Me and my brother was like, 'Damn, that's fucked up.' That was some bold shit. Now I'm a little bit older, I understand that it was just the addiction—not that he was trying to hurt us or that he was like, 'Fuck you all.' The drug addiction had gotten the best of him, man.

"I had always had a distant relationship with both my father and my stepfather. I resented my father 'cause he was never around. Then when I get ready to go into high school, I'm thirteen years old, this nigga trying to come around trying to establish a relationship with me. I'm going into high school. I don't need you, what you coming around for? After he died I kind of felt bad about not trying to establish that type of relationship with him but that's a different story, I'll talk about that in a minute. But with my stepfather I resented him because I was like, 'Damn, why does he have to be here? Why can't my biological father be here?' That's basically what that was. Yeah, I resent both of them. I had distant relationships with both of those niggas.

"But about my real father. I went into high school when I was like fourteen. After I was thirteen, the nigga just tried to start coming around regularly, trying to spend time with me. I remember school was getting ready to start. I must have been in the eighth or going into the ninth grade. He wanted to take me shopping to get me some school clothes. I said fuck him and those school clothes. I told him, I said, 'Fuck you, man. I'm getting ready to go into high school. After all these years, you want to come around and try to start playing daddy?' I wasn't even buying it. My uncle said I shouldn't be like that, that that's my daddy, and I should still respect him and give him a chance and bullshit like that. But I wouldn't even buy that. So I was like, 'No, man, I don't want your clothes, I don't want your time, I don't want any of that, you can keep all of it.'

"That was 1985. Maybe a year or so after that, he got shot twice in the back by police officers. Trying to steal, man. There was some controversy about why he was shot in the back. I don't know if there's some law or rule or regulation that says police officers can't shoot people in the back, but my grandparents, his parents, tried to take out a lawsuit or something, saying that he was wrongfully killed 'cause he was shot in the back and some other bullshit. But, yeah, he was shot in the back for trying to break into a crib in the suburbs. I kind of regretted it for a minute or to a certain degree, not trying to establish that relationship with him. But I didn't cry, not one time. I maybe was a little shocked or stunned but, nope, I didn't really cry. Like I said, I kind of regretted not trying to establish that relationship, but I didn't really miss him, man. Because you can't really miss . . . I mean, he was never there so how can you miss something that you ain't never had? That's all that was.

"My stepfather is dead, too. He died after my father died, of cancer in 1990. I was pretty much indifferent, man, 'cause like I said, relationships with both of them were distant and resentful. My stepfather was there, but I knew that he wasn't my biological father. I don't want to talk bad about him, I'm just trying to be honest. Personally, he was cool and I don't think he treated me any differently than he treated my brother. I think he treated me just as he treated his own son but I knew that he wasn't my biological father. And I was resentful towards him because of that. Because he was there and my old man wasn't. He treated my Moms good. They argued like a motherfucker but he treated the old girl good. He worked, he had a job. He took care of things—until he got to that point where shit just started getting out of hand, with the stealing and stealing things of my mother's and stuff like. But I can honestly say that I know he loved her and cared about her—but with both my father and my stepfather, their downfalls were their drug addictions. Both of them were addicted to drugs, man. And that's it in a nutshell."

TIM S., 18: INMATES, NOT INTIMATES

OMAHA, NEBRASKA—Tim lives closer to his father now than he ever has. He wishes he didn't.

Both men are currently doing time inside the Omaha Correctional Center. Both men are inmates, Tim serving a three-to-five-year sentence for a rape he says he didn't commit, his father for reasons Tim's unsure of. And Tim, who's been in jail for the rape since he was fifteen, doesn't care either. After eighteen years with no father, Tim would rather not take advantage of their time together in this new home.

On the outside, he had seen his father only twice since his old man left when Tim was seven. He's seen his father more often here, but he refuses to speak, to say hello even. He'd prefer to behave as though his father doesn't even exist, as though it's not the both of them scrapping to stay alive and sane behind the prison's bars and barbed wire. He says he doesn't care what happens to his father, whether he lives or dies, goes crazy or maintains.

"He came down here since I've been here, about four months ago," he says. "He knows what's up; I know what's up. He knows it's me; I know it's him but he don't have too much to say to me and I know I ain't got nothing to say to him. Ain't nothing to say. He ain't did his job; I'm here now. I said, 'No, it's too late.' I'm grown. I don't need no father now. I'm grown. It's too late."

When his father had the chance, Tim says, he threw it away. He chucked any hope of a family, of a son, when he walked out on his son and girlfriend. When he had the chance to be a father, the man of the house, he chose instead to while the time away drunk, to beat Tim's mother mercilessly.

"That was the only thing that ever traumatized me," says Tim. "That just gave me a different outlook on women and how men abuse them. It was all the same—hit, kick, punch her."

It was always the same pattern: His father'd drink, he'd smack Tim's mother, he'd get angrier, he'd leave. One day, he never came back.

After that, the closest his son would get to him would be on the opposite side of the prison lunchroom some eleven years later.

"I was in the cafeteria eating, and I looked up and all the new people had just walked in," recalls Tim.

He says he squinted at first, just to make sure. But he knew the face, the walk. Even with the fog of the years clouding his recollection, Tim knew who it was. After all the years, his father had just joined him in jail.

"I saw him and he was with this older guy. The guy was like, 'Hey, that's what's-his-name. Ain't that him?' And my father was like, 'Yeah, that's him.' I was mad 'cause he's here. I don't want to be around nothing like that."

And just as Tim has refused to acknowledge his father, the father has yet to make any overtures toward the son.

"Nothing. He ain't said nothing yet," says Tim. "I ain't going to say nothing to him. I see him around, but we haven't talked since I've been here. And I don't plan on it. What is there to say? Ain't nothing to say. It's too late for all that.

"My mom came here and saw him. She was like, 'There goes Pa.' Stuff like that. But I don't keep it no secret. He knows where things stand. I don't know why he's here or for how long, but he knows not to say anything to me. He ain't no dummy. He knows I ain't got too much to say to him. What can he tell me? I don't need no friends."

BRIAN JOHNSON, 15: HIS HERO

MIAMI—Like many of the young men in this chapter, Brian comes from a home cleaved by a failed marriage. His father and mother split when he was young. But his father never abandoned his son, never shirked his responsibilities. In fact, in the years that would follow, he became more than a father. More than his friend. Dad is Brian's hero.

"His courage and his manhood are what I admire most," says Brian. "My father is about five-two, and to make a living he drives eighteen-wheelers, moving. I was with him this summer and we drove all the way from New York to Atlanta to Orlando to Tampa and to Boca Raton and drove back to New York unloading furniture. And just to support his family, he goes through all of that. He didn't have to do that, he could have left his family and just supported himself, but he supported his family and all of his kids. That's manhood. Unless you can support your family, and respect a Black woman, you are not a man. My father dropped out of school when he was fifteen to take care of his family. To me that really shows a lot of manhood 'cause my father was only in the tenth grade. He worked two jobs at the age of fifteen, not making a whole lot of money. I don't know exactly what jobs he worked, but I know he worked one at a grocery store. And to be at fifteen . . ."

Brian seems truly awed as he recounts his father's struggles. His eyes light up. His face grows solemn as he tells of how his father fed and clothed his family on a pittance. For an instant, Brian sees himself in his father, in the stories. Then, a second later, he realizes he's wrong. He sees the man he hopes to one day be—and in many ways, the man he hopes he doesn't have to become.

As much as he admires his dad, he doesn't want to have to follow in all of his footsteps.

"I'm fifteen and know that right now, I wouldn't be able to do it. It would be too hard on me, but my dad, he knew what he had to do and he went ahead and did it. He didn't think twice. He didn't procrastinate about doing it, he went ahead and did it. Because he knew if he didn't do it, somebody else out there on the street was gonna do it for him. He didn't want that.

"I watched my father a lot. I watch him because of where he came from. I don't want to have to go through that. I want to live a straight life. I want to live the fullest life I could live."

Brian doesn't know why his parents' relationship failed. And he's not seeking any answers either.

"I was small when he left, about two years old," he says. "I don't really know why they got divorced because I don't really want to know that. I don't ask my mom. I don't want what she has to say about my dad and what he has to say about her to give me any bad feelings towards either one of them. I respect them both. It's not that they don't like each other. They talk a lot. They are just like friends, like nothing ever happened. They are real close, but they both live their separate lives."

As he's gotten older, Brian says, he hasn't been able to see his father as much as in past years. He doesn't get a lot of chances to make it to his father's Brooklyn home. But when he does, he cherishes the visits.

"I went up there this year," says Brian. "And then there are the times he comes down here to drop off, say, a load of furniture. He'll come by and see me. And it's not the gifts that he gives me. It's just knowing that he cares enough to come by and see me. He doesn't have to call, he doesn't have to do any of that. But I admire my dad for calling and coming by to see me—and caring about me."

CHRIS WALLACE AKA THE NOTORIOUS B.I.G., 20: A MESSAGE

BIG says there's not much to say about his Pops. Not much he can tell. He never met the man. He wants to, though. He's got a message for him:

"I don't know my Pops. That nigga gone. If you see him, tell him he owe me eighteen thousand dollars. Really twenty thousand. When I was eighteen years old, I had the plot. Me and my boys would be in my room and I used to think that nigga was foul—just left me, left my Moms pregnant to handle her only child. I used to say that when I turn eighteen, yo, I'm going to get my guns and shit and I'm going to go find that nigga. I'm going to get a thousand dollars for every year that nigga wasn't there. That was eighteen G's, and I was going to take it. I was like, 'We going to get that nigga.' And now I'm twenty so I want my twenty G's. If you see that nigga, tell him he owe me twenty thousand dollars. If I ever, ever do happen to see him—or if he would know that I was famous and he came to me and told me he's my father—I would break his jaw. I would break his jaw. I don't know what my niggas might do to him, but I would definitely punch him so hard in his face that I know his jaw breaks.

"Only thing that I was bitter about is this nigga left a lady. My mom was from Jamaica, she moved here when she was fourteen years old, struggling. Bumped up with this dumb-ass nigga, he busts a nut up in her and leaves her. He's a foul nigga. I ain't never seen this nigga a day in my life. I seen pictures of the nigga from when I was born, at the christening on the roof and—but what I'm saying is, I don't know that nigga. You know where he at?

"As for father figures, I was more into brothers my age. Most of the niggas I fucked with was only children, like me. Most of my close, close friends are only children or if they ain't they don't fuck with their brothers at all. They'd rather be an only child, they wish they was an only child.

"So my crew is my heart, man. I can't breathe without my peoples. My peoples is my heart, man. I got plenty of them, man."

REYNALDO POLK, 22: DRIFTING APART

ATLANTA—Reynaldo misses his father.

Not that his dad has gone anywhere physically. He's right here in Atlanta, working as a police officer as his son attends school at Morehouse. They're a short visit away from each other. But emotionally, Reynaldo complains, they're as far apart as they've ever been. Something about him, about that special part of him that energized his relationship with his son, is gone, says Reynaldo.

The son is not sure how to win it back. He's not certain he even can.

"All the conversations we have had lately are just, 'How are you doing?' 'What are you doing?'" Reynaldo says. "Quick conversations. We don't go to baseball games, movies, out to eat anymore in the past five years. That has a lot to do with school and me working. It is hard. And I have a lot to do with our relationship not being as up to par as I would like it to be."

The love, of course, remains. But time is opening between the two men a gap that neither cares for and that both seem powerless to stop. Reynaldo's growing up, taking on new challenges, developing new interests. His father, meanwhile, is as hard at work as ever as a cop in the Atlanta PD. He's always worked hard, says Reynaldo, often seemed like little more than an intermittent visitor to his son's life. Somehow, though, they found the time for a ball game here and there, a little catch in the park, maybe, a few jokes.

"My earliest memory of him was that my father was always a jokester," says Reynaldo. "He liked to have fun with me. He always liked to joke with me, have fun with me in the limited time that he could spend. And he got me introduced to baseball. He used to throw the baseball with me and watch baseball games when he was at home. As far as education, he commented on my grades, making sure I was aware of them and that he was aware that I did have responsibilities as a student. If he could help me at homework he would try but . . ."

But inevitably, the responsibility for homework and the like devolved to his mother, with whom Reynaldo confesses he's developed a much closer relationship.

"My mom always showed me how to do my school work," he says. "My pop was really . . . He tried to teach me the manly things, about taking responsibility, doing chores around the house. He really hasn't played as much of a role as my mom has in my life because I have always been around her. Whenever I'd get home from school he was gone to work. I haven't been around him as much as my mom so it's hard to comment on what he has done for me in my life. Financially, he has supported me, he bought me clothes and my first car. He basically supported me up to right now. He still does by letting me stay there at the house even though they want to get me out of there."

Reynaldo laughs at this last remark. He wants out, too, but only because he feels it's time to strike out on his own. When school's over, so is his stay at his parents' house. But he doesn't look at his imminent departure from the nest with total eagerness; he's a bit sad, too. Leaving home will be just another step away from the family he loves so dearly, still more miles between him and Pops, one more toll exacted by the demands of growing up.

"Time constraints put a restriction on us," says Reynaldo. "It's been hard. We haven't been the friends I wanted us to be. Now I'm not sure if we ever will be."

JEREMY K. MORRIS: ON MENFOLK, LESSONS AND LEGACY

JACKSON, MISSISSIPPI—They are bridges, the ties between us and our fathers. They are passageways to legacies that, one way or another, shape our destinies. Oftentimes, the bridges are washed out by the raging waters of our struggles, the ties lost in maelstroms of absenteeism and bitterness and intergenerational ignorance. But even amid a growing phalanx of ghetto bastards, of Black boys who've never even seen Daddy, let alone been allowed to make room for him, there are plenty of bridges that remain. Through it all, there persist in our communities healthy bonds between father and son that stand as reminders of our inextricable links to the menfolk whose pasts are our crucibles, whose lives are the dies from which our own experiences are inevitably cast.

Jeremy stands at one end of one of those bridges. On the other side are Jeremy's father and his uncles, Morris men all, the aggregation of nearly everything the Jackson State University overachiever admires and aspires to. They've raised Jeremy the way conventional thinking demands Black men rear their boys: with firm hands, heaps of wisdom and common sense and a grasp of heritage that, Jeremy says, ensures he will never forget who is, where he comes from or why he's here.

At their feet, Jeremy's learned of his family's sojourn through the South, of the Morrises' indomitable ambition, of his family's hard-headed inability to work for anyone save themselves. As he recounts his lessons, Jeremy's voice fairly brims with pride and confidence. He knows his family. He knows himself.

There is a reassuring beauty in listening to a young Black man lay out his family history, in knowing that, for all the atrocities slavery inflicted on Black families, there are quarters where our collective memory has avoided erasure. And in this knowledge, Jeremy has found humility, clarity and a comforting sort of power. He's a Black man, a Morris man. It stands to reason, then, that he can accomplish almost anything he chooses.

"My father and his brothers are very ambitious," he says, propping his head on the palm of his hand as he tries to recuperate in his dorm room from a hectic and exhausting day. "Hopefully I have that instilled in me. At our family reunion, they said that we were from a tribe called the Yoruba, who were warriorlike and they didn't take too much from anybody. That's part of my culture, part of my heritage. Men in my family don't accept just anything. They all control their lives and work for themselves. It's that warrior spirit. I think that's basically why we are as ambitious as we are."

He pauses briefly and ponders the wealth of his family legacy. To Jeremy, it's like looking out onto a vast plain, one that stretches well into the horizon. African warrior tribes. Former slaves. Great-grandfathers. Fathers. Uncles. Sons. So many stories. So much struggle. A rare and beautiful and powerful thing, connectedness.

Jeremy: "Oh, man, where do I start? . . . Okay, my great-grandfather was in New Orleans, Louisiana. And he slapped this white man. This was back in the day when you just didn't do that at all. He slapped him. The man was trying to call him out of his name. And, like I said, my family just don't take that kind of thing. We're independent and think we belong here just like anybody else. So he slapped this white man. After that, they migrated to Winterville, Mississippi, to escape the wrath or whatever."

From then on, defiance and dignity would define the Morrises' history in Mississippi, especially the history of the men. His grandfather worked his own land, grew his own food. A graduate of Jackson State and the graduate engineering program at the University of Cincinnati, Jeremy's dad worked in the Delta Health Center for a while, but he quit. (Jeremy won't say why; Morris men are taught to guard family secrets, you know.) His uncles struck out on their own, too. One owns his own real-estate company, another his own law firm. The men in his life set a standard that reaches back hundreds of years. The second of three brothers, Jeremy knows better than to fall below the expectations his family has established.

"They expect a lot out of us," he says. "They push us all, especially the boys in my family."

They ought to. They invested a lot. Jeremy grew up as they did, working his family's land, learning to do for himself. His father taught him the value of land, its importance to any pretensions of freedom and self-sufficiency.

"My dad, after he resigned from the health center, he decided that he wanted to start farming. He has been doing that ever since. I was probably around seven, eight when he decided that's what he wanted to do. I definitely remember when we were not farming. We used to go a lot more places. We used to, as a family, go a lot more places. Vacation. It was just understood. But when he started with farming, he got my brothers and I into it with him. I did everything from picking cotton to driving a tractor to castrating horses. It was nothing stressful but it was there and we did it. We complained about it but we did it. My dad is a very strict person. He is strict but he is quiet and he was always able to get what he wanted out of us.

"We were his sons."

He says his father was always fair, but he was also quite firm with his boys. Even after the boys had grown well into their teens, Jeremy says, their father kept close watch and a tight rein on them.

"Firm, but fair," repeats Jeremy. "I remember once, my brother, who was in college at the time, came home from school to visit. While he was home, my younger brother did something, got into some kind of trouble, but he wouldn't tell us that he did it. My brother was in college, seventeen, eighteen years old. Would you even believe that my dad still whipped us all until my brother confessed to what he did?

"That's my dad. He hasn't allowed us to make too many mistakes. But if we do make a mistake, he's always there. I think I would be the same with my kids. I definitely will be."

There were tough lessons about race taught in the Morris home, in those fields as well as in the living rooms, where relatives gathered afterward to eat and play and bask in the warmth of familial love. There, Jeremy learned of his peculiar burden as a Black man, of the blood and sweat and tears that merely living in this country would exact. He learned early that there are many white folks who would gladly undermine him and anything he sought to achieve. Jeremy wouldn't grow up unaware, his father vowed. He wouldn't be taught lies about the insignificance of race. His history wouldn't be blotted out in the name of some false sense of harmony. He would learn to get along, but going along was another matter entirely.

He remembers Winterville.

"That's where my great-grandfather worked and died," says Jeremy. "So did my grandfather. That fight between that white man and my great-grandfather set a tone." He pauses for a second and then laughs. "My family is technically full of 'racists.' My uncle hates white people. My dad can deal with them but all my uncles hate them."

Only the naive or ignorant would seriously suggest that racism spurs the Morris men's disdain for the whites, who, Jeremy says, seem to be a constant source of irritation for the men in his family. Racism would tell Black folks to surrender, to do as told. But the Morrises stood their ground. Did as they pleased. Still do. It's about pride, pride and a dogged sense of survival. No one was going to cheat this family again. And no one was running them away. They remember New Orleans, Winterville.

"Dad gets along well with everyone," says Jeremy, "but there will always be some type of hatred in all Black people for white people. I can't see that disappearing. It is evident today, and it will continue to be evident. You don't let go of four hundred years of slavery like that.

"My uncles, they blatantly showed their prejudice toward white people, especially my uncle Ajax. He almost attacked this white man because of some lumber. He had incorrectly billed my uncle and called him a name. My uncle nearly choked him. In fact, he might have even had his hands around this man's throat. I heard that story. Then, too, they live in Cleveland, Mississippi, which is mostly white. That's probably why they've had more problems like that than my dad."

But Jeremy says his father's agreeability couldn't mask his suspicions about white people, suspicions he passed along to his son. He kept Jeremy alert to the politics of the world around him, took whatever chance he could to explain to his son how the dynamics of oppression worked to grind Black spirits to dust.

"When we're traveling around the state, he shows me all this land that white people are farming now that used to belong to Blacks," says Jeremy. "He told me how even the FHA really have done some things to some Black farmers in the Mound Bayou area. Some things we bring on ourselves, through mismanagement and that type of thing, but it has come to a point where a large amount of land that Black people initially had has gone into the hands of white people. My dad would always say, 'We got another white person who has by some underhanded means taken land away from an old black guy.' He always says something like that, especially when we are traveling around."

Enlightenment is a heavy load sometimes, though, and Jeremy says the lessons his family has taught sit hard on his shoulders. He admits that he doesn't interact as well with white folks, partly because he knows too well what their coming has meant to Black families like his. He remembers the Yoruba. Remembers New Orleans. Remembers Winterville. Remembers Cleveland.

He's not complaining, mind you. He's simply honest enough to speak what most Black folks feel. He has to. There's a collective memory he's beholden to, a standard he's obligated to uphold: Do for self. Speak truth.

"From what I've learned from my uncles and father, I don't think that I effectively deal with whites as well as I deal with blacks. That is common. I can see myself talking to a black person sooner than I can see myself talking to a white person. I don't have a desire to go up to a white person and start talking to him. I will always know that white people are not my friends, but I think that I will be able to deal with them better than my father and my uncles did. I will always know that they are not to be trusted at all, though.

"I know that from history—and, like everything else, from my uncles and my dad."

The

4

Daddy Trek

At first, I was too scared to move. As I felt the blanket full of reddish-brown flesh squirm in my hands, I drew a deep breath and stood frozen in my ex-girlfriend's living room—and thought fast. *Damn, what now? How do I get outta this?* I was seventeen, a year older than my ex, had been a high-school graduate for all of one full day—and here I was meeting for the first time my newborn daughter.

More than scared, I was confused. I didn't know what to do with her or me. And it would be years before I would begin to figure it out.

I hadn't planned on Natasha, of course. I didn't even believe she was coming until after she'd arrived. Yolanda had told me she was pregnant, but she said it only once, and so casually that I thought she was just kidding. I mean, she wasn't showing, even after she was telling me she was seven months. Besides, my pathetic reasoning went, I'd "pulled out" ahead of time.

This wasn't the first time I'd been forced to contemplate fatherhood. Just over a year before Natasha's birth, another girlfriend had come over to my house and, teary eyed, explained to me in full detail why she'd been missing periods and puking up her Corn Flakes for the past few weeks.

When I told her I didn't want any kids, she exploded. She wanted the child, she said, and no matter what my protests, she was planning to have it. I threatened to dump her. She threatened to slap me with a paternity suit.

I was barely sixteen, but appropriately frightened. Long hours of listening to brothers around the way bemoan the expensive treachery of "the baby's mama" had left me with a stubborn determination to avoid child support. As this girl and I talked, I kept envisioning myself hustling french fries at fast-food joints to meet the $8-a-week payments to the Friend of the Court. I was bitter and, like I said before, appropriately frightened. My dreams of college and career, I feared, were doomed.

A week later, the girl called to tell me she'd miscarried. I was quietly elated. Even as I tried to console her, I was plotting viciously how I'd dump her the following week.

Relieved, I promised myself an end to the unprotected lovemaking that had become a pattern in my short sexual history. But by the time I hooked up with Yolanda, my promise, along with the anxiety of the first girl's pregnancy, had long since faded.

A year later, I had come full circle. And now, as my arms cradled the latest consequence of my carelessness, I tried hard not to tremble.

THE DADDY TREK

Once again, I found myself overcome with anxiety about the Friend of the Court. Never mind that I'd brought another person into this world. I was worried about my wallet.

Like my peers, I'd adopted a warped view of fatherhood. To me, fathers were somewhat of a luxury, an "extra" parent of sorts. My father had left when I was an infant, gone down that same road of abandonment most of my other friends' fathers had taken. His idea of parenting was to fly me every few years to wherever he was living at the time and, in the guise of offering wise counsel, harangue me about the way my mother was raising me.

Of the fathers I knew who still lived with their kids, few had ever left me feeling they did anything more than split time between the auto plants, east-side bars and the flats where they carried on poorly concealed extramarital affairs. When the grown-ups gathered to gossip, I'd hear them complain about what dreadful fathers some of the men around the way were, but I never got any sense of what constituted good fathering.

Not surprisingly, I started off just as poorly, as the kind of father to my daughter that my dad was to me—which wasn't much of one at all. Though I lived only a few blocks away from Yolanda, my visits to her and Natasha were sporadic and short. I loved my daughter, but I didn't know how or why I was supposed to be there for her. I just didn't know.

Through it all, Yolanda remained as understanding and supportive as she knew how. She never asked me for money. She never criticized my absences. And she never questioned my love for Natasha, though I was spending far more time at school and in the streets than with my child. Far from playing to the malevolent "baby's mama" stereotypes, Yolanda began rearing Natasha alone and with a quiet pride.

In a colossal show of immaturity, I started coming around less and less. Even as she sweetly debunked every ghetto myth I'd harbored about irresponsible teen moms, I was callously fitting myself for every caricature of absentee teen fathers. As she took odd jobs to buy Pampers, I was closing up the after-hours spots around my way.

As she ran headlong into the challenge and excitement of nurturing another person, I steered clear of them for fear of being asked to inconvenience myself.

I hadn't yet learned that babies were meant to be loved, not feared. That whatever drain they placed on your resources, they returned tenfold to your soul. How could I know? I wasn't around.

The sins of my father had indeed been visited upon the son.

By the time I'd graduated college and taken my first job, in Los Angeles, I had long since surrendered any aspirations to being a decent father to Natasha. I thought that one day, I'd simply start anew, with the wife and picket fence and whatever else came with the nuclear package. I entertained grand dreams of raising up a healthy, politically conscious Black family in the name of "nation building." I tried not to think about how I was so flagrantly contradicting my beliefs by shirking my duties as a daddy.

Consequently, I tried not to think about the little girl I'd left behind.

That is, until the envelope came. It arrived sometime in 1990, with no return address. When I opened it, I saw a note and a wallet-size photograph inside. It was a picture of that ball of flesh I'd first picked up at seventeen and last seen when she was three. She was now a bright-eyed five-year-old.

I read the note: "Darrell, this is Natasha now. She's growing up. She's getting ready to go to school now. She's really smart. How could you not want such a beautiful, sweet little girl?"

Staring at the picture, I fell back onto my bed and beat back tears. For the first time, the anxieties, the fears, the mindless fun I'd opted for over quality time with my child all seemed so small. Looking at my five-year-old daughter, I began to understand for the first time the weight of bringing another human being into this world, the diligence needed to give that human life meaning.

I hadn't been ready to be a father. That was man's work. I had still been a boy. But I'd created a man's responsibility and was way overdue in shouldering it.

I decided not to put it off any longer. That night I called Yolanda. As always, she was kind and understanding. She explained that she didn't write to burden me or take me away from anything. She knew I'd worked hard in school so that I wouldn't miss out on whatever I believed life had to offer. She just thought it was a shame that, despite all that, I was still missing out on life's best part: my baby girl.

Then she put Natasha on the phone.

Again, my mind began racing: What'll she think? Will she like me? Will she remember me? Does she even know my name?

She spoke softly, slowly at first. Then she called me "Dad." Then she told me she loved me, a slight speech impediment giving her enunciation an Elmer Fudd effect.

"I wuv you," she declared.

My heart turned to goo.

She didn't care that I'd been gone nearly two years without so much as a hello. She didn't mind that I'd hung around her for a total of about two months while I was in college. She just wanted to know her daddy, wanted someone else to love in the unconditional way only babies and parents really can.

When I got off the phone, I knew I had some growing up to do.

Over the years since, I've worked hard to build a relationship with my daughter. I've sought not merely to meet her material needs, but to respect and understand her as a person. When we talk, she tells me what's on her mind, in her heart. I listen as closely as I can, and try to speak as honestly as possible.

And where I once worried that material support was too much to ask, it now seems so minimal, so inadequate.

It disturbs me that too many black children, particularly the offspring of my generation, can define their fathers only in terms of material gifts. Ask a kid what his Pops does for him, and, if he can say anything at all, he's likely to tell you about the Adidas or GI Joe Daddy just dropped off. My daughter can give the same responses, to be sure. I just hope they're not her first ones. I'm working to ensure that, if someone asks my daughter what her daddy gives, her initial response will be "an ear, time, love and every lesson he's ever learned walking this earth."

But whatever the answer, little can match what she gives me:

the joy that comes with watching my little girl grow. And as Natasha grows, evolves, so do I.

It's proven to be parenting's sweetest paradox: The daughter has made her father more of a man.

Of the many indices used to divine Black male attitude at any given time—the tone of our music, the sag of our jeans, the ratio of brothers on Rikers to those at Morehouse, etc.—few provide as compelling a head check of Black America's men-children as our takes on fatherhood.

As daddys, we tote the range of the good, bad and contradictory traits of a generation growing up under the gun. There is resilience, courage, maturity. For many, rearing our children is the most significant measure of manhood. We recast our entire lives to make room for baby, abandoning old dreams, kindling new ones, hustling, bustling, doing whatever for Similac, Pampers and a roof that don't leak. What kind of man doesn't take care of his? we ask.

Still, selfishness, irresponsibility and cowardice abound, too. America makes shirking daddy duty easy, with the twisted non sequiturs it establishes between manhood and income and power. We predicate our worth on our wallets and wardrobes, not on how diligently we tend to matters such as our families. This done, fatherhood ends at conception, allowing us to make and forsake children with a callous abandon. Our babies become a burden to be jettisoned, not a resource to be nurtured. What father can take care of a child when he can't even care for himself? we ask.

Even when our intentions are good, even when we determine that we will be the fathers we can only wish we'd had, we find ourselves overwhelmed by the task and grossly unprepared. We talk of fathering without talking health care or good elementary schools or college funds. We talk of roofs over our children's heads, but not of good light for our first-graders to read by or a spotless floor for junior to crawl across. We tally fatherhood on a balance sheet. We complain about paying out child support and plot ways to dodge it. We find excessive pride in buying our babies new outfits and jewelry, teaching them to value the cover more than the book. We show our children how to become consumers rather than producers, slaves rather than masters of their own destinies.

We become fathers trying to get by, sometimes forgetting that the real struggle is to get up and over.

The profiles that follow offer a patchwork of attitudes on rearing children, from fathers and non-fathers alike. There are teenage fathers, married fathers, fathers-in-waiting. There are brothers who want children, brothers who eschew kids like the plague. There are fathers eagerly meeting the challenge of loving what they've conceived, men who've left college, taken odd jobs, risked their lives and made whatever changes appropriate to care for their babies. There are brothers who haven't seen their kids in years and brothers who barely know their babies' names.

Their postures and circumstances differ, as do their notions about what they should and shouldn't do to raise babies. All, though, seem clear on one central reality about fatherhood: Something very precious is at stake.

LARRY HARSLEY, 21: SACRIFICES, TRADE-OFFS AND DIVIDENDS

PRINCE GEORGES COUNTY, MARYLAND—Larry says he hated to go, but his future was calling. As a kid growing up in Lynchburg, Virginia, he had fallen in love with aircrafts, their beauty, their power. Now, with an offer from an aerospace-design school pending, he had a chance to study them. Thing was, the school was in Oklahoma—and Larry had a fiancée and baby in Lynchburg. He found himself torn and afraid. Scared to leave. Scared to stay.

Finally, his woman helped him decide: He would court the sky first.

So, at eighteen, Larry left Virginia—left his first love and their newborn daughter—to pursue aeronautical design in the Dust Bowl. Before he took off, he promised his fiancée that he'd come back for her, their child. He'd blow through his studies, grab up his degree and be on the next thing smokin' back home, he vowed. All he needed was four years.

He was back within two.

He hadn't graduated from the school and had no concrete plans to. Larry didn't really mind. The stars could wait. His family couldn't—and neither could he. He and his fiancée were married almost as soon as he returned.

"I felt I was leaving a big part of me back home" when he left for Oklahoma, Larry tells me as we sit in the office behind the barbershop he now manages. "I felt that I had missed a big portion of my daughter's life. I wasn't around to see her crawl or her first steps. I wasn't there to change any Pampers. I missed that. But my daughter is four right now, and she's to the age where she can understand that her daddy wasn't around 'cause he was trying to do this. But he's here now, so she doesn't have to worry about that."

Of course, Larry doesn't at all sound like the young Black fathers presented (or conspicuously not presented) to Americans daily through TV, magazines, newspapers and music videos. No great revelation there. Conventional "wisdom" programs us to believe that young Black men don't stick around to raise their kids, that they bolt with that first whiff of responsibility and inevitable sacrifice.

Sadly, some brothers—far too many—do indeed cut and run. But many others, like Larry, hold their ground. But while absentee Black fathers make for fodder for every forum from telejournalism symposia to kitchen-table chitchat, the Larry Harsleys of our communities, young Black men who find a nobility in dreams deferred in the name of hearth and home, generally wage their struggles in oblivion.

But they're there anyway. Just as some men find a perverse virility only in conceiving children, others take pride in seeing the job through to the end, in what we call "taking care of what's mine."

"A man can't say he can't be [his child's] father right now," says Larry. "I think he can. Being a father doesn't consist of materialistic things. It consists of love and caring. That's all the father she needs."

THE DADDY TREK

The love and caring that brought Larry home from Oklahoma also sent him away again, to Washington, D.C.—but this time with his wife and child. After coming home and earning his barber's license, Larry says, he left Virginia to manage the barbershop, which is housed inside the Prince Georges County Mall, a few miles from the capital. He and his family moved into a rowhouse with his mother-in-law, and now they're looking for a house of their own. Larry also hopes to open his own barbershop in the near future.

The sky has been put on hold indefinitely.

Larry says he saw the sacrifices coming long before he left for Oklahoma as a teen. When he learned at seventeen that his girl-friend was pregnant, his heart understood that eventually he'd have to relinquish something to the demands of fatherhood. Anxious and in sore need of a boost in confidence, he turned to another woman in his life: his mother.

"I was like, 'Man, I'm going to be a father, I don't know the first thing about being a father,' " he says. "I sat and talked to my mom about it and we discussed what plans we were going to make, and we went from there. She was disappointed, but not upset. I had a bright future ahead of me. I was on my way to college."

Admittedly "no angel," Larry says he hunted briefly for loopholes out of his relationship with his then-fiancée, even raised questions about whether he had truly fathered the baby she was carrying.

"I basically knew it was mine and nobody else's," he says. "I just did that to throw a loop over it. Most men throw that up just to put a damper on things, just to have something to argue about so they can get their head together. But it was never a situation where she was alone in any way. I was always by her side."

His loyalty and sacrifice has paid some simple, sweet dividends, he tells me. In addition to his daughter, Larry and his wife now also have an eighteen-month-old son. And with each new addition to their burgeoning clan, the bonds between them all—husband and wife, parents and children—continue to crystallize.

Says Larry: "It's like something every father dreams of, for the daughter to be able to come to the father and talk to him. She actually asks me how my day is going at work or says that I work hard. She asks if I'm all right, if I need my slippers. We have a real nice relationship. I've had to give up a lot for it, but it's worth everything. It's like a fairy tale."

GREG CARTER,* 20: NO FRIEND OF THE COURT

DETROIT—"I wasn't using protection 'cause when the 'rain rains,' you're narrow-minded. I didn't think she would get pregnant. Didn't really care because I was young, at an age where the most important relationship was the sexual experience. So if you're about to get it right there, and you got to go around the world to get a rubber, you probably won't. It's being careless. Not really worrying about it, you know what I'm sayin' . . .

"What am I facing with child support? I'm facing possible jail if I get caught. I owe between three and five thousand, probably one or the other . . ."

Around my way, you couldn't approach fatherhood without someone warning you—too late, of course—about the bill.

"Kids cost," the fellas would say. Get the wrong girl pregnant, and she was taking you to the bank. (Naturally, most any of the teenage girls we wound up knocking up were the "wrong" ones. Why else, we thought, would some girl you fucked casually and either lied to or ignored the rest of the time even think about having your baby unless it was about latching onto you and your wallet for life?) With all the hostility and resentment we could muster, we likened the teen pregnancies that complicated nearly all our lives to a stick-up attempt—and child support was the gat at our back.

Everybody, it seemed, had a friend who'd fallen victim to the Friend of the Court, that brother who'd been ordered by some

* Not his real name.

judge to kick down eight dollars a week or do jail time, that brother none of us envied. On the balance sheet with which we selfishly undervalued the worth of our babies, that brother was written off as "caught up."

To some around the way, Greg Carter might seem one such brother. He might even view himself this way. Certainly, his conversation about paternity is laced with heavy doses of frustration and bitterness at the financial burdens that care of his three children— payments, he calls them, to the state for the mothers' welfare stipends—have placed on him. He says he has amassed paternity debts in the thousands and can't pay. Moreover, he's irked that he's being asked to.

At times, Greg's rueful take on child support seems unfair— some would say ridiculous, even—given the Herculean effort sisters invest daily in nurturing Black daughters and sons. Still, Greg insists he's not some deadbeat grown calloused to the needs of his children. An aspiring rap artist, Greg says he's struggling, and he's trying. Where he can't give money, he offers love to his children, caring, a sense of family. But he worries that to a social services system that measures a man by his bankbook—and to his children's mothers, who he says does the same—he is branded useless.

Mostly, he's a young man juggling demands, demands of youth and of fatherhood, of nature and of nurture.

"I had about a year left in school when I just kind of dropped out. I was going through a lot of stuff during the time: I got this girl pregnant. I was still staying at home with Moms. The girl was pregnant with twins and was planning to have the babies. My Moms was like, 'Well, you're gonna start taking care of the babies and this type of stuff. So I just got into skipping class, trying to make loot. I found myself working a job and, next thing you know, leaving school.

"Later, my mother felt I needed to be getting my own place: 'You'll be eighteen in a bit. It's about time for you to go.' So I had pressure at home, was supposed to be working a job and be the dope man of the hood. And you gotta figure I had to go through things that most children have to go through. I used to get into arguments with my Moms, get put out, have to walk around, be gone for a week, hanging and eating in somebody's crib or in the street or wherever the fuck I can go. Then I'd have to worry about calling and beggin' my way back into Moms's house.

"I stayed with the twins' mother for about two years or something like that. She was kind of materialistic, but back then, I was kind of the same way because I could hustle and make money. Then when I finally started seeing myself getting put out, I had to flip and trip out with her every time she'd get mad. I started wising up and elevating my mind. I finally saw myself growing away from her. I started seeing that reflection—and it used to be me!—still in her.

"We started not seeing eye-to-eye about the kids.

"When you are not married to a woman and you're not the husband and stuff in this society, she usually tells the kids what to do, and if Daddy's a part of it, he's a part of it. If he's not, he's not. And when you are mad at Daddy, everybody gotta be mad at Daddy. It's kind of messed up.

"I think she's damaged my relationship with the kids a lot. As I started seeing myself and understanding what a man is, I saw that when I'm trying to discuss something with her, she can't understand it. I'm trying to tell her that we need to have more respect and talk better because we got kids. With her, it's, 'F you.' It's to the point that every time we talk, it's, 'I don't want to talk. Do you got some money? That's all I want.' The kids start seeing that every time Mama see Daddy, it's for some money. And then you have the kids thinking that all Daddy is, is for money.

"She uses the kids, in a sense, to manipulate. It's like, 'The kids need new jackets. I got some money, but I need sixty more dollars.' Yeah, she uses the kids, thinkin' the kids are a shield: 'The kids can get their way with their Daddy, but I can't.' She can't understand that I'm strugglin'. She doesn't want to understand that. It's like, 'Bunk beds!'

"Her attitude is, 'Well, the welfare check isn't enough. You should be kickin' in some.'

"I feel we both should have priorities with raising the kids. I think we both should be able to financially support the kids without being on nothing like no welfare. But see, I'm going through a struggle, trying to find a job and do music at the same time. She wonders why she should have to work. You know [mocking his ex-girlfriend]: 'I'm getting a free welfare check, and he's going to have to pay the money back.' So we don't see eye-to-eye. And she can't see where I'm trying to help in any way. I definitely think, you know what I'm sayin', that we should reach a point where she should be able to financially support the kids also with, you know what I'm sayin', me, you know. Working together.

"But she can't want a welfare check plus some money from me, you know . . .

"I have another baby. He's two, almost three. This one was definitely [conceived] the same way. But with this one, it was like sometimes the mother was taking birth control and then sometimes she would stop. I wouldn't be knowin'. Plus, I still wasn't using a rubber.

"I was working plus selling a little stuff. I was giving her a little loot so even if she did get pregnant, it was like, 'Go get an abortion!' I didn't have many girlfriends who had them. I don't think abortion is right, but back then, I didn't want to get stuck with another kid. I didn't know any better. Then I started realizing it's mine. Imagine if my Moms didn't have me. I wouldn't support my girl having an abortion. That's why you gotta be, as a Black man, you gotta be careful, cautious. Too many men are running around having too many mates. If you're sleepin' with one girl and you're using careful protection or methods to avoid her getting pregnant, she's not going to get pregnant. A lot of people don't sit down and think about that. It's always a physical attraction . . .

"I try to spend as much time as I can with my kids. I try to get them all together, so they can grow up together. I try to teach them a lot of stuff that I wasn't taught by my Moms. I can see the same thing happening in their household that happened in mine: Their Moms didn't know; she's receiving a welfare check. You look around and you think, I just need money. That's the most important thing to you.

"Well, I think anytime one parent doesn't have respect for the other, children're gonna feel it, that Mom is the type who should get the respect and Daddy shouldn't. For instance, I could be talking to the kids and she'll be in the background saying, 'Ask him does he have any money.'

" 'No, I don't have any money now.'

" 'Hang up on him! He ain't never got no damn money!'

"You feel like, 'We can't even talk. You talking to me like this. You disrespecting me in front of my children. How can you expect them to have respect for me? That's all you think about is money. You don't think I'm striving, hustling just like you?'

"So I look at it like this. She sittin' back in, as far as I'm concerned. At least she's getting a welfare check. She's staying with her Moms, not paying any rent. Not more than what she would pay if she was in a house somewhere.

"I'm not working right now. At my last job, relations got bad because I was working for Koreans and I was brought in and made them money. It's just like any business—when it get slow, they be like, 'Well, somebody gotta go.' I guess I got to the point where I was into my music thing and doing so much stuff, I might miss a couple of days. I couldn't see myself staying there selling clothes or how this was gonna pay off for the rest of my life. I gotta do what I love, what's in my heart, what's in my soul. And I was just gambling with it.

"I figure I could sit back and just go in the 'system' [for a job] and just bring about the better things in life. I could try some imaginary white people stuff, you know what I'm sayin'. Or I could go out here, do what I love, make good money at doing it and take care of my family doing what I like. I don't care what you doin'. You can't do anything unless you feel right about it, unless you're into it. Some people try to tell you, 'Well, you got three kids to think about.' I say, 'I gotta worry about a job that's only paying three thirty-five and I can't even afford to pay my rent.' It's still gonna be the same way with the music, so why not try to do that, something that I like . . ."

THE DADDY TREK

. . .

He winds down briefly, and I wince inwardly as, in the back of my head, visages from 'round Moms's kitchen table rise in outraged indignation and affronted womanist pride. Images of old girlfriends and grandmothers and great-aunts and cousins shout inside my head.

"Triflin' boy needs a job!"

"Hmphh. Shoulda thought about how he'd do his music before he had them kids!"

"Now ain't that selfish? Expectin' her to pay for those children alone while he's off somewhere rapping!"

I'm sure Greg has heard similar choruses. For all of his inspired talk of a music career, he knows he can't defer the obligations of parenting without risking calumny, disdain, a cell even. I ask him what he wants, needs, to right his debts to his family.

He runs a thin finger through the stubby dreadlocks sprouting from his head and thinks for a second. He tells me he needs time, time to make his dreams happen. With time, he could make money, make changes . . .

"Number one, if I made money off my music, I'd pay off these so-called 'mister man' debts, like this child support crap.

"You see, in this society it's like all the weight is put on the man, even though I used to hear back in the days that 'y'all both laid down to have it.' But still, if the brother stays around and he's willing to take care of it, you still need much support. It's not easy for a Black man trying to raise one kid, two kids or three kids. So you gotta figure it takes more than just some 'lil three thirty-five an hour McDonald's job to raise one kid. Both people are going to have to be working and they'll be strugglin' still.

"It's messed up that in this society all that weight is threw on the Black man, as many struggles as the Black man has. Problems are being thrown at the Black man to set us back even further and destroy us. Child support is just another plot. You have to understand, when the women get on welfare, they don't receive any of that child support money. All you're doin' is paying back your so-called government. That's all you doing, paying them back. And while you paying taxes, you just paying them back. Because they want to get they money back. So, I just think that it's kind of messed when some women get on there. Like mine. When she got on, the first thing she was like, 'Well, I'm not going worry about it because I'm only gonna be on it for a little bit.' A little bit done turned into a couple of years, three years, four years, more years.

"The child support people, the system, are being unfair. The kids' mother, she's being unfair to me in a sense, too, because she's not open-minded. It's kind of frustrating sometimes when you start seeing yourself sometimes trying to broaden your horizon but when you can't take her even halfway. She's so materialistic that I can't share certain things with her. I feel that if she was more broad-minded, she wouldn't be after me about the money. Then she would be one of the women to be like, 'Well, yo, check this out. I see what you goin' through and I understand. We gotta try and work together.' She needs to be more independent.

"In this society, when you have a child whose mother has four kids, lived off the state and worked and did hustles or whatever, you know what I'm sayin', and the child is going to go the same thing. It's like it's still another cycle. And the thinking is like, 'A baby is access. I got easy money for my baby. His daddy's messed up, I'm pregnant. I'm a keep my baby.' It's just like if you wanted the fat shoes that I got. I got them for thirty dollars while you seen them for sixty. I'll be like, 'I'll tell you where I got it from.' You're going to want the scoop. So you got other women, or men for that matter, saying, 'All you have to do is just get on that welfare and they give you money. They give you this, they do that, they pay your rent.'

"The system should be to the point where the families are tighter, where children shouldn't be brought up thinking that money is the only important thing.

"You gotta figure that America is very greedy. I think the child support system is like that. We waste so many million dollars on doing other things, and you're trying to tell me that you tryin' to sweat the Black man for this? Now, I'm pretty sure that with all the millions of dollars they waste on testing chemicals that's going to hurt you, they don't have to take these little pennies out of my pocket."

Back at my mother's table, the sisters' shrieks grow too loud to ignore. Some questions demand to be asked outright: Okay, so what do you want? What do you want people to do? Are you saying that taxpayers should support your kids without asking you for anything?

". . . Well, yeah.

"It's like when you have your little family. When you have your little family, when you have a party or whatever you have, everybody is, like, committed. We're a whole family, you know what I'm sayin'. When you have a baby, your aunts, uncles, everybody is giving you presents. Stuff like that. They are all, like, in. And we can't feel that we are a part of that in this society when there's billion dollars being wasted on different things. It's like, 'Well, I'm sorry, but we can't be taking care of your children because you're being lazy and you're doing this. You're sitting around watching soap operas, not working, not doing this, and we're losing too much money.' I'd rather for the next man to say, 'Okay, I don't have no money now, but if you can loan me ten thousand dollars to take care my family, when I get on my feet, I'll look back at you, and I'll know that I can handle it.' If I know I have faith in this man, that I can get it back, then why not? I don't want to see his family suffer or see his family die.

"So what things are important? Are the children's survival important?"

As our talk winds down, I can't help but wonder if around some kitchen table somewhere, they aren't asking him the same questions.

KERRY MASON, 22: "I TAKES CARE OF MINE"

DETROIT—The streets still hold an attraction for Kerry, same as they did when he was running them all times of night only a year or so ago. Hell, yeah, he'll tell you, he still likes to party and roll with his crew. He still likes to hang and fire up them spliffs and play ball with the fellas. Life's young yet, and at twenty-two, he's pimping it for all the raucous good time he thinks it's worth.

But Kerry's drawing lines these days, too. He's got boundaries, limits on the wild shit. He's put a moratorium on the worst of it, the fights, the hustling. It's getting old. Jail? Done that. Stabbed? Done that, too. The streets offer a lot to die over. A fiancée and a daughter, however, have given him something to live for. He's got his own place now, a townhouse, and a car, too. He's working two jobs and doesn't seem to have as much time for the clubs and street corners. Kerry's lived for the moment. Now he's planning for the future.

"Man, having a baby calmed me down," he says. "'Cause I've taken care mine since she was two weeks, man—change her Pampers and shit, do what I gotta do, man. I said, 'I got to cut something out.' I'm still doin' what I'm doin', but I'm gonna take care of mine. And then, dig it, man, right now I'm working two jobs, killin' myself, really, man. I don't got no social life. The only social life I have, I have to have when I come home from work. I could do stuff at twelve, but I'd be too tired. I'm goin' to school soon. If I have to work two jobs, go to school to take care of my family, that's what I gotta do, man."

Sometimes, Kerry argues, doing what's necessary isn't the most palatable choice. Fatherhood, he contends, can occasionally demand some near-Machiavellian decisions.

"I'd advise any brother: Don't have no kids. But if you have 'em, take care of 'em, you know what I'm sayin'. You gotta do what you gotta do, you know. I don't knock nobody for sellin' dope, but I think you should try to get a job. If you ain't got no education and you got to sell dope to take care of your family, do that. I know a lot of brothers doin' that. I mean, do everything, do anything you have to do, by all means. If you gotta do it, you got to do it. It's better than being a bum."

Caring for his child has forced Kerry into a crash course in adulthood, but he admits he still holds love for the streets, for the days spent blazing joints with old-school friends and partying late into twilight. Now, though, he's also giving the old school a few new lessons.

"You gotta have some type of fun," he maintains. "I like smokin' buds, man. It relaxes me, man. But I'm chillin', smokin' my bud. I take care of my family, chill, go to work everyday. My fellas come over. Fellas respect what I do, man. They laughed in the beginning, but I takes care of mine, boy. Got to. I want my little girl to be like, 'That's my daddy; that's my daddy. And if he ain't did nothing else, he took care of me.' "

While Kerry admits to streaks of carelessness and irresponsibility, to falling into occasional regressions into the "wild shit," he's openly contemptuous of men who don't own up to the obligation of parenting.

"They're suckers, man," he says. "And especially niggas who complain about child support. Man, it's like this: If you have it, pay for it. Not just for the money. That's money towards your child. It's yours, take care of it. You know what I'm sayin'? You're not suppose to be dodging paying child support. What you doin'? Knockin' it off, gettin' high. Get your daughter, and try to get custody. The way I feel, I'd try to get custody. I feel [a mother] ain't no better than me. I can raise my child better than you. Give me mine. If I can't [get custody], I'm gonna take care of it. I'll go to court if it's mine. What's mine, I will take care. That's how I feel, man, if I had to be around me and my little girl. But I feel like this, man, I will stick by her mother. I will try to do it, anyway. 'Cause I love mine. Niggas, man, they some suckers. They don't wanna take care of their child and mad about child support."

His passions leap like flames as he continues, his voice rising and his eyes narrowing. Kerry shakes his head disgustedly and stares at the terrace floor. He seems genuinely dumbfounded at how some brothers could turn their backs on their duties. Yes, times are tight, and jobs tend to leave the ghetto faster than they make their way into it. But Kerry's about survival—and his child deserves no less.

"Get a McDonald's job, man. You gotta take care of your baby. Your baby's gotta have Pampers, your baby gotta have clothes. You can't be sitting at home 'cause you don't have a job. That's a poor excuse. Hustle up on a hundred and fifty dollars, buy you some bud, and roll. Sell bud. Stick it to a guy. Do somethin', man. That's an excuse. Like, if I was a bum on the street, man, I won't be a bum for long. If I had to gank somebody or whatever to live, man, to eat, wash my butt . . . If I had to get a McDonald's job, I'd be walkin' down the street with my McDonald's uniform on. Forget y'all, 'cause I would save money."

He laughs at the thought of strolling up the block in his burgundy and blue Mickey D's outfit, then shakes his head again. No, it's not the most distinguished job in the world, but he's seen tougher feats pulled off. He grew up, after all, watching his mother.

"My mother raised three boys. You know how tough it is to raise three boys, man. I said, 'If she can do that, I can do anything. 'Cause I know my Moms can do anything if she raised three boys. With all the hell I was takin' her through! So niggas who don't take care of theirs need to get smacked. But all in all, niggas that're like that are going to get theirs in the end, anyway."

CHRISTOPHER S., 18: FOUR IS ENOUGH

JACKSON, MISSISSIPPI—Chris eyes his baby girl wistfully as she plays near his legs, tugging at his cuff and darting in and out of his line of sight. He wants so badly to pick her up, to chase her around this little hospital room on the antiseptic third floor of the Methodist Rehabilitation Center. He can't.

Chris has been in a wheelchair for nearly two months now, paralyzed from the waist down by a bullet someone fired into his spine outside a nightclub in rural Mississippi. Barring a miracle, he'll never walk again. But that's merely torture. He can handle that. Tougher to deal with is the realization that he will never get a chance to be the father he now feels he needs to be, that hands-on man who teaches his sons how to drive, his daughters how to fling a Frisbee or a football. This, says Chris, is more than mere torture. This is hell.

He confesses, though, that without his injury, he may never have been even the father he's striving now to blossom into. He wasn't a dad. He was a baby-maker, fathering four children between age fourteen and now. He never spent much time with them. Shit, he still can't spell all of their names.

But he's trying harder than he ever has to make matters right. They see him daily in the hospital. And when he gets home, he's going to make good on his vow to marry his girlfriend, the mother of all four. It'll work, too, he promises. He's going to see to that.

For now, he's paying penance, catching up on some long-over-due debts to his babies. Hopefully, he says, one day his hell will become a little easier.

"That's what worst," says Chris, erect in his chair as he forces a smile he hopes masks the despair and resignation in his tone. "I can't be there for my kids. God, I just hope they never end up like this. It's rough enough just being eighteen with four kids. You gotta buy them a lot of stuff." He laughs and waits a beat. "And then I'm in a wheelchair. They probably won't understand me, not now. They're little. One is five, one is three, one is two and the other one is a year old. My five-year-old may know something, but I don't think she totally understands. But I'm still gonna be there for them."

He wasn't early on, though. Chris says he was too involved with having fun with his friends to consider the enormous responsibilities he was piling up. No one had ever told him about obligations. "I gave money to their mom. That's about it."

He faults his upbringing. He grew up poor, in unstable homes, being shuttled between his grandparents and his mother. Nobody, he says, ever really took the time to sit with him and explain the joyful burdens of fatherhood—or much of anything else, for that matter.

"I'd just be in the streets, lettin' the streets come first," he says. "I called myself having fun, drinkin', shootin' basketball, just stupid stuff. My Moms, she's there for me now, but she, all in all, should have been there when I was young. I stayed with my grandparents when I was real little, when I was growin' up. That's how I got so wild. 'Cause my grandfather, he's a alcoholic, and my grandmother, she is on the scared side. She was scared, she didn't try to discipline us or nothin'. She's afraid of everything because my grandpa, he used to beat her up a lot.

"For me, that meant I just did whatever I wanted to do, go out and steal, gang bang, everything. To this day, I don't know why my mother left me with them. I just don't know.

"She start to being a mom when I was gettin' older, but I was in the streets then. Once you start the streets, you can't just change in one day. And I didn't really wanna change, anyway."

Chris points to the dead weight that now passes for what's left of his atrophying legs.

"This is what made me change, right here. Until this, I didn't think none of that. I didn't never think about takin' care of them. When I got older I started thinking about it a little."

The fun's over now. The streets won, taking his legs from him during a shootout that erupted when rival gang members saw Chris throwing up his gang's special hand signals. These days, he's found time that he never knew he had. He plans to use it a lot more wisely than before. After all, if there is a silver lining to be found in the cloud of his handicap, it lies in the irony that now, he stands a far greater chance of being the man he couldn't even fathom being to his babies a few short months ago.

"Yeah, I think that I can be a better father now," he says. "'Cause I was living fast. I didn't even think about the consequences of having four children. To my friends it was like, 'Yeah, he got four kids. He's all right. He's gettin' his.' They admired me, thought I was getting a lot of coochie or whatever. But this slowed me down, man—a lot. I believe it was the Lord trying to tell me that I need to slow down."

It cost him all motion and feeling below his waist, but, thankfully for his children, at least, Chris is at last listening.

DONTA LAVON FORD, 24: STEPDADDY

LONG BEACH, CALIFORNIA—It's not easy for any man to come into a family's life as a "new" father and rookie husband—and for a teenager, the task can be rendered near-impossible when compounded by the inexperience and immaturity of youth. None of this, though, daunted Donta when, at nineteen, he married a girlfriend and assumed responsibility for helping her care for the boy she'd borne shortly before their meeting and hasty marriage. He took the job proudly, confident that he could step in as a capable stepfather.

That was then. These days, that confidence is dwindling.

Now closing in on his fifth anniversary, Donta says he's still waiting for a full opportunity to show what he can do. His campaign for acceptance within his wife's family, particularly by her child, has not gone as smoothly as he'd hoped, half a decade back. He blames what he calls an "ornery" mother-in-law, who he fears is trying to destroy his marriage. He thinks she might be turning her daughter, Donta's wife, against him. And, equally as distressing, says Donta, she's fomenting a rebellious streak in his stepson.

"I can't deal with her," he says, his voice almost a whisper. He shakes his head as he lolls back in an old overstuffed armchair at a friend's tiny home. A knit skull cap is pulled down tight over his head, complementing a black T-shirt and jeans. "She got her daughter brainwashed now, and she turned against me 'cause her mother don't like me. She's a crazy woman, and she's trying to get her daughter away. But it's not working and she's mad. She told me she felt like I took her from her. She just don't like the idea. She lies. She would lie and say I pushed my wife's son and that I was mistreating him. My wife started to believe her . . . I had to tell her that I'd never push on a little kid."

But the allegation was enough, says Donta. He doesn't feel comfortable doing some of the things a father should. He can't chastise the child, he says. Can't really make demands of him.

"You know what he tells me? He tells me that I ain't his daddy. His grandmother puts those kind of thoughts in his head. Now, I been with him since he was two months. I take him to the park, McDonald's, buy him shoes and clothes and stuff like that. But she would be telling him that and he'd tell me, 'You ain't my daddy; you don't tell me what to do,' and things like that. It hurts me . . . so I just leave it alone."

But the boy needs disciplining, Donta says. Badly. Unfortunately, no one takes much time to steer him right. Donta's wife tries sometimes, but to little avail. He fears the child's problems could soon grow out of hand. And with the streets of Long Beach and south-central Los Angeles filled with potholes for wayward boys, Donta is understandably anxious over his stepson. And he also feels powerless to help.

"It's getting to me," says Donta. "I tell my wife to tell her mother to stop spoiling him and letting him get away with everything. He's running cussing, calling people bitches and flicking people off. He's on punishment sometimes, but it doesn't work. I have to stay on his butt. There are plenty of nights when he wants to sit up and watch TV, but he can't 'cause he was cussing. My stepson, he cussed and tell his mama, 'You don't tell me this.' And they won't do nothing.

"When I try to get on him, it doesn't work. Even his mama would whip him and he would run to his nanna and she would get him cussing at her. She is the problem. I don't like her."

Donta also has two children from the marriage—a two-year-old son and a two-month-old daughter—and says his stepson's behavior has been rubbing off on his elder child.

"He started to pick up a lot of his habits," says Donta. "But I got on him as much as you can get on a two-year-old. I don't want to have to spend his childhood trying to break some bad habits.

He's mine. I can raise him the way I think I should. My stepson, though, I don't feel like I can give him the guidance he needs."

Donta says he's seen the way children, particularly boys, can imperil their lives when they aren't led by a lovingly firm hand. He cites himself as a prime example.

"I met my father when I was seventeen years old," says Donta. "He came to my mother's house, and I didn't even know who he was. We walked right past each other. I didn't even know that was my father until they said he was."

Donta says that his mother tried, but couldn't control him by the time he was an adolescent. By fifteen, he was spending long nights out drinking and gambling with friends in his old neighborhood in Compton, California. He also ran with a gang, the Dodge City Crips, and thought seriously about joining. After losing some friends to drive-bys, though, he changed his mind.

Still, the streets cost him. Donta says he wound up dropping out of school and spent much of his teens drifting from job to whatever job a young Black man without a diploma can grasp.

At seventeen, he met the woman who'd become his wife. Their relationship wasn't enough to transform him overnight, but falling in love helped him consider certain adjustments in his lifestyle.

"When I first met my wife, it was like love," he says. "I used to make her laugh. She used to make me laugh. We had good times together. I guess it was love, so I decided to ask her. I cooked her a big meal and we sat down and talked. She was shocked. She said she was waiting for me to ask her. Before that, I really didn't want to get married. My uncle was going through problems with his wife and I was just like, 'Man, I will never . . .' But the way things were going on between me and her, we got along real good."

His marriage didn't change him overnight, he confesses, but he knew it would eventually. Slowly, Donta has begun to realize that he needs to pull more of his life together to keep his family afloat.

"I love her," he says. "And I want to do what I have to, to help us make it. See, now I feel kind of bad 'cause I'm married and I don't have a job. My wife is going back to school because she didn't finish. She's trying to talk me into doing the same. I thought about it and I said, 'Well, I might as well go and get my diploma, so when they do come home I will know something instead of just, "Oh, I don't know." ' "

But he's not certain if that'll win over his mother-in-law and his stepson. He's too embittered at her to care what she thinks. But he does want the boy to love and respect him. Further, he wants to be able to reach out to his stepson, to direct him properly before America's streets turn five-year-old naughtiness into something far more ominous.

"Black children need direction, man," he says. "I want to be that for him. I really want to be as good to him as I am to any of my other kids. I want them all to go to college, get a good education, be able to take care of themselves. He shouldn't have to struggle like I did because somebody doesn't want him to have a daddy. I just want to get that chance. All I can do is just try. That's part of being a father."

RONALD ALCIDE, 20: PLANNED PARENTHOOD

NEW YORK—Separately and together, Ronald and his girlfriend have imposed on their lives an urgent sense of orderliness. There's college now, undergrad for him, post-grad for her. After that, he wants a career in communications and, hopefully, a business of his own. If they stay together through all that, maybe then they'll talk marriage, a home. Right now, though, they're pushing too hard toward career goals to give more than passing thoughts to the snugly stasis of domesticity.

Nevertheless, they've already had to talk children.

She got pregnant last year. Both decided she wouldn't keep the baby.

In the process, both learned the hard way that making such a decision is easier than carrying it out. Choices are often funny that way, no matter how pro you are about them.

"I believe in a woman's right to choose, definitely," says Ronald.

THE DADDY TREK

"Abortion is my main thing in a situation where you have an unwanted pregnancy. But it's tough when you remember that this is your kid. I don't think it's wrong to abort, but people can't take it lightly."

He never did, he says, but even so, Ronald had no way of fathoming the emotional drain the procedure would place on him and his woman.

"It was traumatic," he says. "You're in there and you're looking around at all these people. You wonder what they're thinking, how scared and guilty they must be. It's sad, really. You know that none of them want to be here, but sometimes people really don't have any other option. My girl, she's career-oriented, too, and neither one of us felt we could handle a kid right now. You have to be smart enough to know what you're ready for."

Even so, doubts thrashed relentlessly in his mind, he says. He thought a couple of times about grabbing his girlfriend and rushing her out of the place. He found himself wonder how the child would look, whether it was a boy or a girl, whether he and his woman had any right to snuff its life. "I kept asking myself whether this was what we really wanted to do." In the end, she went through with the abortion.

Ronald has no regrets about her choice.

"I can't even take care of myself yet," says Ronald. "I'm like what they call a young man. But I'm not the full 'man.' The word itself, you can't apply that to me 'cause I'm not stable economically. I'm not finished growing—so I can't take care of somebody else. It makes no sense to me. That's why I practice safe sex all the time now, to make sure it doesn't happen. I want to take care of myself first. Grow up, make sure I grow up well. Kids are cute and all, but I can't be playing father like that, and that would be unfair for the kid."

Even so, abortion poses a moral dilemma for Ronald, the product of a devoutly Christian Haitian home. He wonders about the spiritual implications of terminating a pregnancy. "Sure, I ask whether it's right or not. Who wouldn't?"

And he's not alone. Like the rest of this nation, Black America remains gravely divided over the issue of choice. For many, the resonance of social conservatism in Black communities—a by-product of the considerable influence religion has had in shaping our lives—makes abortion unacceptable. Thou shalt not kill, we've been told. Further, something about such a choice reeks of selfishness, suggests a lack of fortitude and scrappiness. More than any bullshit about pathology or superhuman promiscuity, these are what inspire many teenagers to keep the kids they conceive. With so many Black children having seen their mothers and aunts and the like overcome the hardships generated by sex and race in this country, it's little wonder that they expect no less of themselves. As a result, many will tell you point-blank that "I ain't killin' my baby."

"I grew up in a religious house," he says. "My mother taught us about God and life and loving your children. But she also taught us about responsibility to ourselves; you have to do for yourself first."

Ronald sees the tolls of premature parenting with each fifteen-year-old who pushes a carriage past him. How many dreams have been derailed by unplanned babies; how many bright lives dimmed by the demands of caring for another life? Besides, he wonders, how well-equipped can children be to bear children? And in the end, might it not be more immoral to bear a child that can't be cared for properly? In the end, he says, simply loving the baby cannot be enough.

"I see all these sisters walking around here with kids and I think it's a shame," he says. "A lot of them can't even do for the kids. And the fathers aren't around or, if they are, they don't know what they're doing, either. So you got all these girls running around complaining about 'my baby's father, this and that.' And you wind up with all these hoodrats running around wild because their parents don't know how to raise them. Personally, I give props to a sister who doesn't go out and have kids when she's young. To me, that takes courage."

Ronald worries that too many young people are having children to compensate for lost love.

"A lot of these guys don't love the women they have babies by," he says. "They leave them. The women probably feel like, 'Well, he doesn't love me, but what I'm carrying in my stomach will.' That's where they get love, from their babies. Brothers have to be there for Black women. Like when I was with my girl at the clinic. If I wasn't there, I think she might've changed her mind. I didn't force her to do anything, but I let her know that I was there to encourage her. She knows that somebody cares about her and that she doesn't need to have a baby for that reason."

Eventually, though, Ronald says, he will father a child—when the time is right. And when it is, he promises to be as good a counselor, provider, friend and protector to his babies as he can.

"I'll be the modern father," he says. "Not too strict, but not too lenient. And I want them to know what's going on out here. I want to be able to talk with them on their terms and to make sure they've got common sense as well as a good education. I think I'll be a good father—one day.

"But that's later. I couldn't be those things now. Fatherhood takes time and work. I have to look out for myself. 'Cause if I don't look out for myself and then start looking out for him, he's never going to have what I wanted him to have—so I'm messing up his life and I'm messing up mine. I have too many other things to do right now. Being a dad would be premature.

"And it messes up my whole plan."

Sex,

5

Sexism,

Sexuality

Springtime, early nineties. We're three deep on the stoop of my partner's apartment building. The night is warm. The 40's are cold. The conversation is getting hotter.

We're shaking our heads mournfully at the news of a friend's ugly and premature death. Caught three to the head the other night. Damn shame. Cops say it was drug-related, but then they always do whenever the hood takes one or another of us under. You know how it goes: "Those who say don't know; those who know don't say . . ." So while the cops talked, a neighborhood scoffed in silence.

The beef had erupted over a woman. She had been working for our partner, doling out crack rocks for him from the back door of her flat. Was fucking homeboy, too. Then, one night, several hundred dollars vanished. She didn't have an explanation ready, but swore she'd get it to him. He kicked her ass like, well, like she stole something—much the way he was prone to do even to women who didn't sling for him. He wouldn't get away with it, though. Not this time. Not with this girl. She rounded up her brothers, their crew. Within hours, my friend was found in the middle of the street, blood pouring from three gaping bullet wounds to his head and face. Only a mortician's miracle spared his Moms from suffering through a closed-casket funeral. As it was, his head looked like a bowling ball encased in pancake makeup.

A few weeks and a wake later, here we sit. Up till now, we've been morosely silent, our exchanges less dialogue than terse complaints about life's brevity sprinkled with solemn stares and "tsk-tsk's." We're sad, angry. We all miss our friend. When talk turns to the woman who had him killed, tongues finally untie.

"Ol' scandalous-ass bitches, man, I'm telling you," fairly shouts Glenn. "They'll set a nigga up every time. You gotta watch these foul 'hoes."

"Hell, yeah," co-signs Paul. "Shit, if it wasn't for these bitches, niggas wouldn't be out here tryin' to roll in the first place. Man, most of the niggas out here selling dope only doin' it to impress these 'hoes anyway. Trying to get some pussy."

Scan'lous bitches, Ice Cube once cautioned, make for happy feds. . . .

I love the brothers, Glenn and Paul and Cube, but I think they're wrong, painfully wrong. I think that there are a bunch of reasons some brothers sell dope, and Black women aren't one of them. Besides, they seem to have forgotten that our friend did indeed beat the dog shit out of this girl. I haven't forgotten. But I haven't bothered to remind them either.

I could just fake my way through with a knowing snicker. Or I could chime in in agreement just to avoid having to articulate how I really feel. It wouldn't be new. At various times, I've exercised both options, knowing full well that each, in its own way, marked the door to the coward's way out.

Besides, I'm not much different, so who am I to check anybody? Granted, I've never been the one to use *bitch* and *woman* interchangeably. I wasn't bragging about how I met this "bitch" there or fucked that " 'ho" then. If I was calling your daughter out of her name, I felt I had a reason. Like if she snubbed me at the party. Or if she wouldn't come over to the Monte Carlo to surrender the digits—to me or to any of the five other boys packed in with me, hooting and ogling. "Oh! Oh! You too good to give your phone number to six goofy, unemployed teenagers with nothing better to do but ride around Belle Isle yelling at you from the bucket seats of a rusted-out lemon? *Biiiiiitch!*"

Yeah, like I said, real airtight rationale.

So with my place within the subculture of Black male sexism so firmly cemented, I've never felt comfortable censuring anybody around patriarchy. But this isn't high school. I'm an adult. More important, I call myself a Black nationalist now, a lover of all things Afrikan and beautiful. (In case you're unsure, this includes Black women.) I'm supposed to know better. I decide, finally, to summon up the courage to act like I know.

"I don't know, man. I mean, damn, he fucked her up bad. If that was my sister, I'd probably have to holler back at the nigga who did it, too."

This isn't the greatest response, I know. The principled position demands we defend women no matter what their relationship to us —wife, friend, cousin, total stranger. Still, I'm looking to strike a chord here. It works, and then again it doesn't.

Glenn and Paul pause, each for different reasons. Glenn's a sensible and practical brother and, when asked to place himself in the next man's shoes, does a decent job most times. I can tell by the way he nods, pensively, respectfully, that he divines the merit in what I'm saying. Plus, he's got a bunch of sisters. He can relate.

Paul is stunned, a little pissed, even. Like the rest of us, he's suffered some real heartbreak in his young life. He's not trying to get over it, either. Instead, he chooses to harbor a deep distrust of women and an abiding disdain for any man who invests in them anything more than the cost of a condom. I've heard him ridicule mercilessly any of our friends who've dared suggest they might be in love or even that they'd rather spend the bulk of their time with their woman instead of the fellas. Paul's is the "jizz and whiz, hit it and quit it" school of romance. Knock boots and break camp. In Paul, Snoop Doggy Dogg has a true believer.

Bitches, Snoop once cautioned, ain't shit but 'hoes and tricks.

And Black girls, whiteboy Mick Jagger once screeched, just want to fuck all night.

But wait. Let me check myself and be clear as I can. Paul doesn't loathe femininity because of heartbreak. He loathes it because that's what sexism teaches us to do. It's not about soured love. It's about a global system of domination based on gender. But damn, how do I get that through to him, to me?

I look quickly back and forth at them and press on.

"Plus, we always blame women for dumb shit men do," I continue. "Nobody made that brother roll. He did it 'cause he felt like that's what he had to do. Last I checked, wasn't no sisters bringing that bullshit into our communities. Wasn't no sisters putting guns to the kingpins' heads making them sell dope."

Indignant, Paul pipes up. "Nigga, they ain't got to put guns to nobody's head. These ol' scandalous 'hoes don't mess with you if you not rolling, that's all, if you don't got money. And how else the average nigga on the street going to get the money to do what he got to?"

Now, a queen's a queen, Jeru the Damaga once cautioned, and a stunt's a stunt; you can tell who's who by the things they want.

"I hear you," I respond. "But you can't blame women for that, and damn sure not Black women. That's capitalism at work, bro. That's America. And if we didn't look at women as commodities we could buy and trade in the first place, we wouldn't be dealing with them from a money standpoint. Look, if a girl is just looking for me to be buying her things, I can't do it. I can't fuck around. If my game isn't tight enough to pull her without me coming out the pocket with knots, she just won't be pulled. I'm not dying to impress nobody. Beyond that, these niggas out here rollin' ain't doing nothing but fucking up the neighborhoods anyway. We talk that 'do what I gotta' shit and still wind up putting Black folks back three steps with all that foolishness."

"Okay, so you mean to tell me that if you ran into the average bitch out here . . ."

"Hold up, Paul. What's the 'average bitch'? Why do women always have to be 'bitches' everytime you speak on 'em? I don't understand."

"I'm not saying every woman is a bitch, man. But there are bitches and 'hoes out there. You know what type of woman I mean when I say *bitch*. You know. Always wearing tight clothes, with her ass hanging out. Always trying to squeeze a man for some loot so she can get her hair and nails done. All loud and drunk. Just like I said, a ol' bitch."

Now it's my turn to pause. I used to think I knew what Paul means. I used to believe in this half-baked nomenclature, too. That was before sisters taught me to view sexism similar to how I see racism. That was before I'd bothered to pick up bell and Pearl and Toni Cade. Before long talks with friends like dream and Lorena and Monifa and Joan. Not that I've conquered anything, you understand. I'm a sexist. All men are. But I'm learning, trying to think differently, to regard sisters as humans, individuals, not as the objects of sex and pestilence they'd been made out to be in everything from the Bible to history class.

I can't be fake, though. I'm still very much blissfully sexist in my own ways. I'm not challenging much of this misogynist music I nod my head to at the parties. As much as I think domestic violence to be some real punk shit, I'm not checking brothers out here kicking their girlfriends' stomachs in. Neither am I actively attempting to embrace my woman as my equal in a whole lot of ways, and am way too quick to dismiss her ideas as, if not invalid, then certainly not as worthwhile as my own. I'm not combating a whole lot. And in my inaction, then, I condone it all. I'm as sick as Paul. But I know, too, that Black male-female relations isn't simply a woman's issue. The matter belongs to all of us, tottering as it is at the cutting edge of Black grassroots politics. I know that ours must be a fight to forge a partnership. I know that for that to happen, I have an obligation to stand up for sisters anytime and anyplace, the same I would for brothers when white folks try to tear us down. I don't have to agree with everything we do, but I'll be damned if I'll allow our humanity to be impugned. Same with sexism, I've learned. I'm sick with it, but I want to get better. I want Paul to, too.

I resort to analogy.

"Paul, look. If the police pulled up right now and saw us sitting here—blue jeans, baseball hats, beepers—none of us sell dope, but that doesn't mean a thing. They instantly make character judgments because of what we got on. Now, don't front. You get mad as hell when they ride up on us, flashing lights into the car and pulling us over, talking that 'routine stop' junk. You know and I know why they do it—because of how we look. Well, same thing about your so-called bitches. How you gon' make a character judgment about a female—'she's a bitch or a 'ho'—just because she's wearing spandex and Daisy Dukes? If you think it's tacky, cool. But you can't just think she's sucking every dick for a dollar because she's wearing something you don't approve of. What's the difference between that and some cracker in blue calling you the dope man 'cause he sees you got on a pager?"

Paul takes a second to soak this all in. He's nowhere near swayed. He's just thinking of how best to counter what he's sure is some newfangled bullshit I picked up from one of those short-haired, cowrie-shell-sporting honeys he used to see me with down at Wayne State.

"Well, women call themselves bitches," he answers a moment later. "My cousins, they always get on the phone talking 'bout 'bitch this, bitch that,' and they're females. They do it. Why can't I? And even my cousins will tell you that that shit some of these chicks run around in ain't cool. 'Yeast infection shorts,' that's what they call that shit that be cutting all up in girls' asses."

"Paul, so what? Women buy into lies about women the same

way Black folks as a whole buy into lies about themselves. Women have been told that sex for them is bad. That their bodies are meant to be hidden. That real respectful girls don't fuck on the first date or shake their asses at parties. They bought in and a lot of them don't even bother to question that shit. The same way knee-grows like Clarence Thomas buy into the myths of Black inferiority. But nobody's running you into the ground just because you got the pussy on the first night. Naw, you're a true mack dad if you knock boots on day one! But her, she's just a low-life tramp. You hang out the sunroof of your partner's ride with no shirt and you think you just giving the ladies what they want. You stroking your ego. But her, she's a bitch with no morals if she flaunts what she's got. She's just out here trying to catch a nigga up in some scheme. Now, no, it's not cool to play somebody for money, but why is that when we do it, we become some smooth son-of-Dolemite type, and when they work a man they're gold-diggers?"

Still quiet, Glenn raises his eyebrows, and half his mouth curls up into a grin. He's not so much on my side as he is enjoying the back-and-forth between me and Paul. To him, we both have points. Stumped but stubborn, Paul shifts on the stoop and stares right through me. He has no answer, but neither is he convinced. He's thinking about his own history, his own raw deals with romance.

He doesn't say anything more. Neither do I. I'm not trying to inflict pain, to diminish what's real to him. We'll talk again. Right now, he'd rather hurt quietly.

His hurt, as much as he tries to conceal it, is real and runs deep. I don't know the details of his love life, but I know it has curdled under his nose more than once. I know that he has been genuinely wronged by women, as have a few other fellas in our camp. And as always, patriarchy is there to justify our bitterness, to tell us how we shouldn't have been dealing with the bitch in the first place, to tell us how we should've known better from jump street, how we'll know better next time.

"You think I give a fuck about a bitch?" Eazy-E once asked. "I ain't a sucker . . ."

And more than affirming specious reasoning, sexism forces men into an equally ludicrous and destructive silence around our wounds. We don't discuss Paul's kind of hurt much. It's not cool to call your boy in the middle of the night crying because your girl dumped you or because you dumped her and can't believe you did something so stupid. We spoof group hugs, ridicule outbursts of sorrow. *Man, what time the game come on? Can you believe the Hawks let 'Nique go? Fuck that Larry Bird shit, Jordan will always be the man.* Even when we acknowledge the hurt that love inevitably brings, we're terse, vague, given to surface optimism. We pound our chests and proclaim loudly that "I'm a man. I'll be aa-iight." Men, and certainly not only Black men, don't place much value on vulnerability. We've got wars to fight, scores to settle. Patriarchy demands we be bulletproof, be God. And vengeance, not regret or remorse or wimpy-ass sorrow, is mine, sayeth the Lord.

So sisters pay. They pay for betrayal. They pay for loyalty. They pay for leaving us, for staying with us, for bearing our children, for having abortions, for attending school, for dropping out, for working hard, for collecting welfare. We don't have double-standards when dealing with our sisters. We have no standards. Flip the coin and it's heads, men win, tails, sisters lose. In the end, we all get cheated.

But it's not just Paul or Glenn flipping. It's all of us. It's nationalist brothers who would tease sexism from racism, as though they're indeed extricable, as though they don't both crush Black folks like ants beneath twin heels. It's the race men who think Black women don't get called *nigger* or lynched or passed over by cabs or systematically shut out of the job market and shunted into the drug economy that is now the training ground for the state pen. It's the Buppies who whine about the mythological "two-fer," that Black woman white corporations are dying to usher into the boardroom ahead of him because she counts as a "double minority." It's sisters who fool themselves into thinking song after song after song isn't referring to them as a bitch, but that other girl instead, because "I don't carry myself that way." It's those of us who think the battle is merely about language rather than perception, about only words instead of a quotidian oppression that we have come to see as "tradition" and "the ways things are." But, yeah, it's also Glenn and Paul.

And, sadly, me.

ANO CROWDY-PEAK, 17: THROUGH THICK AND THIN

OMAHA, NEBRASKA—Ano's torn. On the one hand, there's his girl, the woman he wants to be with. The woman who, at seventeen, he's already strolled through the fire with. Their relationship has endured enough drama for two adulthoods: domestic violence, infidelity, her pregnancy with a child that Ano didn't father.

Still, they're together. She cheated on him, but they're together. He's been faced with countless fights with her old boyfriend, but they're together. In months, he'll be helping her care for a baby that's not his, that she conceived even as she was proclaiming love for Ano and him alone. Still, they're together.

But there are other considerations, ones that may soon imperil the investments he's made. As much as adversity has reinforced his bond with his girlfriend, Ano admits that his hormones, his notions about manhood and sexuality, now threaten to undo what even their emotional roller-coaster ride could not.

"I keep questioning this," he says, shaking his head. "I keep asking myself whether I want to be with her. Then I'm like, 'No, I'm seventeen years old, I ain't gone through my phase of fooling around yet.' I only had like four girlfriends in my life, and I had sex with five people. That's what I always bring up to myself. I'm like, 'Why do I need to do this? Is it a male thing?' I don't know. I'm seventeen and I'm like, 'I got to get around a little bit.' But I think about the diseases going around, and I know I need a steady girl."

It truly disturbs him, this question of monogamy. AIDS is real, even here in the heartland, and it haunts him to no end. He's trying not to have to grapple with HIV. But he's seventeen, and his glands are coming into their own. Why should he be tied to one girl, particularly one who herself "has been around"? Why, with his young life on the verge of busting loose, should he be asked now to tie himself down?

"I just don't know," he mutters.

But for now, Ano is tied, committed. His sweetheart needs him, and he plans to be there. It's tough even looking at her, though, watching that stomach that's swollen with another man's child. Ano was angry when he found out she'd messed around. He'd been tempted to dump her, or at least to cheat himself. He didn't.

"She really likes me," he says quietly. "She thought that she could never actually feel for a person the way she likes me."

Then: "She got pregnant while we were fooling around; she was messing with two other dudes. She says she was young and dumb. I think that's one of the main reasons why she really likes me. I'm still talking to her. I'm still with her despite the fact that she's pregnant, even though I know she's had sex with a lot of people. And a lot of things that I talk to her about, things that concern me, she tells me, 'Nobody has ever said that to me before.' In many ways, I've changed her life, the way she used to be and her way of thinking. But it's not just because she likes me that I'm still with her. It's also the type of person that I am: I can't picture that person with somebody else after they have been with me, so I try to hold onto them. I guess that's wrong. I don't know what I'm going to do about that. I'll probably be with her for a long time."

Ano is torn.

He doesn't understand how he reached these crossroads. He figured he and his girl would never make it this far. Their love almost didn't even make it out of the starting blocks. When they met, he was crazy about her, the aspiring engineer tossing caution to the wind for a shot at dating the girl whose rep evoked snickers and sneers from his buddies. Her boyfriend at the time was considered (mostly within the dank corridors of his own inflated ego) a tough guy, a gangsta. Ano felt she could do better—namely with him. He told her as much.

"She was in a real abusive relationship before me," he says. "But she liked the guy. The first time I tried to talk to her, she shook me off for him; she thought she was in love with him. I don't know why they thought they were in love, because they were screwing everybody else and then coming back and screwing each other. I was like, 'Man, that is real stupid.' "

He persisted, though. He kept calling, kept dropping by. Eventually, Ano won her over. But he'd won only her heart. Her old boyfriend, the young brother Ano thought he'd finally helped her get over, was still laying claims to her body.

"That's the dude that got her pregnant," he says.

It seemed to be a recurring theme in his burgeoning love life. Ano's first girlfriend—his first love—dumped him because, she said, his friends meant more to him than she did. He doesn't believe that was the reason, but he no longer wastes his time wondering why. Later, he learned that another girl he was seeing had been fooling around the entire time she and Ano were dating. Even his first sexual encounter, he says, was a bust.

"The first time was a mistake in my life 'cause it was the wrong person," he says. "It was one of those things. The person was there. Sometimes it just happens. The person is there so you do it. Many times I regret that I did it. She had been around. Friends and I always talk about it and they're always like, 'So what that a girl got around? As long as you wear a jimmy, you're all right.' But I just don't like having sex with a girl that has sex with a lot of people. And that's something I run into now. . . ."

But Ano's holding up under the stress love has brought to his life. He says he's making the most of his current relationship, despite his concerns, despite the continued presence of the young man who's made loving this girl so much harder.

"He still comes around," Ano says. "He's a real ignorant dude. He has done a few things to her, but he ain't never put no real bruise on her. They used to fight, though. He'd throw her around and stuff. Now, he'll be throwing a tantrum: 'Don't let that nigger touch my baby! I'm going to get him!' One time I was over there, he called up some of his homeboys. He was there for a while, sitting on the bed, talking on the phone, being ignorant. I wasn't going to interfere. I was like, 'This is their thing. They go through this all the time.' And then he left. He came back ten minutes later with his homeboys and they come in and get on the phone and try and get somebody to come up there with a gun.

"He came over maybe twice acting stupid. She never wants me to come up to him 'cause she knows I got a short temper toward that dude. I ain't got no like for him. I don't hate him 'cause he ain't never done anything to me, but it's the way he pushes himself toward me. He didn't have to come off the way that he did on me just 'cause I got his girl now."

Knowing that gives Ano a satisfaction that he says is enough to keep him from fighting the guy—for now. As long as he doesn't hurt her, Ano says, there'll be no trouble. But the first sign that he's put his hands on her, and it's on.

It wouldn't just be because she's his girlfriend, either. Domestic violence disgusts Ano. And while he may abide tough talk from his peers—"I always hear guys talking about 'Give that 'ho a smack' and 'Fuck that bitch up' and things like that"—he says he wouldn't watch any man beat a woman, especially a Black woman.

"Black men should stand up for Black women. We are all in the same boat. If I saw a girl getting smacked by her man, I think I'd get into that. If I was the only person there and I saw it happening, I would get into it. There's a rule that if a female is big enough to hit somebody, then she's big enough to get hit back. But I'd never hit a woman to show off. It's wrong. What could she ever do . . . ? I could understand if she is like six-six and a body builder and he was this little skinny guy. But just sitting here beating on this girl . . . ?"

Without much hint, perhaps unconsciously, his talk turns to his own situation, to the rage in his own heart that he's had to keep in check. She cheated. She could've exposed him to a deadly disease. No matter. He has no right to touch her.

"Maybe she did have sex with another dude, but see, now I'm starting to think. You can't hit people for those things. If your girlfriend gave you AIDS or something, you can't take that out on somebody. It's like, Okay, she was screwing around and I got it, too. It may be her fault, but you can't go nuts and just try and beat the crap out of her 'cause that ain't going to change it. I think it would be wrong either way."

So, for the time being, anyway, he stands at his woman's back, by her side, wherever she needs him. Ano's faced a lot for her, and he's willing to take on more. He thinks her baby could draw them even closer. He looks forward to helping her raise the child. But he's still young yet. He doesn't plan on having children of his own for years to come. He's got a life to lead, people to meet, experiences to enjoy. Which way to go on these crossroads? He's got some ideas, but Ano's never certain.

The only thing he knows for sure is that he's torn.

ANDRE S., 18: BONNIE AND CLYDE

OMAHA, NEBRASKA—Sitting inside an office in the Omaha Correctional Center, Andre can't help but remember the good times. The wild times. The ugly times. Lisa (not her real name) was the best, his girlfriend. One of his best buddies. One of the best crime partners he ever had. They did it all together, from goofing off at the mall to burglarizing rich white folks' houses in upper-crust Omaha —such as it is. To their minds, they were outlaws, anti-heroes, lovers. Lisa played Bonnie. Andre filled in admirably as Clyde.

Then they got caught. He protected her, though. Told the cops she was an unwilling accomplice, said he'd made her tag along. She wound up with probation. On May 24, 1993, Andre, a former member of one of the tens of Bloods gangs that have sprung up around Nebraska, was flushed into the heart of the penal system, sentenced to a four-and-a-half-to-eight-year bid on theft, criminal mischief and burglary convictions.

Their relationship, in effect, ended that day. He was going away for a long time. He couldn't ask her to stay tied down. With more than a little influence from her parents and his gang comrades, they broke it off. All that remains now are an occasional phone call and some searing memories, bittersweet recollections of what was, what might've been.

"We were friends before we started messing around," says Andre. "I met her around my neighborhood. About eight or nine months after we met, I started trying to talk to her.

"She's a person who can make you laugh. I always thought she was a hard person, but I think sometimes she would try to use that against me. We always had a good time together. We would go out places and every day we would usually go to a movie or something, go out to eat. Something."

Lisa's mother and father openly worried about the relationship. They didn't see what their daughter did, didn't know what she knew. They didn't see in Andre security on the streets or safety in a ghetto filled with drive-bys and gang fights and stray bullets. They weren't giddy over his stride and sangfroid and raw humor. To his girlfriend, Andre meant thrills and excitement and good times, common magnets for the young women who dare forge at basement parties and parks and housing projects love affairs with those flint-eyed Black boys the rest of the world fears and shuns. "I gotta get a roughneck," MC Lyte explained, summing up the heart's desire of so many teenage ghetto girls. But Lisa's parents saw neither unreconstructed cool nor stout heart; only daughter saw fly-ass gangsta, roughneck. Parents sensed trouble on the horizon.

But Andre swears he never meant to bring trouble to their doorstep. He tried to keep his girlfriend out of his shenanigans on the streets. He didn't want her caught up in his criminal activities. He and his friend had been robbing houses for several months, in addition to slinging a few rocks on the street and fighting relentlessly with another gang just across town. Lisa was his refuge from all this. He didn't want her involved in his troubles. But then, she came searching for them.

"One day I was about to go out with my homeboys and do some 'business,'" he says. "And she was like, 'Let me come.' I was like, 'No, you don't know what you're doing.' She was like, 'What are you talking about, those burglaries you've been doing?' I was like, 'How do you know?' She said, 'Chad told me.' She was like, 'I can do it.' And she started doing it."

Andre says that he and Lisa hit close to thirty houses over the next several months, making off with thousands in TVs, VCRs, jewelry, money, firearms, china. They never robbed houses in predominantly Black north Omaha. They always went to the rich, white, west side of town.

"I don't like breaking into a brother's house because, for one, they're a brother," says Andre. "White people, you know, especially rich white people, they got money and they got a lot of stuff that is worth value. So we decided to go out there."

Andre says the burglaries raised the stakes on their romance and drew them closer to each other. She was now a part of the full scope of his life.

"After that, we just went everywhere together. For a while, before I moved in with my homeboy, I was even living with her and her older sister. Then she moved back with her parents, but we kept getting closer."

Then, one cool night in '93, it all came apart.

"We walked out of the house and we went out and did some burglaries at this one house and we left," Andre says. "Then we went to eat and went to another house. When we were leaving the other one somebody must've seen us. We were driving away, and the sheriff was right there! So they turned behind us and chased us."

Ten minutes later, the car chase ended when Andre crashed the van they'd stolen for this night's burglary jobs into a light pole. A foot chase followed.

"She hit the window and they got out, her and my homeboys," says Andre. "I tried to get out my window, but it was jammed, so I had to climb all the way over and get out. I had to go my separate way. My girl got caught."

Twenty minutes later, so did Andre.

When they went to court days later, Andre says he told the judge he had masterminded the burglary, that he'd forced his girlfriend to come. He just couldn't bear the thought of wrecking her life the way he felt his had been. "Why let her go there? I would rather go down than her, so I took the blame. I told them that I just took her with me, that she couldn't really do nothing to stop me."

He'd hoped he'd be tried as a juvenile. His hope was in vain. He couldn't even get a plea bargain. Worse, he says, his girlfriend was not allowed to come to his hearing. Depressed, defeated, he pleaded guilty. His girlfriend was outraged when she learned the outcome of his case.

"She was mad at the judge and stuff for not letting me get tried as a juvenile and not letting me get a plea bargain," he says. "She was upset about that, and then when I got my time she said she couldn't stand those white motherfuckers. 'That's all they do is try to hang brothers, and if it was a white person they would have spent some time . . .' and everything like that."

She was loyal to the end, Andre says. And they might've even worked their romance out, might've convinced her parents to not be too hard on him—had his friends not tried to shoot her.

"My homeboy thought it was her that was talking, snitching, thought that was how the police found out that we was doing it," says Andre. "So they did a drive-by on her house. That's fucked-up. They ain't only hurting her, it's her little sister, her little brother and her mom and dad there, too. Luckily nobody was hit. But her little, little sister is only like two years old. She could have got hit.

"My girl was mad at me for a while. She asked, 'Why did you have your homeboys shoot at me?' I didn't. I didn't know what she was talking about and then she named him. I didn't even know it then."

Two weeks later, Andre says, that friend came up to the county jail where Andre was being held and the two of them talked about the shooting.

"He was like, 'Yeah, I got her for you.' I was like, 'What are you talking about?' I felt like fighting him, but I didn't. I don't know why."

Though he and this friend aren't as close as he and Lisa, Andre admits that some male friends just mean more to him than a girlfriend ever could. Girls are temporary. Homeboys, he tells me, are forever.

"With some friends, we've been friends ever since we were little. When he had trouble, I am there; when I am in trouble, he's there. It's been like that ever since we were little. It is like, if I get in trouble, if I had trouble with my girlfriend and we end up breaking up, I can always get another girl, but friends . . . It's harder to break away from your friends that you knew ever since you were little. There is just that bond. It makes it hard."

After the shooting, Andre says, his romance nosedived. Lisa never cut off contact completely. But the calls, the visits, the letters, they came less frequently. And she wasn't home as much. They never even said their love affair was over. Instead, the two of them just drifted apart, let their hearts figure it out for themselves.

"I know she's messing around," says Andre. "When I met her, she was going with somebody else, and she broke up with him to go with me. So I know. And you can tell how a girl is acting. She tried to act like she ain't doing nothing when I ask her a question. She says she's always at home. But it's kind of hard to believe because when I wasn't in jail, she always went somewhere. If she wasn't with me, she was with her friend or at a club, somewhere or something."

Andre says they're still friends, though, and he misses her. He questions, though, whether he was ever really in love.

"I think I love her, but I don't know. I liked her a lot. I don't think I love her, but we will always be good friends, no matter what. We still talk every now and then. And I think we'll still have some kind of relationship when I get out. I just don't know about love."

In any case, he looks forward to seeing her when he's out, and he hopes to be back home in another year and a half. He wants to show her a better man than he was when he came in here. He's finishing up courses to earn his diploma, and he's taking up various trades around the prison yard. He's done playing Clyde, and he prays Bonnie's learned her lesson, too.

He knows that, together or apart, they can be so much more than they were en route to becoming. Even so, however, Andre will always reminisce over what was.

C. TONY WELLS, 20: GAY FOR THE FIRST TIME

WASHINGTON, D.C.—Somewhere between fourteen and fifteen—he's nonchalantly uncertain about the exact age—Tony lost his virginity. His first, he recalls, was a quiet and gentle man, a twenty-four-year-old clerical student Tony had met at a local church months earlier. There were few preliminaries to their first, and only, encounter, few discussions, little wooing. There was a date, a quick trip back to the rectory, a kiss . . .

The encounter only confirmed what the boy had long suspected. Still, acknowledging his homosexuality hasn't necessarily made accepting it an easy thing for Tony, a Catholic since childhood. He admits he still wrangles with himself over the Bible, over the Church's sundry interpretations of his sexual orientation as an abomination. But acknowledgment, he says, has afforded his perspective a certain amused frankness about being gay. Though to his family he's still "in the closet," Tony seems offended at the level of the Black community's silence around homosexuality. His indignation is expressed less in outraged protest, though, than smirking scorn at what he views as ostentatious, but thin, charades. He can't believe, for instance, how many drug dealers lie about liking only girls. But he's also genuinely irked by what he regards as unfair charges of excessive homophobia among Blacks, particularly poor Black people, who he believes to be far more tolerant of gays than most white Americans.

Which isn't to say Tony isn't scared for himself many days. He is. It's never, he says, truly safe to be young, Black and gay. But he feels that living with himself is much easier without confusion fogging his sexual identity. That fog has been lifting for some time now, he says, starting one evening with a secret kiss in the recesses of a Catholic church . . .

"The first time I messed around was when I was going from the ninth grade to the tenth. I was like maybe fourteen, fifteen. It was a guy much older than me. He had to be about twenty-four at that time. I had met him in church. He was studying to be a priest. He was a brother. I would never tell on him because I knew this is what I wanted. I didn't think it was molestation. It was what I wanted. A lot of boys that tell about molestation later on in life, I think that is what they really wanted anyway. I find out with a lot of guys, the main guys that are going to hurt you are the ones that have something they need to hide from you.

"Like this one guy at my job. He suspects I'm gay, so he's always bothering me. He says he's not gay, but he is the type that can be had, because a friend of mine told me any man can be had. You just have to work at it. I asked him, 'If a gay person approached you and didn't even touch you, you would feel you got to beat them up?' He's like, 'Yeah!' I said, 'Why? He hasn't touched you. Why do you have to touch him?' If you say no, then most of the time gays can accept that. Sometimes they go overboard and that's where you get negative types of stereotypes, but most people are going to leave you alone. They might have some smart comment, but they are not going to touch you. They might be scared of you.

"But anyway, about this first guy. One night he asked me to go to the movies, and so I was like, 'Yeah.' I knew what I wanted to do that night anyway. I knew it wasn't the movies! He said he needed to eat, so he had to go back to the rectory. We got there and this was the first time I had ever been there so he showed me around. We went to his room, and he closed the door, so we were just standing there. Then he just kissed me. When he finished, he said, 'I'm sorry.' I said, 'No, it's fine. I wanted to know what it feels like.'

"After that, we did it.

"I was like, I'm never going to do this again because it hurt so bad! It was always the thing in the back of my mind saying, 'What if it was just him?' I got with other people and it felt better. I enjoyed it. It didn't hurt. I guess because it was my first time and I was so nervous and tense.

"I never told anybody. I didn't feel like I had anybody to tell. I just started coming out to people and being comfortable. That was the beginning.

"A few years later, I was about eighteen and went to work at the

Signal, this clothing store. It was a guy that worked in there, he was real flamboyant and didn't care who knew about him. He was like, 'I think I know you from somewhere.' I was like, Oh, God, he knows. Everybody knew about me because of him and he got fired or left and then everybody knew about me and they used to help me out.

"So, yeah, I started getting more comfortable. But at the time of that first time, I was more nervous than anything. I'd heard it was wrong, but I didn't think so. I still don't think it is wrong.

"I profess myself to be a Christian and a lot of people in the Church say this is wrong, and I know that there are certain parts in the Bible they can pick out and find a place that says homosexuality isn't the right thing to do. I am thinking, Is this because the Bible was written in those days and the rules were so strict? Jesus Christ never addressed the subject, but you see it in Corinthians where Paul addressed it. I think maybe in the New Testament they had something about it. I don't think Jesus ever addressed homosexuality, so I don't think that it's wrong. Paul was a man just like I am. I'm not doubting his divine inspiration but he was making the rules because he was a pope at the time. He is known as the first pope. That was his day and his era. I think it should be different now. Being gay is socially acceptable.

"The preacher preached against homosexuality one time and I didn't know how to feel. I called some of my other friends that go to the church and asked them how they felt. They said it is because this, that—and none of them had a concrete background. I really would like to know if this is right or wrong. I don't want to die and go to hell, but I still think I would go to heaven because I think I am a good person. I don't know. I think I would go to heaven. I think everybody has sins and just because of that one thing, I don't think God would hold me from seeing His kingdom. I've done so many other things good in my life. I always try to be there and help people. That is the main thing. I like helping people, especially women. Women just don't do anything for me. As friends they're fine. I can tell a woman when she looks good but it is not a thing where 'She is bad!' I don't look at them that way. I look at a woman in terms of whether I can help them beautify themselves. One time

I was thinking about becoming a hairstylist. As far as women and relationships, I don't think it could ever happen. Then again, it could. I could get saved.

"But I don't hate women, although some gay people do. They're not going to deal with them, so they got to always insult them. They feel like women are taking all the men. I don't feel that. To each his own. Gay men already have an attitude about women, and then a woman will come and say, 'You're gay,' and that will just make them snap. The woman will just be left to cry. They shouldn't have started it. Gay people don't bother anybody unless they are bothered. I don't know if it's jealousy of women, but I wouldn't think gay men would be. They're going to get what they want anyway. Are they jealous because women can be more open with affection toward men? I don't know. I wouldn't hold a man's hand in public but I don't resent a woman because she can. She can hold his hand out in public during the day and then at night he could be going to bed with a man. Where does she stand?"

Tony's not very interested in changing. What concerns him more is his security in his identity, his safety. I ask him whether he feels threatened much, either because of his race or because of his sexual lifestyle. Racism he sees. And it scares him. Homophobia, he says, is less of a threat—if only because homosexuality still generates so much silence in Black America. But, says Tony, our collective stasis around the issue belies the prevalence of gays in our community, even down to the roughest roughneck. But as comforting as he sometimes finds it, Tony says, that silence needs to be broken.

"Homophobia doesn't really concern me the way racism does because a guy in Southeast, those guys can accept gay people. I know they can because a lot of the hustlers mess with gay guys. I have never messed with one but my friends have. I hear the biggest, biggest drug kingpin that was arrested—I'm not saying his name 'cause I ain't trying to get shot—a big queen around here is known to have messed with this guy. I think hustlers might use them for their body and stuff. They're still gay. I don't think just because a guy tried it one time and says, 'It is not for me,' I don't think that automatically makes you gay. If a hustler is doing this and he likes it, I think he is.

"There is a big percentage of gay drug dealers, from what I hear. I don't know. I don't get into the drug scene. Most people think I'm a mama's boy. I've never seen anybody get shot. One time I heard gunshot and I was really astonished—even though I lived in Southeast. It just is something that has never been around me. But, yeah, a big percentage of hustlers mess around.

"They do it because they have so much, they need to go on to another level. I don't know."

Tony may not have sex with cocaine peddlers, but he admits that he's "been around." He says he's had his share of one-night stands and off-and-on flings with regulars at pick-up bars, clubs and other gay night spots. But some of those relationships were years ago, when he was even younger, headier. The thought of promiscuity doesn't thrill him much anymore. And the threat of AIDS, he says, absolutely terrifies him.

"Yeah, a musician friend of mine, I just found out that he has it. This is the closest it has ever struck. I messed with one person who died of AIDS and I took a test. It was negative, but ever since then I've been scared to go back and take another one. It was like two years after I messed with him that I took the test, so more than likely I wouldn't have it from him. Ever since then, I've been having safe sex.

"For this past year I have been celibate, because it's the same thing with men and women. You know how sometimes men just want women for their bodies? Men want men for their bodies. Next time I lay with somebody I want it to mean something. I know after sex I feel bad. I do it because it didn't mean anything. A lot of times I get urges but I got to think, Do you want to feel like the last time you finished? That [is] what has made me last for a year. I want a relationship. I think it's the same as men-women relationships. I think sometimes men can love men more than women and men can

love each other. A man knows what another man feels. I can identify with some women, how they feel about men because of the way
I am. But I think men can identify with men better."

CARLOS WILLIAMS, 22: SEX & THE SINGLE CHRISTIAN

ATLANTA—Carlos isn't a virgin. He wishes he were, though. He
doesn't like what sex has taken from him, from you, too. There's a
sacredness, a purity that ends up wasted in premarital sex, he says.
A devout Christian, Carlos believes his God has established an order for our sexuality, a framework that we flout at our own moral
risk.

He's run that risk himself. Carlos lost his virginity in his teens,
but in the years since, he's decided to hold out until he's wed.
Coincidentally, he's not dating either. He wouldn't mind a girlfriend, he explains, but she'd have to honor his commitment to
abstinence. She'd have to be Christian, too, and willing to share his
decision.

So what's an ascetic, born-again brother from Albany, Georgia,
to do? Carlos has hurled himself full-bore into his studies. He's a
sophomore at the Morehouse School of Medicine, and earnestly
chasing a dream of opening his medical practice somewhere in
Black America. He studies. He prays. He keeps holding on—and
holding out . . .

"I've never discouraged relationships. I have always encouraged
a healthy emotional relationship with someone that is there for you.
I was recently in a relationship for three years. That was the longest
relationship I had been in because I usually don't stay in long-term
relationships. Me and the individual grew very close. We were there
for each other emotionally. She was a spiritual young lady. She
helped me out a lot in understanding the spirituality of life. I attribute some of that to her. I believe that a good boy/girl relationship
is healthy, no matter what you are going through. People say you

don't need a relationship when you are in medical school. That is fine for those who can't handle that relationship. If she respects you and loves you to not hurt you when you need her most, then I think that there are no absolutes in life. We have absolute morals that I think you have to stick by. It can work if you put in the effort to make it work.

"The woman I was with for three years, when we first started out it was basically a relationship where we were just dedicated to each other. We were more or less around each other in a way that we were friends. We were friends for a long time before we ever got in a relationship. It was basically nonsexual. That's what is hard to believe. I learned through life that there are a lot more important things besides just having sex and being out of a relationship. So we managed to abstain mostly. I guess it is the result of what an individual wants to do, too. It was successful to the degree that she had a strong background. She has eleven in the family and she had a strong spiritual family. As a result of that it wasn't too hard.

"I really hadn't gotten into a *relationship* relationship until I got into college anyway. But I've always been a boy so it's no big deal for me. I am not saying you don't think about sex, 'cause you do, but I wasn't exposed to sexual relationships until I got to college. At this point in time, I look back at it and I tell anybody: Don't get involved sexually yet, before marriage. That is from experience; you lose what you should gain from marriage. To me, when you first get married, you're the one to have a bond with that person only, and only that person. But if you start sexually from the get-go, then you may lose faith. I don't lose faith with people as a result of that. If I choose to do that and you choose to let me do that and we choose it together, that is something that we chose. But a lot of men lose respect after they get through. 'Wham bam, thank you, ma'am,' and they keep going on. I'm not like that.

"Through time and through the pain of losing a relationship because of unfaithfulness, I learned that sex was something you can get anytime. When I first got in college it was a new experience for me. I saw a whole lot of women and it was like a kid in a candy store. You don't know what you want. I had lost a little bit of the sense of faithfulness."

Carlos returns for a moment to his comment about boy/girl relationships. He reminds me, that, despite his abstinence, he's still a great fan of sex, just within the framework of marriage, is all. Men deserve women and vice versa, he says. But that's as far as he takes it. Boy/girl. Boy/boy, he tells me, is sick, an offense against nature and God. He's appalled by what, to many, has come to be known as the "gay nineties," at the way the gays have placed their agenda at the forefront of national politics, at the gall they show in trying to equate their struggle with African-Americans' civil-rights battles. God, even if men must fornicate, he wonders, why can't they just find a woman to do it with?

"I see a lot of men just out-and-out stone homosexuals. Some people beat them up. I've never done that. I'm the last person to lash out at another person for who they are. But I strongly disagree with homosexuality. I don't condone it at all. I believe that one of these days that person will have to come to the realization that he was wrong. You can't make someone think something is right. A lot of people who are part of the spiritual, who are saved and fifty years old, they can't tell me that they knew everything about God fifty years ago. They had to come to the realization that 'I need someone who can give me everything I need besides the material things.' Most people knew that there was a God, but one day they came to realize it themselves. I can tell a black kid to go to school every day and get his education, but until he realizes it himself, telling him means nothing. Same thing goes for homosexuals. They have to get to a point where they realize it is wrong.

"It is not my teaching. I grew up believing that men and women have kids. Men and men don't have kids. Men and men have nothing.

"There's been a lot of publicity about gay rights, but gays don't have rights, as far as I am concerned. I don't mean that in negative terms. For example, there is the recent issue about gays in the military. They keep talking about how Blacks were segregated in the army, but there is no correlation between Blacks and gays. They want to put gays among the minorities, but there is no correlation. They are a small group, but they are not a minority. They want to compare us to gays. No! There's nothing wrong with being Black. It's not a sin. I was born the way I am. Don't lock me up with someone who's not normal. That's not normal.

"I know some gays say they were born the way they are, too. I was thinking about that the other day. I'm not so sure that all people aren't born confused. It is their decision to know that their confusion is still wrong. They need to abstain, to try and go right. You may never be in a decent female/male relationship—and I am not trying to make you be in one—but I think you need to come to the realization. I don't have a problem with someone doing wrong. That is not for me to tell you. I may not condone it, but I don't have a problem with you doing wrong. But I don't like when you try to make what you are doing wrong seem right. Don't try to condone it. A lot of people who are gay call themselves Christians. I am not saying you can't be gay and be a Christian. I say that because you can be a murderer and be a Christian. One sin or another sin. Being a Christian, you got to put forth the first foot to come out of the wrong that you have been in. They don't put forth that effort, and they try to condone it and make it right. You can't make it right."

God has his place for everything, everyone, says Carlos. And it's not for men to try to buck that order with their lusts and perversity. Neither, he says, is it a woman's place. Carlos says that he doesn't ascribe to the sexist notion that a woman's place is in the kitchen or behind her husband, but he does believe that God anointed man head of his household. His is a hierarchy among equals, if that makes sense.

"It's hard to say if women have a set role in life because women have had to rise to the occasion. Traditionally, women do have a role in society. Women have a role as being homemaker. Don't get me wrong. They can do anything they want to do. They have the same mental capacities and everything that a man does. They are not inferior to men, but I do think that we have made women do things they weren't 'roled' to do. Women being head of a household, they are not roled to do that. They are not roled to take certain positions in society that they have been forced to take. It is kind of hard to touch on a situation like that 'cause I don't know how deep the particulars lie. I think a woman can be a politician if she feels she has that talent.

"In a good home, the father is supposed to be the man, the leader of the home. He is the person who's looked at as being responsible for what goes on in the home. That is the burden of the head of the home. In a home setting like that, a woman should be the homemaker. Have a job, but know that your husband is head of the family. He should have a sense of leadership in the family. A lot of times, men aren't the leader so they leave and seek out other places because they don't get the respect as the head at home. If you're a man at home and you have a sense of 'This is my place and I'm responsible for these people,' then you stay there. Why leave the kingdom that you rule? Most of them are not doing fine at the kingdom at home, so they go and seek somewhere else that they can leave and go out and say, 'Hey, I got something good.' Most of the times families don't make men feel like 'I'm good at being the father; I am good at being the leader.' Most of them don't, and the problem is a lot of women can't do that. They have been put in the position that they're in: They've seen women who have had to raise the kids and pay for this—and they don't know how to be a part of and not be head.

"I don't consider myself a sexist. I believe a woman can do anything in the world that she wants to do. Women have always been discriminated on, even before Black folks. Women couldn't vote for so long. So, yeah, I believe women should have the same rights as men, and when I get in a relationship with a young lady, I don't get into a relationship to rule her, but to gain from her. We are walking together; I'm not ahead of you and you're not ahead of me. And when I get married, I'll want a girl who's in the same mode."

MATTHEW MIDDLETON, 23: HEARTBREAK

WASHINGTON, D.C.—At a glance, Matt Middleton doesn't look like an easy one to hurt. Brother's diesel. Thick arms and a barrel chest stretch his white Howard Univeristy T-shirt. His squarish face—lit up with a grin that lies somewhere between sly and shy—is mounted atop a neck that would do any fullback proud. Even his T-shirt exudes an air of rugged assuredness, emblazoned on the back with what could be equal parts life's motto and upward-mobility crib notes for the future attorney: "Work hard, get good grades and live very large."

But as we lounge inside a log gazebo perched on a knoll about one hundred yards from the Howard University Law School, where Matt is in his third year, he makes it clear that he's not so invulnerable after all.

His voice marinated in a thick, Harlem-bred accent, Matt tells of heartache deep and unrelenting. After months of infidelity, fights and a slowly disintegrating sense of trust, Matt explains, he and his girlfriend decided to end their three-year, off-again-on-again romance—this time probably for good.

Truth be told, Matt expected as much. After all, law school is a demanding mistress. What he wasn't ready for, he admits, is the pain the breakup has left him with.

So even as workouts strengthen his body and law school enriches his mind, Matt Middleton's heart struggles slowly to heal . . .

"The worst heartbreak that I've had to deal with is the one I'm dealing with now. This is a sister that I've been dealing with for three years. That's the longest time I've ever dealt with anybody. You know, I'm only twenty three, so I'm not old or nothing, but that's the longest time I've ever dealt with anybody. I've known her ever since, like, 'eighty-seven, when I came to Howard. We were friends but didn't actually start dealing with each other till my junior year.

"I remember when I was in undergrad, when things were going well, I thought that this was the one.

"I had been with mad girls when I was in undergrad, but it was like I ran into a brick wall when I started dealing with her on that level. Me and her really had it going on for like a year and a half.

"We met at Howard. She went to Howard; she was a freshman. I was a freshman, and we had mutual friends. We all used to hang out, but you know, me and her didn't start dealing like that till junior year. That was in 'ninety. So me and her were together for a while, you know. We lived together at certain points. We used to always talk about whatever, like how it would be if we got married.

"I had never been in a relationship that serious. I've been confused and frustrated 'cause I don't know if it's because I'm growing out of her, I'm growing older. The trust factor was one of the things that broke our relationship down. A lot of things she did broke down my trust for her, and a lot of things I did broke down her trust for me, y'knowwhatI'msayin'? And it's not even always about her cheating on me or me cheating on her; it's just the fact that the one incident—whatever she did that was wrong and whatever I did that was wrong—it messed it up. And it's hard to repair that. Once the trust is gone, I think the foundation of the relationship is gone. You can't repair that, 'cause as much as you try to forget about it, it's like everytime you always second-guessing. And you can't really have a productive relationship if you always second-guessing.

"When I got to law school, my time was gone. This was a new thing to me. I got introduced to stress. This is what I've been trying to do ever since I even started thinking about school. I felt I wanted to be an attorney, and I got to law school and my time was gone. Things just went on from there.

"A part of [the breakup] was I was also meeting other people. I was meeting sisters up here who were on another level. They was trying to go to the next step. So I think the main part about it was a lack of trust. I didn't have the same amount of time to spend with her. We struggled with it my first year in law school; we struggled with it my second year in law school. We weren't even really together my first and second years, but it was just on and off struggling with it.

"This week we just came to terms that, you know, it isn't gonna happen. But the confusing things to me is that I don't know if it's just 'cause I'm in school. 'Cause like, everytime school is over, like during the summer or the break, I feel like that could happen.

"But I think we've both realized that, this time, this is it."

JOHN COPELAND, 24: BUPPIE LOVE

MIAMI—Of course, John Copeland's heard the question, ringing, as it has been, in the collective ears of at least two generations of African-American men. Where are the good Black men? Sisters want to know. For years now, they've watched their sons and boyfriends and husbands carted out of their lives through one mishap after another. They've watched their men rot in prisons, watched them abandon their families, watched them kill themselves with drink and drugs and each other. Books have been written. Talk shows have been aired. Still, the question persists: Where are all the good Black men?

For those Black men still alive, sober and not incarcerated—that is to say, the majority of us—the question raises eyebrows, ire and still more questions. Most commonly contemplated,/ obviously, is the definition of "good" here. What, we ask in response, constitutes a good brother? Too often, the answer returns with any number of variations on the same, tired patriarchal theme. A good man has a good (read: well-paying) job; a good man is socially connected; a good man is powerful.

Now, hand this answer back to most Black women and they're likely to deny that they limit their ideals to so obviously materialistic and shallow definitions. They'll tell you, sincerely, that a good man is also sensitive and caring and warm and gentle. They'll tell you worldly possessions mean little in the measurement of a good man. But keep listening and plenty will also admit that they haven't checked for him lately at the car wash or the security-guard booth or the drive-through window. Mr. Ideal, to popular thinking, wears a suit to work, not a uniform with golden arches stitched into the sun visor. He draws big bucks, sweet benefits and has a few pretty trinkets to show for it all. Power, even the appearance of it, is an aphrodisiac in contemporary America, no matter whether its wearer deals in cars, crack or certificates of deposit.

And it has, to hear many Black men tell it, driven a wedge between them and the women they fear harbor a standard that most of us could never rise to. White men have choked off the avenues to power to most of us. Rare is the good job, upper-crust education, high-octane Rolodex. We are shut out of the game or, at best, permitted to play only along the sidelines. Still, we fear, our women cannot understand this. They don't know how hard it is for us, we complain. They want us to match the white boys achievement for achievement, without ever enjoying the resources available to them. So the ringing continues: Where are all the good Black men?

Enter John, who at twenty-four doesn't necessarily walk alongside the power brokers in his native Miami, but is doggedly stalking their footsteps. A Harvard-educated marketing exec by trade, John swapped a prestigious position with the McKinsey & Co. consulting firm in Boston to head Miami Partnership for Progress, a nonprofit organization dedicated to strengthening ties between the city's business community and the Black consumers it has so flagrantly neglected. Instantly, John became point man for the gripes, ambitions and worries of a community he still considers himself very much a part of. He's also high-profile, well-salaried and, stigmas be damned, Black and urban and professional.

He is, in short, many sisters' answer to that burning question.

Not that he tries to be. Not that he has ever tried to be. He's too caught up in his career and community work to squander time fashioning himself as a ladies' man. But the fast track hasn't blurred his observation of the obvious, either. He knows the sort of success he represents, to Black people as a whole, to Black women in particular. He knows his obligations to the good-man question, and, very much an admirer of beautiful Black women, John accepts the challenges of Black bachelorhood with both good-natured cooperation and half-embarrassed modesty.

Still, he says, it's tough sometimes finding suitable companionship. He's not a stickler for résumés or pedigrees, but he wants a woman who can understand him, his singular pressures and circumstances. Finding her has been an interesting study in trial-and-error learning for, even on the cozy frontiers of Buppie love, he's been hard-pressed to carve out a lasting and fruitful relationship; in any event, he's got enough to keep him occupied while he sorts through the field.

"I think there are some things that I need to take care of, and I don't want to have to compromise my relationship with anybody in order to do that," says John. "So I think I unconsciously have been trying not to necessarily go that deep into any one relationship. With the position I am in now, being out there in the public and everything, I get a lot of attention from women. That tells me it must be pretty bad out there, if you think about the laws of supply and demand. I think I get an inordinate amount of attention.

"Back in my younger days, I probably would have leveraged that for all it was worth. Now, I think I'm a lot more settled and a lot more mature. My overall perspective is that women are pretty nice people and I'm trying to find somebody that is a good person.

"I used to be into—especially coming from Miami—the big butt. I'm not saying I'm relaxing that a whole lot," he adds, laughing, "but a sister has to have some substance. Recently, I went out with somebody who I had gone out with in high school and—maybe I am the one that has totally changed 180 degrees—but it wasn't all that fulfilling. I probably am the one who's changed, but I have come to definitely respect women for the aspects of them that are particular to them being women, for their intellect and for their conversation. I may be the one who's done the 180 degree deal, but

I really do value a lot of that kind of interaction. Harvard probably did it."

In high school, John's aims and standards weren't quite so high. He got around, he says, trading on the popularity that comes with doubling as a two-sport athlete and honor-roll fixture. Of course, he wasn't looking for the qualities he values now, either. Ask him about it, and he'll tell you that he was in it for good times, props and some cheap, if scintillating, thrills.

"I don't know, you probably could call me a player back in the day," says John, amused at the memories of himself in his wool Kangol caps and purple suits, a far cry from the sober, navy-blue corporate armor he dons these days.

His field was broad and open, uncluttered by responsibility and social politics. His tastes were always fairly parochial. He loved sisters. Still, his attentions ranged at times.

"I went out with a few white women in high school," he says. "I never did that in college. But in high school, there was so much curiosity. And besides, I didn't really think about race like that at the time. These were the folks that I'm in class with; these were the folks that rooting for me at the basketball game or the football game. It was a deal where they asked me and I didn't say no."

His parents, major influences on his social outlook, nearly said no for him. I ask him about his parents, solid, working-class pillars in Black Miami, and their responses to his dips into interracial romance. Like a lot of Black parents with ties to the South—with remembrances of Jim Crow and lynching and race wars and separate bathrooms—his parents could hardly stomach his dalliances.

"Pops almost died," says John. "It was interesting. I ended up having to try to apologize to one woman. She decided she was going to come to my house to pick me up so we could go out, but my father just was not as nice to her. I can't remember what he said, but, in effect, it was probably 'I can't believe my son is going out with you.' That is not the most accepted thing, particularly where I grew up. I guess it gets back to the mistrust Blacks have of whites."

He says his parents' response bothered him, but it would

prompt, in later years, John's reexamination of his consciousness, the obligations to that burning question. By college, he'd determined that he was one Black professional who was going to enjoy a Black family.

"In college, I never even thought about dating non-Black women. I suppose if I had I would have pursued it if that's what I wanted to do. By then I really . . . it wasn't something that I thought I wanted to do. Nowadays, I'm just going by what has worked for me so far. I don't think personally I would feel comfortable with somebody who wasn't sort of like me. Which means able to get along in both worlds. I don't think that white women out there get to know me that way. The woman I marry I want to be truly and completely comfortable with. That's a big part of who I am."

Again, that hasn't been easy. He covets balance, he says, for much of his life is spent walking tightropes, be they stretched across his career path or his personal life. He's formal in that way of aspiring professionals, but he detests stuffiness. He's often precise in his speech, but he cherishes what he calls being "down home." And his job is the most demanding high-wire act of all, shuttling as he does between the profit obsessions of the business sector that pays him and the calls for justice and opportunity from the Black community that raised him.

Big butts are great, but he's desperate for someone who'll tiptoe that tightrope with him.

"Intellect, I probably overplayed that," says John. "It's not like she has to be a rocket scientist or an Applied Mathematics major. What I meant by that was somebody who I relate to in both worlds. Somebody who can even get down home if you need to or cut to the chase. That is part of who I am and what I have to do every day. I go home and I live at home with my family and we don't speak proper English at home. It is Black Miami. I want to feel comfortable when I'm at home, and I want to feel comfortable when I am out. I'm going to functions with CEO's and big-time people. I need somebody who can feel comfortable there, too."

John says station matters little when weighing the substance of a woman. He wishes, though, that more Black women would give Black men similar consideration. Far from cashing in on what he knows are some desirable qualities, John seems genuinely disturbed that some Black women refuse to date men with menial jobs or low wages. In the ambitious pinstriped circles he travels, he says, this attitude is common.

"First of all, a lot of women don't go out with anybody that makes less than they do and sometimes that's hard," he says. "They don't want to go out with anybody who is at a lower station. For example, if you're a fireman and they're a lawyer, you don't count. I think there may be something to it as far as a lot of Black males are involved. I think some sisters are looking at some of the wrong things. My thing is, I'm looking for somebody who feels comfortable doing the things I have to do. I'm not looking for somebody with a law degree from Harvard or who graduated with a 3.9. I don't break it down. I'm not looking for somebody who makes what I make. Those are things I think you have to work around.

"On the other hand, I'm looking for somebody who is progressing and wants to get somewhere. That is not . . . They can start from anywhere. I think there is something to it 'cause I don't see a lot of brothers like me who are out there. If what [Black women are] looking for is people that are like me, that's a pretty tall order. I don't think you'll ever have a lot of white people or Hispanic people [successful] like me."

He's not boasting as much as he is running down the sad reality for large segments of Black America. We're choked off, under the gun. And a people in struggle can't afford to fixate on titles and prominence.

John says he'd rather seek maturity. As a result, he tells me, he often winds up going out with older women. But even that isn't always satisfying.

"I've gone out with women ranging from a year younger than me up to thirty-four. So . . . it was interesting. Part of it is, older women don't perceive me to be as young as I am. A lot of them will ask me out, then over the course of whatever, they'll say, 'Well, how old are you?' I think they have a sneaking suspicion that I may be younger, but they probably give me credit for being at least twenty-eight. Definitely, there's a different mentality as far as what is going on. I sense an urgency of looking for somebody with people that are a little older. The people that are younger and are closer to my age, it's more, Let's go out and have fun. I don't get the sense that we're there for a reason or there's an agenda. I guess, in the end, I prefer the flippancy of youth. I'm pretty flippant myself. I suppose my age works to my advantage, but I don't know.

"Really, I'm not all that worried, though. My attitude now is that when I get married, the woman will fit the bill. But in the meantime I am going to have a good time and meet people."

And, of course, he'll keep working on the answer to that ringing question.

VICTOR BROWNFIELD, 22: LOVE FROM BEHIND BARS

OMAHA, NEBRASKA—The hardest part isn't the bars that confine Victor to the grounds of the Omaha Correctional Center. The most maddening frustration that hounds him doesn't come from thinking of the time he's done or the time he has left or the regrets over the assorted crimes that landed him here.

The worst part about being in jail, he says, is missing his fiancée.

He feels he let her down just by being here. She'd urged him to chill with the drug dealing, to ease up on his preoccupation with gang banging. He'd been jailed before, but only for short stints. Those, though, were enough to spark her concerns. She feared Victor was accumulating some bad karma to go along with his lengthening rap sheet. He wouldn't keep getting off with probation and other warnings. If the bullets didn't take him, she feared, surely the bars would.

Victor didn't listen. He wishes now, of course, that he had. He was incarcerated two years ago and is due out in early 1995.

"She was madder than a motherfucker at me when I got locked

up," he says. "I disappointed her. I called her and they said, 'Collect call. Will you pay for it?' She said, 'Yeah.' Then she was like, 'Where the fuck are you at?' I said, 'I'm in jail.'

"She just started crying. She said, 'I told you to get a job.' "

Victor says he could only cringe. She's a good woman, he says, not like the others he's dated. Her peoples got a little money, a cabin somewhere in the woods in Iowa, a boat even. She's from Sioux City herself, doesn't really know about ghettos like the one in Minneapolis where Victor was raised. She thought, still thinks, she can help him overcome whatever he's got to deal with. He tells her all the time that she has helped, she has made a difference.

But here he was calling her to bail him out after he'd been busted selling marijuana. As usual, he was sorry. As usual, she got his back. She showed up and posted his $1,500 bond.

"I went home with her," he says. "She was mad and crying and shit and she was like, 'You know you're going to get prison time for this.' "

She didn't want to believe herself, though. Throughout the trial, Victor says, she supported him. She touched him lightly in the courtroom, whispered to him that things would be all right. She prayed and hoped and hoped and prayed. In the end, in September 1992, Victor got one to three years.

"The motherfuckers sent me to prison," says Victor, still incredulous. "She started crying, 'Don't take my baby; don't take my baby.' She was crying, she was hurt, but she is still going to be there for me. I got one to three. She wrote me a letter last night saying, 'I'm waiting.' I got it yesterday. She said, 'I'm still waiting for you and I love you and I want to marry you still,' and shit like that. I wrote her back a letter and I told her I got fifty-six days left till I am going to see her."

Victor says he doesn't worry about losing her while they're apart. He's realistic about the demands on sisters with men in jail. He expects her to wait, to be faithful. If she doesn't, however, he'll understand.

"When I first got locked up it went through my mind whether

she'd still be with me," he admits. "But she promised me and I trust her word that she would never . . . If she did, I couldn't do nothing about it. If she doesn't want my dick, it's open."

He doesn't believe it'll come to that, though. He's holding on, too. He doesn't have many choices, but the ones available to him he says he's eschewed. He's avoided prison sex, the homosexual unions that he says so many other men turn to when behind bars. For Victor, it's strictly nude magazines and the occasional letter and phone call from his girl.

"It's hard," he says. "You sit in your cell and you're watching TV and you see they got these bitches—'cause they rent movies for us on Fridays, Saturdays and Sundays. I just reminisce all the time. I'll be like, 'Damn!' Remembering and shit. Listen to a little Keith Sweat, you know. Honestly, sometimes I got to get my toss on with my hand."

He pauses for a second and chuckles, slightly embarrassed at owning up to masturbation. But more than this, his laughter, I suspect, also serves to keep him from crying.

When the chuckling stops, he lowers his eyes to reminisce a bit more.

"It's hard for me," he continues. "It's really hard."

ON SEXISM

I FEEL a special need to address the issue of sexism as directly as I can, given my limitations as a beneficiary of the oppression of women. I raised this issue specifically with brothers who exhibited admirable degrees of Black political consciousness because I wanted enlightening dialogue and monologue on what I consider one of the most critical matters facing progressive Black men today: that of the continued brutality, oppression and disfranchisement of Black women.

One of the most insidious side effects of the victimization of Black men in America has been our inability to understand ourselves as victimizers. By this, I don't mean to call on the white-dominated media's sweeping images of us as pimps or crack dealers or other forms of urban predator because, juxtaposed next to white folks, we remain very much the injured party here. But rather, most of us have failed to see our role in the continued domination of the one group of African-Americans less empowered than Black men: our sisters.

Like most men when it comes to matters of sexism and patri-archy, we just don't get it. We tend to process our hand in oppress-ing sisters much the way most white people process their role in the maintenance of white supremacy: We act as though we don't see it. Sexism is a foreign notion for many of us, taught as we are that race supersedes gender in matters of struggle.

Black women have gone hoarse trying to explain that this shouldn't be so. For the most part, they've been shouted down as betraying the race, as attempting to impose white women's con-cepts of feminism on the Black community. We level such charges as though sisters can't think for themselves, as though Black women don't know the manifold nature of their oppression as well as con-scious Black men understand theirs. (Oftentimes, Black women are themselves among those promoting such foolish, dangerous accusa-tions.)

But there are some brothers who have listened over the din of reactionary male egoism. There are some who've paid attention to Alice Walker and Pearl Cleage and Ntozake Shange. There are young Black men who recognize that the widening gender divide in our communities represents an immense threat to our continued existence here, as much as crack or poverty or teeny-bopper assas-sins.

This isn't to say there are any among us who've broken the grip of our oppressive constructs of gender relations. None of us have. All men are sexist. But some young Black men do indeed recognize this, grapple sincerely with it. So even as rampant misogyny in hip-hop caricatures us all as unfeeling, domineering, at times hateful brutes—even as much of male-driven Black culture foments bitter-ness and disdain across sexual lines—other brothers wage war daily with themselves and the power unfairly bequeathed us by virtue of our maleness.

Bilal Allah, a member of the Five Percent Nation of Islam and an editor at the hip-hop magazine *Rappages*, and Ras Baraka, poet, teacher and cofounder of the Black activist group Black Nia Force, have both thrust themselves full force onto this battlefield within. Neither of the brothers presumes to have figured out a whole lot about this issue of patriarchy and domination, admittedly bounded by the blinders that inhere to membership of overlording power groups. Each admits he makes mistakes, that his thinking on sexism and his idealizations of Black women are not always consistent. But like many of us, in the name of a sweeping love of Black people and an intense desire to resist oppression irrespective of its forms, Bilal and Ras keep fighting.

BILAL ALLAH, 24

"OKAY, basically how I see it is like, my whole perspective on women comes from two areas: what I seen at home with my Moms and Pops and based on what I've learned through experience and what I have read and how I interact with my own peers and my own demographic. It's like I definitely want to be with a sister who is dope. First and foremost, she has to love herself more than she loves anybody and anything else, then definitely a love for me. She has to have her own life. Definitely, I want her to be domestically inclined as far as being able to clean the house, make food and all that. However, I got to be up on it as well, I got to be able to equate that on the same level. I have to be able to clean, clean the food, whatever, so we can build together.

"I feel what happens is that, as the mother, she's going to be able to bring a special vibe when she cooks dinner that night. She's a woman; she got that special spiritual connection and she got that mental vibe where she knows how the family wants it, more so than I'm going to bring to it. She's more in tune with her thing inside than I am. Then that's what I have to learn about myself; then we can learn from each other.

"I think the roles should definitely be shared.

"I feel a woman has to have her own career, her own life, her own thing so that I can check her out. There's going to be days when I just want to chill, and just peep at what she's doing, check out her career moves, see how she thinks, see how she moves and shakes or just doing mine. It makes it hectic as far as having a family because then if both people are out of the house the majority of the time, it's hard to raise a family and raise kids, but that's the challenge. And because I want to, because I see myself as god, however, I want a woman that's a goddess, you know what I'm sayin'.

"She is the same as me but she is feminine. She is the same as me, but I'm just masculine. And it's like that whole issue of duality so, you know, Allah, God, is not male or female, but it's representative of the two entities, masculine and feminine, and it's manifested as a man or woman. And so I don't feel like a woman should dress in a head-wrap all the time and all that. I mean, that's cool, I think, if a sister want to do that, but I'm not trying to make her do that. A sister definitely has to be refined: I don't want to see her in cut-off Daisy Dukes, either.

"I would very much prefer to see her in business attire, sophisticated, dress pants, shoes, an eloquent woman. That's my utmost concern. That the sister that I'm with is very eloquent, articulate, intelligent, spiritual, loves herself more than anything else. It's disastrous, man, if she doesn't. It's like she has no self-esteem. And then all types of things happen. You won't be able to say that if something is to happen to me, things are going to go on because I know she loves herself and she's going to know that the kids, the family, the house is going to be straight; that she can replace me for someone who can handle their business; that if they're not like me, they're similar, where things are business as usual. That's what I'm looking for.

"I don't need this traditional woman, in the house waiting for me, and then when shit gets crazy she crumbles and then I trip on her while it crumbles. And then playing mind tricks, like she suckered me in, whatever. I don't want to go into any of that bullshit, you know. She is just as important as me. She is different, she is special. Of course, she is going to look to me for certain things and I'm a' look to her for certain things. Because she is tapped into certain intuitive instincts that me as a man, I've been socialized to be disconnected from. So I'm going to learn and be proud, you know.

"So there is going to be certain things that I'm a' have to check and learn from her. I'll have to straight be her student. And then the same as me, if I'm really on mine, if I'm secure and strong, then she is going to come to me and support and let me be the man who I am. But I have to learn to be in touch with my feminine side to deal like that.

"I think that being in tune to the feminine side is being in tune with your intuitive mind, meaning listening to your inner voices and letting them decide what's right and wrong. Rather than basing it on external shit. Macho, bravado. 'Yo, they trying to play me so I'm a' react like this' rather than say, 'No, fuck that.'

"Like a perfect example: I'm in a situation, right? I'm in a verbal interaction with a brother that I know doesn't like me. He's trying to play me. And I'm feeling embarrassed. Rather than playing myself and reacting off of his shit, I'm like, 'Yo, this is a bad vibe. I need to bounce.' And I don't care if I look like a chump to some other brother. I'm willing to survive—and that's the inner tune, intuitive, feminine side because I'm listening to my inner voices rather than saying, 'Fuck that. I don't give a fuck, I'm not going out like a sucker,' and then wind up really getting hurt or getting sent back to prison or something. That's dying, you know what I'm sayin'? That's killing yourself because you are making the wrong chess move. It's checkmate and it's over—'cause they just got the king. So rather, that's one aspect of it.

"And also, being in tune to other people, being in tune to other people's feelings. Rather than saying 'I don't give a fuck what nobody think. I'm going to tie this motherfucker by the ears . . .' and *boom, boom, boom,* not realizing that I'm catching this person at a down moment. I could really just distort their energy right now and their whole self-esteem. So I chill and be more critical and constructive and then see them when they are more of themself. Then I can drop a real bomb on them. Being in tune with these things, being in tune with certain people's feelings and be like, 'I know this is a bad time, I'm not going to say this right now, I'm just going to say it like that.' That's being in tune, it's basic things of, you know, how moms and grandmoms say you treat others how you want to be treated. It's basic down-South shit. That's what we knew.

"I think sometimes even being sensitive and trying to deal with sexism, though, become a game we get caught up, become something that get dominated by our masculine side. The majority of brothers are verbally gifted in certain areas. Talking to a sister has become a game. So that's what we do. Even us college-educated brothers, we come with game—where we are 'not sexist' because we've read the latest Terry McMillan book or Toni Morrison or Alice Walker. Suddenly, we're really in tune with Alice Walker—and we went to the last bell hooks lecture, you know what I'm sayin'. We come with these games. That's the twist that we bring to it.

"European men, they don't give a fuck. They in control of their women. And they straight with that and they don't front. They straight up with theirs. Like, 'My wife's a bitch, and I bring home the money and she knows what her job is.' 'Okay, I'm a' let her work and bring home so money, 'cause we're in the nineties—taxes are high—but she still know her role.' They don't care. The brothers, you know, you might have some brothers that are from the old school and they'll be on that vibe as well, but you get this whole new breed of brothers who say things like, 'Nah, we aren't like that.' Whispering and *boom, boom, boom.*

"They put a whole twist on it, but then they still doing the same shit. And they don't have any real respect for sisters' liberation struggles. We may not overtly hit our woman, but we'll hit them with something else, you know. And that's the difference, admitting you're a sexist in order to really deal with, and admitting it only to cover it up. That's where your feelings stop being truthful and honest.

"Now, I make a distinction between sexism and misogyny that a lot of sisters don't make. I think that a lot of sisters are tripping on this whole misogyny kick, like all brothers hate women. I think the majority of brothers really are sexual and you definitely have a silent sector that is misogynist; based on their own upbringing, they hate women for whatever reason. But I think that sisters that are flipping over that are doing it a little too often instead of dealing with the fact that we are sexist and that's bad enough and we need to focus on that. We don't hate them. But we do have a problem because we have been socialized to think that we are the only thing that is the shit and that the woman is a tool and that is it.

RAS BARAKA, 24

DD: How do you place yourself within the power relationship defined by sexism?

RB: I'm a sexist. I grew up in America, and capitalism breeds sexism. You're taught that from the time you're a baby to adulthood. It teaches men to be sexist, to be overpowering to women and to look at women as inferior or less of a person than you are. There is no way to escape it, but you have to try to fight it and recognize it in yourself. When you fight it you're fighting it personally at the same time, being around sisters that are not tolerating it most of the time.

The first thing is, when you're younger, you view women as being just weaker than you. You feel like they just can't do nothing. It's like, "You got beat up by a girl!" "A girl beat you doing this; you mean to tell me that you let a girl beat you?" That is the worst thing that can happen to you, being defeated by a woman, as if women are such low creatures that they don't have any skill or talent comparable to a man's. That's the first thing—so even when you are angry with a girl and you think that girl can beat you, you avoid that fight. If you get beat up by this sister here, that's trouble.

And then we feel like, women, you are supposed to have them, not just one of them, all of them. You can have them here, there and there, and you can do and say anything you want to them. That's how I grew up. I wasn't raised in my household like that. The family is not divorced from society, though. A family can't raise a child. A whole neighborhood, the society, raises a child. In the community, your brothers and stuff, they're telling you, "Look, in the summertime you can't have no girlfriend 'cause you have to get all the girls you can 'cause they are out in shorts. You got to get a girl in the wintertime 'cause it's cold and you get one girl to be up on—but when the summertime comes, you have to dump her." You don't have any thought about her feelings or what it is she thinks about this move you might have pulled on her 'cause, to you, you're not even looking at her as a person who has feelings, like a human being even. It is like pick and choose whatever you can do. Whores and bitches. It's reinforced. It's not like we pick it up out of a vacuum in some strange way. It is reinforced through your education, through the radio, through the television, through books, whatever. The exploitation of women in all ways. You got to get yours; you learn that women are evil. You learn. When I was growing up, I definitely had those ideas about women, and some of those ideas I still have.

I would say I'm not as sexist as a lot of brothers—not in tribute to me personally but in tribute to my mother, to some of the sisters that I'm around now who constantly make you aware of what it is that you're doing. Simply 'cause I'm trying to become revolutionary. My thinking is changing in the sense that you become more conscious of what it is you do or what it is that you say. You catch yourself: "Man, I wouldn't believe I said that." You think that if your boy said something, it's one thing; a lady said it is something different. I'll be with my boys and with my girls, and my boys are more important than my girls. If my girl got something to say, then she is not respecting me because my boys come first.

You're taught like this. We hang with boys. Your boys are going to look out for you on the streets. If you get in trouble, you don't call your girl. You call your man and they come fight for you. They rescue you if need be, tell your mother if she's got to get involved in it, but it don't ever have to do with a woman. That is why we have those feelings that way. Somehow Mother is even different. You look at Mother sometimes different than you look at a regular woman. You can't even make that relationship. It's getting so wild now that even Mother has become some strange thing to people. It is getting so bad. The girl intervenes with something the boys want to do and she doesn't like what you're doing with your boys, then something is wrong with her. She is being selfish, is what I think a lot of times. You got to check yourself.

DD: Yeah, those sort of self-checks are important. But we need some sort of construct that allows us first to recognize what needs checking and then that permits us to get beyond that macho shit that doesn't allow us to change. How do we begin to go about checking self?

RB: You stop and you think about it and you give her a call and be like, "Yo, you're right." You become more conscious of it and it makes you more conscious. It affects women, too. A lot of women reinforce it. They feel the same way, that men are there to get them out of whatever. Male domination in the society reinforces this kind of thinking. Capitalism uses the exploitation of labor so women are necessary twice—not only for their labor but for their reproduction 'cause they can reproduce labor, as in slaves. Slave women were worth more money than men because not only could they work for you, they can give you about five or six workers. So they cost more money and so women would be exploited twice and black women would be exploited more than twice. They are black and women and the fact that they are workers at the same time means they would be exploited as much as they can be in this society.

We use women to sell things. We play on the bestiality element in men. We sell cars, sell things that don't have nothing to do with women or people. You use naked women to sell the product, to make the money, and it just trickles down into our community, into everybody's community. It manifests itself in different ways. At the base of society is economics. So at the base of this society is capitalism and everything comes from that. The social structure of your family and your neighborhood and your community is set up based on your role in that society. Women in this society, in this advanced stage of capitalism, have no work to do. Supposedly, the man is to provide the function of the family and the woman is supposed to do whatever she can do to help him in any way. It's always secondary, even in the conscious community when we say, "Respect and protect the Black woman." That's a little sexist, too, and brothers use that because in the sense that we say "respect and protect," it's like they can't protect themselves.

In terms of respect, we want to put women on a pedestal, and that gives us a way to be like, "They're women, they might hurt themselves, we need to protect them." But really it is your idea that they can't do it no way. That they are not physically fit to do the things that you can do or whatever. So that becomes perverted into sexism as well. In Black Nia Force, we might have the women work out and then there are people who are opposed to that. They say, "Well, we don't want the women working out with the men; they might hurt themselves; they got to have babies. We need to protect them for having babies." That is that reproduction line coming in there. But if you are trying to fight something that you think is oppressing you, and it might even kill you, then what is the purpose of saving her to have babies when she might not even be alive? "We need to save our lives in order to allow her the time to have some children." It becomes perverted that way 'cause it's not really fighting the root of sexism, which is capitalism. Once you get involved in it like that, you become more revolutionary in the sense that you are looking at it in its proper perspective as opposed to like some sick type of weapon. Anything else is your coloring what society is doing now. You're putting the shade on it so it can look pleasing to you. Sexism might not be cool caped in white supremacy. Do you understand what I'm saying? But it can be cool caped in Black consciousness. You put a color on it.

DD: I know you've done work with progressive women like Sister Souljah. Tell me a little bit about how relationships like that impacted your dealing with sisters.

RB: I never had a woman as a friend when I was growing up. Not as a close buddy. I don't know too many buddies who say it. It is just your fellas. One day, women can't do nothing for you. That is what these rap songs say. They can have sex with you and please you, but that's it. My relationship with Souljah is she is not only a comrade, my partner; I love her, I'd go out for her and I believe that she would go out for me the same way. I never looked at that relationship like that with a woman before. It is usually your brother. Souljah and I did the welfare hotel children. We had a camp. We took some kids from New York City down to North Carolina and had a camp for the children. We had to teach for them, cook for them, clean them, all types of stuff. I got a lot of respect for the sister 'cause I've seen her in action and I've seen her speak and behave and have more courage and ability and more wit and intelligence than a lot of the brothers that I know. More courage than brothers who are on the street. When I see the sister I'm like, "Damn." Even if we disagree on certain things, I look at her as my friend. It has definitely impacted my relationship with women 'cause you say, "Wow, you could have a relationship with a woman like this that is not sexual." Even sometimes you have a platonic relationship with a sister, but you still want to have sex with her. It's still there regardless. It ain't because [Souljah's] not attractive or nothing, 'cause I think she is attractive or whatever—but it's just that my respect for her is on another level.

DD: I want to go back to something you said. You said that sometimes sexism is cooler when it is caped in Black consciousness as opposed to white supremacism. How do you think Black men process sexism as opposed to mainstream America? Do you think there are any differences, and if so how do they manifest themselves?

RB: I think a lot of the stuff is very similar. It might be different because your relationship to production is different, meaning how you make a living, and everything surrounding that is different. The only relationship difference would be that. The sexism in rich white America would be different in the sense that the women have more privilege, and because they have more privilege, I think it would manifest itself differently. With the brothers, it becomes, it might get, a little wild even 'cause your relationship to production is different. The society is set up, it's so wide. It is the separation of the men and the women, period, in this society. But when it comes into our community in terms of jobs, in terms of who is working and how much money they are making—like women who make more money than you—they are uppity bitches because you can't make any money, 'cause the society hasn't provided a way for you to make money. We'll start something to say that women are making all of this money and the men ain't making no money and the women are trying to hold men down. That's such a bunch of bullshit, really. They have nothing to do with you being in the position that you're in, to be honest. Like most people who are on welfare, a man can't be in the house. You can't have an able-bodied man in the house and get welfare at the same time. The relationship between the man and the woman is strained because of that, too. How brothers act toward them is different. They get angrier. When they come in the house, they had a hard day's work, this thing and that thing, and the women are less tolerant 'cause they have less privilege and less relaxation time [than white women]. Everybody in the household is tense and tired because you're working all day. Brother told me a few days ago he worked sixteen hours three days straight overtime. He's tired. He came home to his wife, she's pregnant and she has an attitude. He don't want to hear it, and she shouldn't have anything to say anyway. "I'm out working." But he didn't look at the fact that she was in the house working for two children, for him and having another baby by him and working and cleaning the house. The house isn't air-conditioned. She can't walk in the back yard and stroll along the patio or something and take a nice reading of a book 'cause she don't got any money to afford maids and a housekeeper. She is stressed out, too, and so a fight ensues and you think that a woman shouldn't talk back to you or say the things that she is saying to you or be upset with you 'cause you did all of this. And when she does you hit her, and if she says something else you might hit her again. You might beat her.

They shouldn't tolerate violence. You wouldn't want nobody beating up on your mother. Brothers, we don't get too upset about it. You feel obligated, but you don't get upset. If somebody hits your sister you might feel obligated to fight. There is a difference if you see him hitting her. You might be mad 'cause you're not looking at it as her; you're looking at it as he is disrespecting you. If a sister gets hit, you might feel obligated to do something about it but you ain't mad. You ain't as mad as if he hit your brother. That's what is different. If somebody beat up on your brother, you go beat him up. If he beat up on your sister, it's more like, "What did he do, what did he say? I find myself in those situations, too, and would I have hit her? She do got a big mouth. She probably said some shit she ain't got no business." After you hit her, you might say something to her. I see some brothers, they even smack their sisters. They might fight the boy and then smack her: "You always talking, get your ass in the house," stuff like that. Even their mother and the mother's boyfriend or something. That is how it is. It is not like, "You have offended her and you are upsetting me." It is more like, "You are offending me 'cause you hit her."

You got to fight it in order to become like, "Yo, you ain't got no business hitting on her in the first place. Regardless of what she said don't mean that you should beat her." The more conscious you become, it does allow you to have more feeling towards her when he hit her because you start to feel like, "That's foul, man, why are you beating her like that?" You feel that way about any woman. You could see a sister getting beat up on the street and you don't care. When you get more conscious you start to be like, "Yo, you can't hit her like that!"

DD: In talking with students, I've urged young people to step up and assume responsibility for attacks on Black folks in the street, regardless of whether they're familiar with all the players or not. When it comes to women, though, the brothers tell me that, if they break up a fight between a guy and his girlfriend, they'll feel foolish because plenty of times, she's right back with him the next week. I tell them to break it up anyway, but even those young brothers who I sincerely believe would are turned off to interrupting that sort of violence when they feel they're sticking their necks out for sisters who they worry will return to the man.

RB: That's true. That happened to me. My sister, we beat up one of her boyfriends before and she got back with him. But it's like, even a child, you might hit a child to stop him from doing something, and he might do it again. You got to teach them until they learn. Women are victims of sexism, as men are. A lot of times, women think they deserve it just like he thinks that they deserve it, and that's what society put on them. They think that "I shouldn't have got smart" or "I know he's got that temper, I knew he'd get mad, I shouldn't have done that, I shouldn't have said that, I knew he was going to hit me on the mouth." Then they think like that is some love in a bizarre way. A lot of women think that if he hit her, he loves her 'cause he got that upset about her—but that is not what that means.

Recognize:

6

The Struggle

for Respect

Somewhere in my heart lurks a vengefully mischievous alter ego, on my "white" side, if you will. Angry though he is, he's not to be confused with the sullen me who stirs on bad days or the righteously indignant me who wades loudly into the heat of political debate. He's not to be associated with any outburst or threat or nationalist polemic.

No, this man is quietly calculating about his arch acts, deliberate and coolly unrepentant in his malevolence. And when he surfaces, it's usually on elevators with white businessmen, on streets where white women clutch their bags as I pass, at suburban 7-Eleven counters when there's only me and that lone, white attendant working the night shift. He's never violent, my wicked twin; he's not even truly threatening. He's merely the boogieman so many white folks expect to see. And when they figure they've spotted him, that's when he loves to come out and play.

Granted, he never looks like he's playing, what with the scowls and grimaces and swift, sudden—but always harmless—hand motions he tends to give. Once, riding an elevator in my old apartment building, my boogieman, bundled as he so often is in a gray Champion hoodie, puffy goosedown jacket and sagging jeans, stood absolutely motionless for nine floors, staring from beneath a Detroit Tigers cap at a white tenant whose jaw nearly fell off his face when he saw I'd be joining him on the way up. The man tried hard to recede into the wood paneling on the wall, but from the sear of my eyes in his back and the occasional frightened glances he'd toss over his shoulder, he knew I knew it would take only one unanticipated move from me to have him shitting in his pants.

I could've said hello, tried sparking the conversation he was too paralyzed to initiate, to make him feel at ease. I didn't. Fuck him and his unfounded fears. It wasn't my responsibility to prove to him that I wasn't the last crack addict he'd seen getting busted on *Cops* the night before. Plus, it'd been a long day, and I needed the good laugh I had when I got home.

I realize I'm not alone in my mischief. I've seen my alter ego rear up in other Black men, though lots of brothers pretend that they don't harbor any such side. I even saw my boogieman in the movies once, in that scene in *Juice* where Tupac and his friends, strolling playfully through a park, happen upon a white businessman passing by. Mr. Pinstripe's fear too obvious, the crew decides to have a little fun: They scream "boo" at the white boy and watch him cower and stumble past hastily.

Mind you, the young brothers had no intention of harming the man. They didn't even give chase. But they wanted him to know they knew.

Some might interpret this behavior as just plain meanness. The more politically astute might see such actions as my higher, "Blacker" self does, as the desperate exercise of a power more imagined than real—and minuscule no matter what.

I concede that my little taunting, haunting games don't do anything to ease the suffering of Black babies afflicted with AIDS. I know that they don't rehab any Black lives crippled by crack. I understand that not one Black elder is taught to read, not one Black woman spared the scars of domestic abuse because of my games. For these of my people I reserve true labor and love.

Still, my boogieman plays on. He plays because I'm tired and, as much as I'd like not to admit it, still smarting from even the oldest of wounds that come with being Black in America. He plays because, in those brief moments, whites must hear the rattling chains of the ghost of retribution future, must snuggle up with the reality of what the travesty each of them has had a hand in making of our existence here and abroad.

He plays because, since America refuses to empower and respect me, it deserves at least to be frightened out of its mind.

But before anyone wails too loudly for my boogieman's marks, understand that young brothers play out similar games among each other far more than among anyone else. In his book *Monster*, from his cell former gangsta Sanyinka Shakur writes about "mad-dogging" passersby, about staring down other residents in his all-Black south-central Los Angeles neighborhood. Prison inmates from Detroit call the game "marquetting a nigga."

Too often, though, some of these brothers play for keeps. When that happens, tragedy shapes the endgame—and no one ever wins.

See, young brothers hear no ghosts of retribution; they haven't committed the sort of inhuman, global misdeeds that warrant such guilt and terror. They hear only the rage that roars in their own warrior hearts and feel only the weariness that burdens those whose people must abandon too much of themselves to "get along" (read: *survive*). To them, the mad-dog stare, being marquetted, represents still another attempt to take from them a respect they're rarely accorded and that, to white men anyway, Blacks surrender too easily.

So, as if bowing and scraping and lying and suffering all the other indignities of the confused and oppressed weren't enough, here comes this other young brother on the bus (or on the dance floor or in the school hallway) trying to take what his peer just ran out of the willingness to give.

Couple this with the self-hatred that comes with being Black in a whites-only nation. Add a misstep, a soiled Nike, then sit back and watch the news flashes fly: A teenager in Detroit shot to death for sitting next to another brother's girlfriend on the bus. A kid in Pittsburgh slain because he called someone the wrong name. A boy in Los Angeles dead because he wouldn't renounce the significance of the blue bandanna dangling from his pocket.

Me, I chose a long time ago to stop blaming the victim. I don't return mad-dog stares from Black men anymore. When I bump a brother in a crowd or step on someone's shoes, I say, "Excuse me" loud and proud.

Two motives determine why. One, I don't want to get shot or into a fight with another brother. Two, I've finally realized that, if an apology for an innocuous misstep will give some young brother one less reason to be pissed at his own, then I'll give it up. If a mere "pardon me" can confer even the slightest sense of respect and collective love on another Black man, then I'll mouth it.

Needless to say, my boogieman will continue to marquette the white folks who look at me as though I've got an ear growing out of my neck. Like the hillbilly white woman in the Nebraska convenience store who, after ringing up my five Snapples, one bag of potato chips and copy of *Sports Illustrated* late one night, wasted nearly three minutes fearfully pretending she didn't notice me still at the counter, glaring at her.

Presumably unaware that she could be no more scared of me than I'd probably be of her and the biker-gang sons I was sure this gnarled, snaggletoothed, tattooed Ma Barker had hiding out from the cops in her basement, she finally decided to acknowledge me.

"Whatcha want?" she snarled, avoiding eye contact and clearly hoping my answer wouldn't be her money or her life.

Her ugly face frozen in my stare, I chortled sarcastically and pointed at the bottles and potato chips and magazine still spread out on the counter.

"How about a goddamn bag?"

Some thirty years back, Malcolm X told our parents that the one thing power respects is power. Over the past decade-and-a-half, a generation of young Black men has lived out a painful and frustrating corollary to Malcolm's observation: The one thing powerlessness disrespects is powerlessness.

The proof abounds in Black America. We've learned well the ways of our masters, internalizing all the lies and misinformation America spreads daily about us, our communities, learning to despise ourselves as our enemies do.

Obviously, the ease with which we debase, abuse and kill one another—even as this country tightens its systemic noose around our collective throats—illustrates the problem. Front pages and six o'clock newscasts are filled with sensationalized reports of our fratricidal foolishness. Self-hatred, we know, is eroding our identity.

Our lack of self-respect is highlighted not only in what we do to one another, but what we will not do for ourselves. Too many young brothers steadfastly refuse to stand for something, anything, that promotes the best interests of Black people. We have little time for the ideals of community, collective responsibility, of being our brothers' keepers. Instead, we bow to the lie of individualism, chasing wealth and the chimera of fame. Our respect and self-worth are weighed most heavily on the scale of acquisition—cars, women, bank accounts. Dope dealers and doctors alike desperately suck up hedonism's fumes, praying it will anesthetize the aches of second-class citizenship.

We've always lived in a world wherein respect is measured by wallet size, but never before have we witnessed such a pell-mell rush down the American Way, one so tragic among brothers and sisters so young. Never before have we died so brutally and in such numbers for the hollow trinkets of makeshift self-esteem. Never before has a generation so betrayed its obligations to history for the few pieces of silver America's always willing to dangle as a diversion to the liberation struggle. The visions of Black Power that have informed our legacy seem, to us, a relic of a bygone era, like glass-heeled dress shoes, leisure suits and wide-collar print shirts. We've settled instead for the mediocre aspirations of Black Prominence—an eponymous talk show, a signature line of sneakers, an eponymous sitcom. After all, the struggles are not as tough, the ideals not as abstract, the salary a lot better.

Power and respect cost, and our generation has tired of trying to foot the bill. Meanwhile, our esteem continues to be ground to powder by the engines of racial degradation.

Of course, it's too simplistic to say that we don't crave respect because some men kill over shoes and chump change, because many of us gratuitously slander Black women, because we fiddle while our communities burn. We want it; we don't always fight correctly for it.

To hear us, though, is to know we desire the regard all men seek. We want our skills acknowledged, our contributions lauded. We want to be liked and appreciated. And we want to like and appreciate. Sometimes, we trade on respect as though it were some sort of karmic credit card, hoping that treating someone right will atone for past or present wrongs. Other times, we just hope that treating the next man right will spare us a bullet wound.

The respect of Black boys can often be hard won, but equally as hard not to court. Who doesn't want to bask in the favor of a generation that gives "props" and "juice," that'll "big you up" and "recognize"? Still, our tussles with esteem are forever waged on shaky ground. There is, we feel, always someone looking to play us, to dis, be it in the workplace or around the way; be it over the maddening trivialities of intraracial skin games or the hornet's nest of human sexuality. So we stay on guard, rationing out our good graces like overpriced caviar.

Too often, though, we still wind up wasting it on the undeserving, the unproductive, the unhealthy. That's the thing about the respect of the powerless: For all the significance and life-threatening gravity we want to attach to it, we still sometimes wind up selling it for cheap.

ANTHONY "COUNTRY" MEYERS, 19: RESPECT AND RECIPROCITY

LONG BEACH, CALIFORNIA—Country accepts that he's sowing a mean wind. He doesn't need anyone lecturing him on the evils of crack dealing. He doesn't need to be told again about the futures he may be ruining, about the Black lives his product compromises. He knows. And he's a man who believes devoutly in retribution. What you do, he figures, will come back to you. And so, Country awaits the whirlwind.

He prays only that he can soften the blow. He tries, you know. Tries to do some right to offset the wrong. He hopes that, when the universe finally exacts its vengeance, his track record will count for something. He hopes that karma or destiny or whatever you call it remembers that he's tried to be a good guy in spite of his hustle, that he's tried to love those he can and tried to respect almost everyone.

Respect, he says, is the linchpin of his conscience. He's not the dopeman stereotype, out here cussing out fiends, cheating them, clowning them in front of their children and friends. He doesn't run roughshod over anyone. He's soft-spoken, lenient, caring, even. He's in this for the money, sure, but that doesn't mean he has to mistreat or humiliate anyone. He gives people their due. He extends a courtesy, a dignity that he hopes will be remembered when the day of the payback he feels is inevitable finally arrives.

"That's the bottom line, you got to have respect," he says, lounging in an overstuffed armchair at a friend's house in Long Beach. "If you're dealing in the dope game, you know that you just can't go out and just do dirt and do so much evil. You got to do good. Although there is so much evil in this world, you have to do good in order to make it up. That's the bottom line. You can't do wrong to others and expect to be treated right. Where I was raised was in the South so it was very strict. Neighbors used to pound on you if you tried to be smart. I was raised with a healthy respect for people."

Reared much of his life in Texas, Country says he was raised to be a Christian, to honor everyone, to wait on God to solve his problems. But when he lost his construction job, Country lost patience with God. He copped a sack and started makin' loot. He still holds tightly to the honor part, though, to that respect thing he was drilled on all those Sunday mornings. He wants God to understand this.

"How I look at it is, I'm doing what I have to, to survive in the world," he says. "I can't do anything better. This is all that is here to offer me. I know I got a good heart. I know God is going to judge me on my heart. Things I am doing are wrong. I'm doing what I can to survive. I am not ignoring God. I know there is a God. I still pray at night. I'm still religious. I feel it is wrong because I shouldn't have to do nothing illegal. I should be patient with God but right now it is kind of hard for me to look forward to that. There are a lot of things that have to be done. I am taking things in my own hands. It might be wrong."

Of course, it's hard. It's hard to sell drugs and claim to respect the people around you. It's hard to respect his young rivals in the game when he knows they'd blow his brains out for a nickel. It's hard to respect the old customers who come to him sweating, begging, craving a hit that he knows they'll do anything for.

Still, Country refuses to be callous. He won't treat his customers like dirt merely because he knows he can. He won't talk to them any kind of way. And if he can help it, he won't let them squander all of their paychecks on his rocks. It's about respect, he says again. It's the least he can do.

"I already know crack is killing our race, but what I do is, if I see the family, the Moms messing up—there's always a problem with the mother or the father—I get the kids what they want, as long as my money is up in front. It is a respectful thing. Nothing bad; whatever they do, the parents and adults, is their business. But I know they got to raise their kids. I help them in the process even where I'm making my money. Like if I get a dime sale, when they give it to me and they got kids who're crying, I'll just give the kids whatever they need. Or I'll give the mom two or three dollars. Sometimes, I have to go to the store for them 'cause you can't trust smokers. I'll buy the family some bread or whatever they need. I talk to them, find out what they need in the house. Whatever they want, I get it for them.

"It's not much."

But it is, he hopes, something.

MARCUS FRANKLIN, 22: COMPLEXION COMPLEXES AND OTHER COMPLICATIONS

DETROIT—I never thought much about the other side. Honestly, I never really knew there was much of one.

For years, all I knew was that when I walked on the playground in elementary and junior high, I was a child marked, the inevitable target of some vicious complexion joke or another. I was the "tar baby" and "creature from the Black Lagoon" and the "black smut." I was "smoke" and "blue black."

I was a kid. I didn't know about the rape of slave women, about how forced miscegenation had stirred our gene pools until lineages of what were once the darkest Africans had found themselves all shades of caramel and café au lait as well as near-indigo. I didn't know how whites tricked us into believing one degree of brown more virtuous than the next. I didn't know any language to justify my hue, to prove that it wasn't some sort of curse or deformity or badge of shame. I just knew I was shunned, dissed.

I hated me.

I knew that to many, especially to many of the little girls I tried so hard to impress, I was ugly by virtue of my skin tone. Even to girls who found me attractive, I was "cute to be dark-skinned," as though my features had somehow conquered the poison of my flesh. And no matter what, I was never as good as the lighter-skinned boys I played with.

I envied those brothers. I marveled at how easy they seemed to get the girls' attention, how their confidence was bolstered repeatedly with remarks about how fine and light they were. They had it made, I thought ruefully. They had it easy.

I was wrong. I didn't know they, too, toted scars from our community's sick skin games, from being measured by the same white supremacist yardsticks that, even in the afterglow of the post–civil rights seventies, many black folks still used to undervalue and divide themselves. Their struggles weren't identical to mine, but they were grueling in their own right.

Many of them grew up feeling insecure in their identity, forever feeling pressured to prove their blackness, their "realness." To be light was to be considered soft, weak, of questionable legitimacy in the eyes of those who thought themselves the standard-bearers of blackness. Moreover, they had to fend off the envy of the darker of us who bought into the lies about the worthlessness of dark skin. We were targets, all of us. Me for being too black. Them for not being black enough.

But again, I didn't know then that they had a side. I didn't know what it meant to grow up insecure, fighting daily to prove that you were down in spite of myths about being "high yella." I didn't know what it meant to worry that friends and strangers alike suspected you of being stuck up because of your complexion, or that girls would date you only because they saw in your sperm the potential for "pretty babies."

It hasn't gotten much better, but a generation weaned on Public Enemy and Spike Lee has nonetheless chipped away at the shackles. Most of us understand, at least overtly, that complexion is no measure of any black man or woman. Plenty of us proudly proclaim our immunity to the sicknesses of skin games. Subconsciously, though, we still struggle with the oppressive iconography that gave us "good hair" and "redbones." We still confound our children.

Marcus knows the confusion these stereotypes breed. He knows the angst that our communities often invest in the fair-skinned, knows the frustration of having to forever show and prove, with having to fight in word and in deed to be respected as a young brother like any other. He knew and he fought. Sometimes he fought at the wrong times. Sometimes he wrongly blamed skin games for his troubles with people. Still, he could never be certain why he got this stare or suffered that insult. So he fought. Sometimes he won. Sometimes he lost.

Either way, he always wound up wounded.

"Did I ever feel the need to prove I wasn't soft? All the time. To this day. To this day. All the time! One, because I'm light-complexioned; two, I'm smaller than the average guy my age. I only stand at five six and three quarter inches, and I'm underweight, slightly underweight. So yeah, all the time, man. That's the root of most of the fights or physical encounters I've had with guys—be it in a bar, in school, wherever. That's where that stems from: 'cause I'm light-complexioned. I don't know what it is. I guess the darker you are, the tougher people think you are. I've listened to a lot of dark-skinned people say that they had problems with being of a dark complexion, some of them saying they have inferiority complexes. But a lot of people don't realize that a lot of light-complexion people go through maybe not the same thing, but the same kinds of shit that has the same kinds of effects. 'You yellow motherfucker.' 'You tar baby, you.' Because you're dark or because you're light, you're either inferior or you think you're the shit, you're arrogant. Motherfuckers automatically think that you have a chip on your shoulder or think that you think you're superior to people whose skin is darker to yours—and it's not even like that with me. But I've had people tell me, 'Oh, you're cool to be a light-skinned brother' or 'You're cool to be a light-skinned person.' And that's just as bad as telling a dark-skinned person, 'She's cute to be dark.' I don't think that's right. They're equally as wrong. And yeah, like I said, most of the problems, physical encounters and verbal encounters, I've had with the brothers, I think stems from motherfuckers trying me.

"And I've had a lot. I'm surprised I was able to maintain the grades that I did as many times as my mother was running my ass up to high school for getting kicked out for little bullshit. And I look back on it now, look back on the fights I've had outside of school or in the club setting or whatever, all the shit was stupid. But people don't realize that the rules are just different. And I'm not saying that the rules are right, but the rules are different depending upon where you live and shit. I may not react the same way to somebody in a professional setting that I would to somebody in a club or in school or something, 'cause the rules are just different. I'm not saying that the rules are necessarily right but you know that's the way it is.

"As far as respect, I don't have a real clear or precise definition of exactly what respect is in either world, but it's slightly different. Like say in the professional world, somebody says something to you that's out of line, you kind of learn to deal with it verbally. Whereas the brothers I know, most of them wasn't going to argue with you. They don't know how or don't want to settle things verbally or don't know anything about conflict resolution. I think that's something that needs to be taught in school, at an elementary level, because a lot of us don't know how to resolve our conflicts verbally.

"And that's why I say the rules are different. You get out of line or a motherfucker get out of line with you in a club or in school or wherever, you're not going to say, 'Let's sit down and talk this out.' Especially in the heat of the moment, know what I'm saying? I look back on all those incidents and say, 'Damn, that was stupid' or 'I could have reacted a little bit differently' or 'I could have walked away.' But in the heat of the moment, you're not thinking, 'Let's solve this.' You're not thinking to yourself, 'Let's solve this verbally' or 'Let's see if we can sit down and talk about this and handle this like two adults.' You're not thinking like that. I'm not thinking like that for one thing 'cause I know nine times out of ten, the nigga I'm getting ready to go to blows with, he ain't thinking about it, either. You're going to react.

"One time, there was this incident between me and this other guy. This was some time in June of 1993, okay. I went to visit my girl. We were kicking it. We weren't going together or anything, but we were kicking it pretty strongly, and we were physical with each other. So I went over there and I was visiting her, and a guy, a brother about my age, maybe a little bit older, knocked on the door. She let the nigga in. So I'm just sitting there. I don't know who he is. She ain't introduced us, ain't said nothing. We're just sitting there and out of nowhere this nigga started saying shit like, 'Well, who is this nigga?' And this goes back to what you asked me earlier about the light complexion and people perceiving or assuming that you're weak because you have light skin. 'Who is this weak-looking motherfucker? Who this nigger supposed to be? This somebody you fucking?' Saying shit like that. The nigga wants to start calling names.

"Again that goes back to the rules of the game—at least where I'm from. I'm not speaking for the entire Black community. I'm speaking for myself and where I come from. A nigga want to start calling a motherfucker 'bitches' and ' 'hoes' and 'sorry-looking niggas' and bullshit like that—that's disrespectful to me. So we went to blows.

"Then the nigga pulled out a razor and tried to cut my wrists. Obviously, he knew what he was doing because he went for my wrist and he cut it. Blood was everywhere. I thought I was going to die. He left after that and I haven't seen either one of them since.

"I had sixteen stitches on my right arm. I had six stitches in my stomach. I thought I was out of there. [He laughs.] Like I said, the rules are different. If you don't get a nigga, he going to get you. And obviously he was trying to get me. He didn't give a fuck about me so why should I, particularly in the heat of the moment, why should I give a fuck about him? If he's going to try to take my life?

"Honestly, I can't say whether that changed me or not. It depends on the situation. If I were in a club situation, or around those type of people, the guys I usually hang around, I'm not going to say that I'd back down. I don't think I'm as hyper or as quick to get physical with a nigga now as I was when I was in high school or when I just graduated from high school. But I still will.

"It's a matter of respect. In that case, I guess it would be respect from him and respect from the girl that was there. And to a certain degree, respect for myself, self-respect, man, 'cause I wouldn't feel right just walking away or just saying, 'Yo, chill out. That ain't cool.' Niggas don't want to hear that brother shit—'Oh, brothers killing each other, and we don't need to be killing each other.' When you are involved in that type of situation, motherfuckers don't want to hear it. Egos are involved and a whole bunch of other bullshit is involved and niggas just don't want to hear that, man.

"Like I said, we need conflict resolution, starting with kids, with teaching kids how to deal with people who are different from them or have views different from theirs. Learning to respect the fact that because this person doesn't think like you or doesn't agree with you doesn't mean that the two of you can't get along. 'Cause motherfuckers I know, if you don't agree with them, then something's wrong with you or you're out of line. Niggas are ready to go to blows, and that's not cool.

"It has to do, to a certain degree, with a warped concept of respect, what is respect and what is disrespect. It's some kind of an inferiority complex that—and I don't like to get into this because I'm no expert or anything—maybe dates back to slavery, when it was instilled in you that you were inferior. And then like a lot of older black people, particularly from the South and stuff, including my maternal grandparents, they have, to a certain degree, this idea: They don't just come out and say that whites are superior but they're always putting Black people down. We're always putting each other down or putting Blacks as a whole down. I think it's part of the reason a lot of us have inferiority complexes. And that's your way of proving this warped or distorted perception or definition of what respect and disrespect is. That's how you prove it by pulling out a gun or pulling out a knife or going to blows with a motherfucker. That's your way of proving that I am somebody, that I may not necessarily be superior to you, but you're not superior to me. I don't have any cut-and-dry answers, but to a certain degree it all— fights, the complexion thing—has something to do with inferiority complex and a self-hatred type of thing."

VIONDI COPELAND, 20: REBELLIONS AND RESPECT

ATLANTA—It was April 1992. Los Angeles was on fire, decades of neglect, white racism and black and brown frustration having dovetailed into a frightening conflagration of human outrage. And the fires were leaping. In Seattle, a community of Invisible Men materialized as though from nowhere to mete out vicious punishments to whites at intersections and in business districts once thought sacred. In Las Vegas, gang members banded together to send white cops scurrying for cover, leaving Silver City simmering even after LA had cooled.

In Atlanta, the future came calling for a debt from the past.

To much of Black America, Atlanta represents a new promised land, the latest whistlestop for a new Black migration poised to return generations to the same Southern soil their grandfathers once fled for the Los Angeleses, Detroits and Chicagos of Black dreams. It's a Black Mecca, a fast-sprawling projection of the African-American dream. A Black city run by a Black administration, home to the hub of Black colleges, to a blossoming complex of Black businesses.

Fittingly, it was the students, Black America's talented tenth in-training, the heirs to the dreams Atlanta had come to symbolize, who took to the streets. They came pouring out of libraries and dorm rooms and chem labs all over Morehouse and Clark and Spellman and AU. They marched at first. Some carried signs. Others toted Bibles. Others found their pickets in debris gathered along the way, in the stones and planks scattered along their path.

Somewhere along the march, the students got suddenly tired. They got tired of trying to explain, to plead, to bargain with white folks for a modicum of dignity. They got tired of being told to turn cheeks and love neighbors and respect even those who disrespected them. They'd seen the videotape. All of America had. Eighty-one seconds of white supremacy unleashed. They saw the batons, the tasers, the boots that crumpled the massive Black man. They saw the cops flailing away as though possessed. They didn't need sound. They knew the words without ever having to hear them. We all knew.

Somewhere along the march, the students got tired of listening. They had something to say.

Viondi spoke that day, as did his classmates and friends. A student at Morehouse, he'd been listening much of his life. He'd been listening when he was told to play the game. He was listening when he was told to get good grades, to get his degree. He'd been listening when he was told that hard work produced change, that success sent the loudest message to the racists who'd just as soon banish him back to the projects in Atlanta or, better yet, see him dead.

He heard all this as he marched in the streets to protest the beating, the acquittal of the white men with the tasers, boots and batons. But his heart roared louder. His heart reminded him of years he had never known. Of years spent in shackles, in cotton fields. Of years at the back of the line, the back of the bus, the back of the burner. His heart recalled, as well, the years he had known: the slights, the skewed stares that followed when he walked into office buildings, the glaze that seemed to coat white folks' eyes whenever his people demanded what was theirs, what was right.

Part of him had always wished the argument would come to the streets. Had always wanted to take it out of the conference rooms and other staid, sanitized forums where he'd always seen the questions of race and power debated. C'mon, he'd wanted to say, let's take this shit outside.

Finally, he and the scores of students who filled Atlanta's streets had succeeded. It was April 1992. Hours after the acquittal of the cops in the beating of Rodney King, Viondi and his peers detonated. For the next two days, they tried to take a little of Atlanta with them.

Viondi's calmer now, a year later, though as we speak the passion is still evident in his voice. In the conference room at the offices of Atlanta's 100 Black Men, where he works, he sits with his legs crossed, wearing a dress shirt, slacks, preppy Mickey Mouse socks and black penny loafers. His eyes are narrow, hooded, warm, his face roundish. From a distance, he could pass for a young Nelson Mandela.

He's listening again. He's returned to the game. He's a student once more, back in the starting blocks for the corporate rat race. He wasn't trying to risk his future in those streets. He wasn't trying to get killed, wasn't trying to hurt anyone too badly that day in 1992. But he couldn't take it any longer. He couldn't stand the idea of white folks getting away with it again. Uh-uh. At least once, just once, he had to let them know.

VC: We had just got finished having our pageant for Miss Morehouse. Everybody was still hanging around campus. Somebody came out and said the verdict: The cops got off. We were like, "What!?" The crowd I hung out with, Morehouse would consider the more radical crowd, more the radical brothers. We went to the room and started talking about it. Telling how it felt from our perspective. "What is it going to take to get justice?" "What must be done?" We came up with ideas that we got to hit them financially. That night we marched from the school downtown to the state capitol. No violent march. There was about thirty-five, forty people. It wasn't violent at all. It wasn't planned. We didn't have guns or sticks. It was just marching to the state capitol. We got there and all we were trying to do was stand on the steps. They clubbed a couple of brothers down the steps, telling us to all go back. We went back to the campus and said whatever we do, we need to plan, 'cause that was just a spur of the moment thing. We need to sit down, have a plan. We did that. The next day it was planned. It was a big thing. Campus had a news conference for all the students on the campus to come out. We said we want to do it nonviolently, come on out. We did that. We marched from the school down to city hall. What happened, locals joined in and from there people began to cause a lot of problems. I'm not downing them for doing it. They began to break windows on buildings, and they kind of pumped everybody up. From there, things just got violent. We didn't destroy no Black businesses. The only reason we did it 'cause we were tired of it. Brothers can't take it no more.

We have been through so much, so any little thing is going to tick us off. We have just been disrespected for so long, and whenever anything happens it just sets things off. White people, they might be more tolerant about certain things. You don't hear about this white man stepping on this other man's shoes and getting shot. They are more tolerant of that sort of thing, which is kind of good, but at the same time it's not. We as Black men tend to have a low tolerance of disrespect, but we should not use that anger on each other. We should know it's about time for the white man to stop doing this to us. Don't take it out on your brother because he stepped on your shoes. Take it out on this other people doing it to us. Throw the hostility that way instead of toward each other.

It is a question of respect. Rodney King, he got disrespected as a person, but that also disrespected Blacks, especially Black males. They should just show a sign that says, "Hey, you can't get no respect around here." The young generation felt the need to vent our hostility and crush that. Go out and take it out on white people personally. I didn't see nothing wrong with that. They did it to us, they do it to us, they still continue to do it until we fight fire with fire.

I took it to the streets. Personally, I started out nonviolent but as time progressed . . . The camera people were trying to get us on the news. We weren't trying to make this out to be no big news thing. We didn't want it flashed across the country. I saw a camera in my face, and I just knocked it out of my face and by mistake it fell on the ground. Also, I threw a couple bricks. Threw some bricks through some windows. Then we went through a couple of local shopping areas, either the Korean-owned or areas owned by the whites. There was a cash register right there and it was open and I just pulled it out. I didn't see no need for it to sit right there when it could be used for something else. I didn't get hit by no cops or nothing, but a lot of my friends got hit and it was awful. Brothers were getting hit.

DD: Did you attack any white people?

VC: Kicked a few, yeah. I wanted to do more than that, but one of my friends was there and he was like, "Let's go, let's get out of here." The next day they moved on campus. They had GBI, they had all those people come in and they barricaded us on our campus. They told us we couldn't leave the area. We were like, "This is a private institution." They got barricades set up around campus, shields and helicopters dropping tear gas down on us on our own campus. They were saying, "You all need to go in your dorms." The only thing going through my mind was concentration camps. All the people in uniforms were basically white. You had a couple brothers out there, but the majority was white. They had all these busses around. They tried to make us go back into the dorm, and we wouldn't go. They were beginning to hit the sisters with clubs and pushing, and that kind of just set it off. We began to fight back with the officers. That's when they brought in the helicopters, dropping tear gas, shooting tear gas onto the campus from the street. Brothers were picking it back up and throwing it back at them. Brothers' hands were getting burnt and everything. Sisters went and got buckets to put water out there so you could flush your face out. I kind of felt good 'cause we were one. They were in the wrong for coming up on campus and doing that. I criticize the commissioner because he had the say so, and [Mayor] Maynard Jackson, because they are the ones who have the directions and orders to do this.

I still have respect for Mr. Jackson because he's a good man. That one incident made me take a closer look at him. You are supposed to be my brother, my Morehouse brother, too. We are supposed to be looking out for us over here, especially as a people. But Black people had all the helicopters dropping tear gas. Maynard did come back and try to make a statement saying, "Hey, I probably called them in but it was for your benefit because things could have gotten out of hand. It could have gotten worse if you had gone downtown. We tried to keep you out of the fire."

I was like, "No, this brother has been brainwashed."

He lost a lot of faith doing that. After that, election time was coming up. He was going back to the poll and that affected a lot of people. We had a large turnout. Everybody decided to take how they felt to the ballot. We weren't voting for another mayor, but if he decided to run again we are going to have to reconsider him.

DD: After all the uprisings were over and all the statements were made, did you feel that African-American people had gained back a little bit of respect that may have been lost?

VC: Actually, I did. Because if we hadn't done nothing they would have felt, Hey, we can continue doing this. If we show we are not going to take it, we are going to get you on the street—hit you in the pocket or physically—maybe then they will reconsider. I mean, realize you got to get your foot in the door. Higher education and knowledge, they are what we can fight them with, what we can also use to gain our respect. They tend to have an advantage education-wise. But if we start going into those books and then go back and challenge them, they will see that we are not just going to take this. We are going to get respected more. But we're also trying to tell them we are not going to take it no more. They haven't stopped fucking us over. They may have slowed the pace, but I say every time something happens, we should take it to them like we did in the streets in ninety-two.

RAKEEM ALLAH, 23; ANDREW KIRKLAND, 19: "NIGGA" OR NOT?

THERE are debates that burn much hotter in our community. There are discussions among Black folks that guzzle far more emotional energy. But few issues lie so squarely at the intersection of language, power and identity as this nagging matter of the word *nigger*.

Older generations have debated it before us. I remember when Richard Pryor announced to thunderous applause that, after a life-time of bandying the term about, he would eschew *nigger* forever-more. He thought it was disrespectful to our time-spanning legacy, our beauty. Black neighborhoods buzzed about that one for days. In the barbershops, we'd roll laughing as Muslim brothers would bust veins trying to explain to the good-natured 'Bama deacons how the white man had locked their brains down by keeping them tied to that word. The deacons never really let on that they agreed with Brother Abdullah and the rest, but whether they followed suit or not, most of the adults thought Richard had done a good thing. Still, you also knew they'd miss it from him.

I don't doubt that the *Def Comedy* crowd would lavish, say, Martin Lawrence with a similar ovation if he swore off *nigger* in a concert film, but among our generation, the new champions of the good deacons' position have gotten a bit more hard-core. Fewer young brothers are relinquishing the word that easily. Plenty of us feel we have a case to be made for Black people calling each other *nigger*. (Of course, whites, as far as we're concerned, are still very much prohibited from even thinking about it.) As always, its meaning is purely contextual, but that context has expanded to construe *nigger* as a sign of ghetto love, a show of camaraderie as well as some level of recognition of our people's common constriction to the barren outskirts of American power. To make it go down better, we drench it with the nectar of Black dialect, hence the volumes of rap lyrics and liner notes (and books) crediting this "nigga" and that "nigguh." To call a friend "ya nigga" is a sure sign of respect and love. At the least, it's appropriate slang.

There are other camps, though, not all Muslim either. Fuck Axel Rose's whiny-ass "Eddie-Murphy-and-other-Blacks-do-it" line of logic. Plenty of young people don't play that shit, no matter what your melanin count's holding at. We'll tell anyone outright, "I'm not ya nigga." The use of the word for these among us remains a cardinal act of disrespect. Stress the *er* too hard, and we might be tempted to swing.

For even the furtherest extremes on the subject, the crux of the issue remains the question of who we are in relation (and opposition) to what America tells us we are, who we are within the context of what our history demands we be. Which is the greater show of resistance? To reject the master's term, Ol' Sam's homemade designation for the victims of his white supremacist viciousness? Or to embrace and then undermine it in that very special way we have with our captors' tongues?

Rakeem and Andrew know the power of words. Both are rap artists, though Rakeem the far better known of the two. Rakeem is part of the brain trust behind the Wu-Tang Clan, an architect of the Staten Island rap mob's "36 Chambers of Death" sound. A graphics art student in Chicago, Harlem-bred Andrew is yet one more talented Black man nursing dreams of rocking parties from coast to coast.

Neither is rabid in their opposing stances on the term, though Andrew still objects to the word far more fervently than Rakeem accepts it.

In the name of Black love, I gotta note one more element about these entries: Though they were interviewed separately and in cities hundreds of miles apart, both brothers' conversations indirectly provide compelling looks at another hotly contested phrase in the lexicon of Black youth culture: *bitch*. Unintentionally, these two entries speak to some of a generation's most commonly held views on sexism and the demeaning language revolving around Black women that reinforce our sexist views. Neither brother was asked directly about the term *bitch*, but both raised it, almost as a companion term to *nigga*. While each understands *nigga* in its historical and contemporary contexts, *bitch*, even when paralleled to *nigga*, gets dismissed as nothing worthy of historical analyses. So while Rakeem insists that he sometimes uses *nigga* despite knowledge of self, and while Andrew ducks the word for the same reason, neither lends *bitch* even that much consideration. Neither bothers to speak to men's diluted concern over language oppressive to Black women as any reflection of our Black consciousness.

I don't at all doubt that both brothers love Black women. But at the crossroads of language and identity and power, their testimonies bear sad witness that young Black men, like the fathers before, and almost certainly the men-children after, still struggle with the concept of oppression as a one-way street.

RA: I'm out of that stage of being bothered by the word. Several years ago the word fucked with me. Now the word is a slang word to me. It's not because I'm ignorant. I got knowledge of it. Somebody calls you a nigga, nigga is a word. *Nigga* don't mean nothing to me. Curses, *bitches*, all that shit, it's now slang to me.

I see that words carry some kind of power with them, but at the same time, the power it carries is from the person who projects that shit. If you hear me saying, "That's a bad-ass bitch," am I dissing her, am I complimenting her? To me, it's the texture of how you use it.

People would argue with me and I'd let them argue by themselves. Semantics. We got to snap out of that shit. We're worried about words affecting us. Hopefully everybody can recognize that it's slang; you just take that shit for what it's worth. If it offends you, then don't use it.

AK: Back home, my sister and her ex-boyfriend got me to understand more things with the Black consciousness movement. I'm the type of person to run away with an idea. I was like a missionary. I'm pro-Black, and I refuse to deny it. I would try to tell brothers, "I don't use the word *nigger*." I don't do that. I understand that it's something that we didn't make up. I know you can say whatever you want about the word, like, "We don't mean it like that"—but it's a negative word. Why would you even use it? Why find an excuse for using it instead of just not using the damn word? I know if I call a sister a *bitch* to her face she's going to have a problem, but I would rather be called a *bitch* than a *nigger*. *Bitch* is so trivial, like if I say, "You 'ho." Just trivial bullshit. Nigger has history to it, and I don't care what nobody says. Our people fought for a lot of different reasons for equality, and I'll be damned if to stop calling me a motherfucking nigger wasn't one of the things. If it wasn't a big issue we would still be called *niggers* on TV, in the news. You don't hear that shit 'cause motherfuckers would blow up. I talk to brothers and they be like, "Oh, I don't mean it like that, you're in on all that Black shit." I'm like, "You need to be in on it, too." It ain't no

Black shit. I deal with racism. I encounter it definitely. I went to an all-white high school my first two years. I went through. I left there because of racism and shit. White people were so funny. They do racial shit and don't even realize it. It is the norm for them. Brothers don't realize it, but they give white people leeway to use that word loosely. White motherfuckers would even ask me, "What would you do if I used the word *nigger?*" I was like, "Don't do that shit. You don't want to know."

JOHN COPELAND, 24: ACADEMICS, ACCEPTANCE AND AVOIDING "ACTING WHITE"

MIAMI—Somewhere early in our lives, Black people start making certain cultural distinctions between us and the white folks we interact with. As a kid, I was always fascinated with, among other things, movement, with how differently white people walked and danced and gestured. I cracked up whenever I glanced at *American Bandstand*, incredulous that anyone could take seriously this orgy in jerky rhythmlessness while *Soul Train* chugged along in some UHF netherworld. I noticed, too, that my white teachers didn't glide the same as the older brothers did around the way, their stiff gaits a marked contrast even to the strides of those brothers who cared little for the pumping pimp strolls the younger crowd spent so much time cultivating.

These differences—as well as that twangy, stilted, nasal sort of enunciation we had long since identified with "talking like a white person"—provided the source of endless jokes among my friends. Look on most any *Def Comedy* stage, and you'll find out that pointing to such differences still make Black folks laugh. By and large, we just don't think white people are all that cool.

Now, though, comes the disturbing argument that Black youth believe good grades and collegiate aspirations to be as much the provenance of white people as *American Bandstand*. Reports have flown about how African-American schoolchildren discourage their peers from earning A's and reading by accusing them of "acting white." Precocious Black children have been rounded up for talk shows and magazine articles to tell how their textbooks have been knocked from their hands, how they get chased home from school, how they suffer merciless needling from classmates—all because, the reports would have you believe, their classmates think good grades and an interest in anything other than basketball or gangs represents an attempt to imitate whites.

Such reports have always struck me as racist nonsense. To be sure, I've met young people who don't grasp fully the importance of education. I've met kids who, out of jealousy or embarrassment, may lob barbs at a classmate who reads regularly or who fares better on his report card. And I've met kids who cringe at the thought of being singled out at a pinning ceremony or an honor-roll call. But this is nowhere near the same as accusing our children of loathing intellectual pursuits because they think only white people should engage in them. I've never met any such Black kids, kids who hate good grades and harbor no dreams of life in a better world. I've yet to meet the Black child who wouldn't like to get an A on his math test. I've yet to encounter the young sister or brother who thinks the honor roll is shameful. I've yet to run across the student who thinks only white folks should have white-collar jobs, high salaries or an Ivy League degree.

John Copeland has all of these. A Harvard grad, he grew up in the heart of Miami's Liberty City, one of the toughest working-class Black communities in the country. He was a stellar student, always finding a place for his name and his grade-point average on the honor roll. He scored fifteen hundred on his SAT's. He was his high school valedictorian and later went on to a career as a corporate executive.

And nowhere along the way, John says, was he ever accused of trying to mimic a white boy.

"I was never criticized about that," he recalls. "People respected my accomplishments. At the free-throw line, they would crack jokes, always calculating the trajectory to the front of the rim and all this type of stuff. It didn't ever really discourage me. I actually kind of liked it. My boys recognized that I was hooking it up in the classroom."

John thinks the "acting white" criticism has less to do with our perceptions of academic achievement than with community standards governing social behavior. Precocious kids can be introverts, and few people of any color, he says, take to hermits. Hell, even white folks have names for scholars who don't place themselves within the active social context of their immediate communities: nerds. John suspects that this is what Black kids mean when they say someone's acting white.

"I conformed to whatever surrounding I was in," he says. "In the neighborhood, I definitely wasn't speaking like I do around the office. I didn't want to go that route. I hooked up the vernacular big-time. I think that I was cool like that, and I didn't have to be pressed with that sort of criticism. I worked pretty hard to fit in. I was a quarterback, was a drum major in the band—so I was out there shaking my ass in everything I did. People respected that, the fact that I could socialize with the community and was doing what I was doing in the classroom. They didn't look at it as trying to be white.

"I think that the individuals who end up getting called that are the folks that tend to not be cool. We are part of a community. You only really get ostracized when you decide that you are not going to be part of the community. It is probably not the people's fault, but if you see another Black person and you look down at the floor and just don't want to face whatever, then that is when people start reacting that way. When you, by the way you act or speak in a roundabout way, try to demean them. A lot of people who speak 'correctly' do it with attitude. 'I am speaking proper English, what the hell is wrong with you?' It is one of those types of things. I didn't take a holier-than-thou approach. It wasn't, 'I'm doing right; you're doing wrong.' For me, it was 'I'm doing it differently. This is how I'm doing it. You can choose what you want to do. That's cool. Let's do what we like to do.' That is less confrontational personality or whatever. I just think that feeling stems from the fact that some people try to put themselves up on a pedestal.

"It's not how well you do in school. It's how you socialize. It's pretty easy when you get in with everybody in the class. I lived in a Black community so I socialized with that Black community, in the manner that the Black community has deemed appropriate. Our community has standards of conformity just like white people have dynamics about their behavior. When you're a part of the community, you get accepted. It's pretty easy, really."

If anything, John says, he had more trouble fitting into the sterilized atmosphere of Cambridge. As excited as he was to attend Harvard, which he'd decided on after winning a scholarship to the school, and as beneficial as he says the experience ultimately proved, John admits he suffered major culture shock when he arrived on campus.

"I went there for the exposure," he says. "When I left here I said I wanted to be an investment banker but, truth be known, I didn't know what the hell an investment banker did. Didn't find that out till I was in school. I thought about going to some of the Black colleges. To a certain extent, they are starting to get a lot of the exposure that some of these more 'privileged' schools have had through the years—but everybody comes to Harvard to recruit. All the investment banks, Morgan Stanley, First Boston, Goldman Sachs, on down the line. You can't help but get exposed to it.

"So I went. I came from Miami, and if you know anything about Miami dressing, that was the first thing about me that stood out. I had Kangols and all that kind of stuff. I'm in Harvard yard with sunglasses while it's chilly, walking across the Harvard campus. Certainly not the typical student at Harvard. I didn't own a dark blue suit. I had a purple suit that I wore to grad night. Just what I had been exposed to was a whole lot different from the ivy-covered walls. I adapted. Some of this is all right. The rest of it I can do without. Like I say, I try to conform to my environment, but I'm not interested in trying to be anything other than who I am—so I don't think I adapted fully. There were certain things that I picked up that were okay and ran with. There were other things I didn't get into."

John says he grounded first with the African-American community at school. There, too, he honored accepted standards his community had schooled him on. He didn't want to be an outsider simply because he was away from home. And, yes, even at Harvard, Black kids can accuse others of "acting white," so clearly, this has little to do with grades.

John is quick to note also that to suggest a community has standards is not to say it doesn't permit diversity. At Harvard, he says, he encountered a wide spectrum of Black life, from the prepschool grads from the East Coast to other bright products of working-class homes like his own.

"I got used to a lot of other folks, even though I come from Liberty City and somebody else may be coming from Manhattan. At Harvard they have what they call Freshman Black Table, which all the African-American freshmen at Harvard go to. So that was the biggest thing.

"After those type of things, I began looking at the rest of the community. I had never been in such a culturally diverse place, and I liked that. I hung out with all kinds of people, ate Indian food, hung out with Indian people, ate Korean food, hung out with Korean people and so forth. I look on it as a learning experience. I went into it with some preconceived notions but I maintained a certain open-mindedness and I'm ecstatic that I went there and had a chance to learn."

But more important, John says, he brought to them a new perspective, one that said he could learn and interact as well as his peers, but he'd forever be that kid in Liberty City who made time enough to both score A's and shake his ass at pep rallies. His academic achievement was as high as anyone else's. His culture, though, was his own.

"At one point during my college career, part of me must have thought that I shouldn't have come to Harvard, but it was a good experience. I know I taught a lot of folks a lot of things about where I'm coming from. I wasn't trying to act like anyone except who I was. Diversity is fine. Black people are diverse. But we know what we mean when we say things like 'acting white.' We know how to make distinctions between being a different type of Black person and 'acting white.' I knew who I was, from high school to college. People looking at me knew they were looking at a Black kid from Miami. I excelled in school and did well in the corporate sector. And I wasn't acting like anyone except myself."

MATTHEW MIDDLETON, 23: THE WARRIOR'S SPIRIT

WASHINGTON, D.C.—As a kid, Matt watched the petty, sometimes dangerous games of machismo that played themselves out among young brothers in his Harlem neighborhood: the malevolent stares meant to chill rivals; the heavy woofin' exchanged between crews; the zero tolerance for the disrespect perceived in such minor matters as stepping on sneakers, bumping shoulders in a crowd, cracking jokes about someone's mother.

A third-year law student at Howard, Matt has outgrown most of the games, but he still sees them unfolding among young Black men wherever he goes. He thinks some of it is silly now and, given the itchy trigger fingers that too many youngsters want to pride themselves on, not worth the risk. But despite the ultimate insignificance and the potential hazards these contests hold out, Matt doesn't view the games as America would have you understand them, doesn't see them as any sort of indictment of young Black men, as pathology plays or atavism. Instead, he defines such one-upmanship as exhibitions of directionless valor, feeble efforts to establish power among the powerless and carve out respect amid the disrespected. In the young men, Matt sees the descendants of African soldiers, the spiritual heirs to the courage of Nzinga, the bravery of the Ashanti, the stout character of the Zulus. He sees the same toughness that survived slave ships and colonialism and dehumanizing cotton plantations.

He sees in Black youth a warrior class.

"A lot of scholars say that Black youths lack a lot of self-pride," says Matt. "Maybe that's true to a certain extent, but I think that there's a certain pride we do have. A lot of brothers I grew up with, they have a lot of pride. Even if that pride turns into ignorance or prevents them from doing things, they have a lot of self-pride and a lot of self-respect. That may not always be good in terms of how they show it, but it's there.

"We take the respect thing a little further. I don't know if that's good or bad 'cause a lot of times that can get us in trouble, but we do take a lot of things to a further extent than people that are not Black. We won't allow a lot of shit. The average brother that I've encountered won't allow certain shit, you know, to be disrespected.

"It has to start with our ancestors; it has to be something that's within us. As an undergrad, I was introduced to so much information about us, man. When I was in Harlem I didn't know nothing about the Black man being the original man, being the Asiatic man, being the first man. I just think it has to be something innate in all brothers and sisters, that's just something strong. We have a certain bond. Whether it's the melanin, whatever. There's just something special about us and people have to realize that. I do think people realize that. I even think white people realize that, spiritually, there's something in us that's rather different from them.

"Take slavery. Those brothers that in the slave era, there was a pride, a strength that they had to have to keep from succumbing totally when certain things were happening, like when our sisters were being raped and stuff. They were being disrespected, slapped, beaten or whatever and that demands a strong character when you can't just always react with physical violence and stuff. That builds up a strong character and that just kept coming on with each movement and each era. Whether it was the Harlem Renaissance, Civil Rights Movement, when they was all into nonviolence, the Panthers. That just kept coming on and on. We had a sense of pride, that we were people and we had a right to live like human beings just like anyone else. That kind of respect and pride has [characterized] a lot of our history."

But Matt is clear that he respects the heart, the burning desire to assert Black humanity, with which our legacy has invested this new class of young warriors. He realizes, though, that somewhere along the way, America found a way to pervert that courage, to kindle within us a self-contempt that turns that character against us. He's distressed by the bloodshed that has resulted, that some of his peers choose to settle differences with .38's rather than dialogue or, at least, an old-fashioned fistfight.

"One thing that immediately jumps into my mind is the sad fact so many of these brothers can't just square off and go toe-to-toe no more, you know what I'm saying? I think it started dying out when I started coming up 'cause it was happening less and less. Brothers weren't fighting one-on-ones. And I believe that if you had a problem with somebody and brothers didn't have all these guns, they wouldn't be so quick to react so violently. 'Cause then, if you had a real problem with somebody, you would step to them one-on-one. If you got your butt kicked, you would think again about starting some trouble over some stupid shit. But brothers got guns now, so they quick to react. It's like a power thing, that 'just to get a rep' mentality. I think that plays a large role 'cause brothers in their environment, they want to be all that they can be.

"I don't mean to go off on a tangent, but speaking of being all you can be, I'm thinking about one of my boys. When he went to jail—he was on the Island, on Rikers—he stayed in jail almost the whole time that I was in undergrad. One summer, I came home and he was out of jail. During that time in jail, he did the things he needed to do to become the big man in jail. So he didn't mind going back to jail. It was nothing out in the streets for him because he was the man in jail. He didn't mind doing something if he knew he was going to get caught and he was going to go back. He didn't mind 'cause he knew he was the man in jail. Whatever he had did. Whether it was he knocked somebody off or whatever. He was the man in jail, and he didn't mind that. He was, you know, back on the streets, he had to go back through the same old bullshit or whatever. But brothers can't afford to have that kind of pride. That's also ignorance.

"I've been in compromising positions before around pride. I've had confrontations with an individual who I knew was off his rocker, who had crazy pride or whatever, who would just flip for the littlest shit. And when you find yourself in compromising positions, it's either your pride that's going to prevail or your intelligence. I feel that my wisdom or my intelligence or whatever—it could have just been luck—made me say the right things or react a certain way to avoid that individual. It's not even a matter of punking out or being scared. It's just knowing that if you get into a certain situation with this individual, it's not going to end until it's fatal. I just think you avoid certain things. Yeah, my pride has been compromised, but I think to a certain extent that has made me a stronger person, too.

"Now, there are certain things that you can't let happen. It's not even a man thing. But if you're just going to live in this environment, in this society, then, I mean, certain things I don't think you can let happen to yourself, man. You can't let your face be taken, you know what I'm saying? Disrespected. Whether it's your family or whatever. There're certain things you have to fight, stand up for. Right is right, wrong is wrong. So it's not always a tough thing. Certain people, if I tell them that I'm from Harlem or if they watch the way I react, they think automatically it's a tough thing. But it's not all about that. It's just about not letting yourself be disrespected.

"But if you're knowledgeable about situations, then you should avoid certain things. If that's compromising your pride, then I don't have no problem with that. I think the strongest brothers are those who can compromise their pride and can shut up at the right times, when they know that they're right, to avoid a situation rather than provoke the situation because your pride is talking. You just don't let yourself be disrespected for any reason at all—but you just find ways to avoid the wrong types of situations. There are different ways to handle being disrespected."

The Souls

of Black Folk

"God is a schizophrenic . . ."

—MUTABARUKA

"When I was 12/I went to hell for snuffin' Jesus . . ."

—NAS

My approach to God has been a shaky, tortuous one, winding as it has through sprawling patches of spiritual turbulence: guilt trips over "back sliding" from the Christian roots that run deep in my household; a gnawing frustration with the church's role as anesthetic for Black consciousness; and teenage bouts with what I once thought was the Devil himself.

The summer of my fourteenth birthday, I was exorcised. The evangelist who performed the ritual told my mother that my spirit had been hijacked by a host of demons, that they had gotten to me through, of all things, the more than nine hundred comics I'd been collecting since I was nine. Moms called her in after my behavior and temper had begun spinning wildly out of control: I was coming in late, knocking over TV's and lamps in fits of anger, arguing with growing hostility with Moms. I was feeling my oats, thought I was a man, was ready to challenge authority in a heartbeat. Moms wasn't hearing it, though. All she knew was that something was wrong with her son, something she couldn't decipher. At some point, she gave up and decided to put it all in God's hands. I know I'm lucky she didn't put my ass out on the street. But what she did do would alter my perceptions of God for the rest of my life.

She called in the evangelist who would declare me demon-possessed.

Absurd as I find this now, I didn't question the minister at the time. I'd been going to church since I was eight and, even though I wasn't the most devout member, had been taught better than to doubt the spiritually in-tune. I had been raised to believe in demon possession and drilled constantly in Sunday School and afternoon services and revivals and watch-night meetings about the evils and dangers of "spirits of the earth and air." So when the evangelist offered her spiritual diagnosis, I went along, even going to the trouble to growl and froth on cue. (Like I said, I believed.) I remember how my mother cried as the woman held me down and smeared olive oil, in the shape of a cross, on my forehead. I remember the preacher, sweating, grimacing, muttering prayers and, after a few minutes, turning to my mom to tell her everything was all right now. The demons, she said, had been cast out. For good measure, the preacher torched my comic books.

There were shouts of joy, peals of laughter. My mother cried some more. I didn't feel anything. I certainly didn't feel "unpossessed." I was too scared, though, to say so. All the incantations, the olive oil, the commands for the demons to be gone—they'd spooked me more than I ever let on. I just wanted all the mysticism behind me.

At first the exorcism scared me, so I tightened my embrace of Christianity. I spent the next several months praying daily, reading my Bible and attending church, well, religiously. I temporarily put a hold on the street life I'd begun to court in junior high, and I permanently calmed my ass down at home. Whenever I felt my faith slipping, I was reminded in countless ways—by stray comics I'd find around the house, by my mother's counsel, by the sermons fired at me each Sunday from our church's pulpit—that Satan was always lurking, always waiting in the shadows to conquer my soul again, always ready to put me on a fast track to the pits of hell.

And I, of all people, knew he was right, didn't I? Hadn't I tasted firsthand the power of Satan to corrupt soul and flesh, of Jesus to cast out devils and redeem you again? The wages of sin is death, and my teenage spirit, I feared, had nearly taken an early buyout. Only Christ would save me.

There were over the years other scare tactics. In lieu of the X-Men and Avengers and the Hulk, I'd started reading Christian comics and religious tracts, particularly the dark, neo-Gothicism of a line of pamphlets known as Chick tracts. Named after one Jack Chick, the tracts I saw obsessed graphically over sin and shortcoming and the ugly prophecies from the Book of Revelation, its art and text scaring the shit out of me in countless, detailed ways through exaggerated depictions of hell's everlasting torture chambers that awaited anyone, man, woman or child, who dared to stray away from God's "word." My eyes bulged at the sketches of burning flesh and eternal agony and torment. I saw people stabbed and beaten to pulps in these tracts and comics, saw some men persecuted cruelly in the name of Christ and other men toiling in well-drawn damnation for rejecting it. For all the evangelist's declarations, never had my Marvel issues seemed prone to such bloodlusts. But this, I was led to believe, was different. If the gore and terrifying images brought you closer to God, further cemented your faith, then they were good things.

As much as dying and going to hell, missing out on "the rapture"—that mystical event in Christian prophecy in which true believers are caught up in an instant, mass teleportation to heaven while the rest of us infidels are left to wait out "the Last Days"— grew to be another anxiety that haunted me when I fretted over the fate of my soul. I was taught that to be left behind after the rapture meant enduring an Earth dominated by pestilence and war and the fascism of the anti-Christ, as per Revelation. Our church sponsored a film about the rapture for a group of young people, gathering us in the darkness of our tiny storefront for us to see for ourselves this all-white rendition of the misery and sadness and sense of loss—and that final pitched battle of Armageddon, between God and Satan—that ultimately await any who dally too long in drinking of the redemptive blood of our Lord and Savior Jesus Christ. I remember, too, poring over a book my mother had recommended that offered a fictional account of life for humanity after all the Christians had been borne away In the book, the protagonist accepts Jesus too late to leave in the rapture and, as a result, must be hounded for his faith by the relentless minions of the anti-Christ, who decrees that his number—666, of course—be stamped on the forehead or palm of everyone under his rule. Those who refuse risk death. One of the heroes of the book is beheaded because he won't be stamped.

These are the images I battled for much of my teen years. Even after my attendance at church began to fall off at 16, 17, I was still haunted by nightmares of waking up to find my mother had vanished "in the twinkling of an eye," to find myself alone in a diseased, distressed world gone mad. Even as I write now, I can feel the dread scurrying in circles in the pit of my stomach, compelling me to rethink the current heresy of my disbelief, asking me "but what if you're wrong? What if there really is a rapture and an anti-Christ and an Armageddon and you're stuck here to deal with it all?" I was taught that to refuse Christianity was to gamble with one's soul. It's a game you can't win, and a bet you can't cover.

It would be years before I could truly snuff Jesus.

Before I continue, I feel it necessary to point out that my mother, who was chiefly responsible for keeping me in church, never looked at fear as the central justification for faith. No, hers was a Christianity of love, charity and sacrifice. She labors today in what she considers "God's army" more because of what it does for her in life than what she thinks it promises her in the hereafter. Nor could the ministers and mothers and deacons and trustees who helped rear me, the working-class Black men and women who stood as quotidian role models long after my father called it quits, have truly imagined the persistent terror they were inflicting with their apocalyptic warnings about the eternal tolls of sin. They just wanted us kids to "get right" and were ready to use tough means to meet that end. Rather than some morbid interest in conjuring nightmares in children, they were far more concerned with escorting us to the moral high ground, continuing Black folks' expansive history of seeking truth and a proper sense of justice in a country that has never seen fit to dole out either to us. They knew it was frightening, this talk of 666's and Armageddon and final destruction by fire. But they wanted to create in us an ethicalness they rarely saw reflected in the world around them. Jesus, they felt, was the bringer of that uprightness.

As I stare at the contemporary political landscape, I see this same Black morality being seized upon and plumped by white racist Republicans in the "religious" right wing, their new smarmy incursions into the Black church cloaking their anti-Black, anti-woman, anti-human politics in Bible babble that their propagandists tailor to our specific tastes. It is this thirst that they try to manipulate when pointing to poll data that reflect Black social conservatism around issues such as abortion and capital punishment. But it's imperative that our churches resist these white supremacists' fake attempts at identification. We need to be clear on who we are, what we truly seek in our quests for spiritual correctness. We want only to be safe in our streets and right with God. We want to be blessed and prosperous and surrounded by Black folks who enjoy the same.

The Black church is the institution that urges Black folks to forgive their white oppressors for continued involvement in the worst crime against humanity the world has ever seen. How could it then side with racists whose only words for disadvantaged Black boys are "three strikes and you're out." The church is the wellspring for charity and love, gathering spot for the elaborate Black extended families that are the ultimate manifestation of the African proverb that tells us it takes a village to raise a child. How could this same church ever side with men who would lock Black babies in orphanages, who would chop off the public's helping hands to the poor? Our churches want freedom. They are not interested in being the tool that promotes subjugation.

But, of course, right-wing zealots have long since been pumping their bile through the channels of Black faith. This, more than anything else, is what set me on the course my mom would come to see as spiritual rebelliousness. I didn't mind the singing and shouting and fiery sermons that filled my ears each Sunday morning at church. But I began to notice, too, that, at home, Jim Bakker's PTL was in heavy rotation on our TV, as was Jerry Falwell and Pat Robertson's 700 Club. On the radio, I was bombarded by such ludicrously right wing (and not-so-subtly racist) "religious" programs as "The Voice of Americanism," on which some crackpot white preacher prattled tirelessly about communism in the South African freedom struggle and the moral wretchedness of Dr. King and other luminaries in the civil rights movement.

I don't think my mother ever bought into the twisted politics that hid behind much of the religious dialogue. She was merely interested in hearing "the word" wherever she thought it was being uttered. But to a high-schooler who'd just discovered a dusty copy of *The Autobiography of Malcolm X*, "The Voice of Americanism" gave yet another ounce of substance to the big "A-ha!" that came with my tardy discovery that white folks were manipulating God in the name of their own selfish political goals. As my sense of Black Nationalism exploded into consciousness just after high school, my mind bubbled with questions. Why had my Sunday School books always depicted Christ and his disciples as white men? Why was I always singing for Jesus to wash me "white as snow?" Why are white people in America allowed to defend themselves and their interests with SAM missiles and Sherman tanks while Black people receive only parables about the power of passivity? And just whose cheeks are we supposed to be turning, anyway, 'cause collectively, haven't me and mine been slapped on all four of ours long enough?

I began to worry that belief in God was a good excuse for Black people not to believe in themselves, in the transformative power of mass struggle. We wait on manna from heaven so that we don't have to organize in housing projects and at adult education programs. We look for the rapture because we don't want to consider the dead ends economic and political oppression have made of our lives here. We speak of Armageddon because at least then we'll be sure to win.

Even when I placed the politics of theology aside, I was beginning to deal honestly with the hollowness I'd always felt where others told me the Holy Spirit dwelled. There were too many things I couldn't reconcile, too many ways that religion just didn't work for me. The God I'd been raised to believe increasingly came to seem petty, insecure, two-faced even. Jesus curses a fig tree for not bearing fruit out of season. Our supposedly egalitarian Jehovah plugs Jews as the "chosen people" and tells women to "obey" their husbands. God grants men free will then threatens them with fire and brimstone if they attempt to exercise it.

I was confused. I'm sorry to report that not much has happened in the way of dispelling that confusion. I still am not certain who or what my God is. I believe in one (at least), yes, largely because I have no other way to explain the worldly wonders I see explored on the Discovery channel each night. How else to understand the hulking grace of wildebeests on the Serengeti or the killer speed of the cheetah? If not a divine one, then in what other context do I place the aerodynamic unlikelihood of the bumblebee, the multiculturalism of bears from panda to polar? Indeed, I believe.

But as opposed to kids I grew up with who went on to become ministers and choir directors, I can't claim to know God's wishes, God's ways. I don't know if He ever revealed himself to Muhammad, if He ever walked the Earth as Jesus. I certainly don't know if He is even a He, though, given masculinity's track record, I am frequently inclined to doubt it. I've been afraid to believe in much of anything concretely, fearful that my soul may be forfeit no matter what path I take. But I'd also hate to think I invested my life in a faith only to find that there is indeed no reward in the form of a Great Beyond.

In the end, I suppose, I'm not certain which is worse: Losing your soul to a Satan whose there or devoting it to a God who isn't.

DATHAN ERICK DUPREE, 16: JESUS IS LORD

MIAMI—Dathan understands that Jesus isn't playing well among his peers. He knows that now, more than ever, his religion is coming under increasing scrutiny, fire, disdain. But at a time when many of his peers are rejecting Christianity as the oppressor's religion, at a time when Black youth culture is crackling with cynicism over the church, at a time when sixteen- and seventeen-year-olds are finding God in Islam and Yoruba and humanism and nothing at all, Dathan Dupree has chosen to stand fast in his belief that Jesus Christ is Lord.

He's not pious, nor is he blind to the ways his religion has been used to deceive and subdue Black people over the past few centuries. Dathan just believes that, no matter how man has twisted the Scripture, his Bible still holds the key to life everlasting.

"A lot of people take the Scripture and they turn it around," he says. "And they try to make it seem like [it is] for what they want to say. People can really use the Scriptures head-on and backwards when they really want to. So they try to turn it around to what they want to say, but that's not what it means. People have to get more study of the Scriptures before they can try to quote it to you because I tell people now, if you can't show it to me in the Bible, and you can't tell me how you came to that conclusion, don't come to me with that. Especially nothing out of the Bible because, right now, people are calling me, like, a Bible scholar."

He's not boasting when he says this. It's true. Some people in his church do indeed think Dathan has come into an understanding of the Bible few sixteen-year-olds are privy to. He lectures, leads services, teaches classes and travels Dade County ministering to his peers. Many expect he'll be a full-fledged preacher one day soon.

Dathan doesn't talk much about what he thinks the future

holds. He's certain, though, about his past, a past spent bouncing from different congregations with his preacher grandfather, a past spent studying the Bible alongside his seminary-student mother. To hear him tell it, Dathan was born to be born again.

"If I had to start with my earliest memories it would have to be two years old: singing in the choir with the adults. Because I have always been a singer all my life. My mom was really big on singing so she got me started in it when I was very young. So, since two years old, I was leading songs in the adult choir and people used to tell me that I looked so cute and everything.

"And my grandaddy used to take me to Pentecostal churches all over the place. He is the bishop now, but he was the pastor. And he used to go to all of these different churches and speak. His church is based in Coconut Grove. It's the United Christian Church of Christ. So, he used to go to all of these different churches and preach and he used to come by the house and pick me up and take me with him. My really best memories of church would have to be when I was young and my granddaddy used to come and pick me up. He used to come get me once a month and we used to go buy a suit for church. A new suit every month for church.

"When he used to buy me these suits, I used to feel important. I used to feel like, 'Hey, I can do anything now, I'm dressed up, I'm lookin' good.' I had on my little tie on my little suit. He even bought me a cane. And, you know, it really made me feel like I was on top of the world, it made me feel like anything that came my way, I could conquer it. And that's really what I feel that spirituality does for you. I think that what church does for you. It gives you a sense of easiness and calmness. I was just telling someone the other day that I don't consider the week to be completed if I didn't go to church on Sundays. Tomorrow night I'm going to church for a prayer meeting. I normally go to church on Wednesday nights, and if I didn't go to different things dealing with the church, I don't think that my life would be as full as it is, because I've been in there so long. It's become a part of me now. People ask me, 'Man, why you always goin' to church?' I say, ' 'cause I like going to church.' "

Dathan says he tries to attend church as often as he can.

"It really depends on what's going on," he says. "Normally, I go to church on Sundays, Wednesdays for prayer meeting and Tuesdays for choir rehearsal. We just had a revival and I was there every night last week all the way up to Friday night. We didn't have it Saturday. So we took a rest. And then I was in church all day Sunday. We had Sunday school. And I teach Sunday school so I had to be there. I teach a high school class. And we had morning service, which was eleven-thirty to two-thirty. We got out of that and we had a program at another church, which we had to go to at three o'clock. We went to that. We got out of that program at three and had to go back to our church at seven. We didn't get out of that program until six-thirty. So as soon as we rushed from there, we just went straight back to our church. So, you know, I go to church pretty regular."

And no matter what his friends may think, Dathan says the benefits of his faith far outweigh whatever it is that their souls lay claim to. In this, he says, he has found a power few others even know about.

"The church gives me a sense of calmness and everything," he explains. "I also think that the church gives you a sense of moral values. You go to church and you sit down with your pastor and you listen to what they are saying. And you listen to the things that the Bible has to say, and when you try to work them into your life, you see the things that you should or you shouldn't be doing and you see the things that you can change. It also just gives you a sense of moral values. I find myself that I have a lot more moral values than my friends that I know of. I would never just walk around and just touch a young lady on her behind and think that it's okay. I mean, I don't even do that to my girlfriend. You know, if I hug her, I hug her around her waist. I don't do all that right there because I have more sense of moral values. She tells me that it's okay, you understand, but I feel that within myself that it's not. So, I don't do that. I would never call a young lady a name, like b-i-t-c-h or a whore or whatever like that because those are names that are given to people that are doing the wrong thing. And really, the way I see it, we need to try to motivate our brothers and sisters instead of pushing them down. Instead of stimulating them, we're depressing them. We tell them what they are and what they aren't gonna be and 'You not goin' to be nothin', you're never gonna amount to anything, you always gonna be a bum' and all this kind of stuff right here. And I feel that when you feed something to a person for so long, what you perceive is what you believe."

For Dathan, his food was the King James Version Bible, the one he studied with his mom as a child, even as she was preparing to enter what, over the past few generations, has become a family vocation for the Duprees: ministry.

"My mother's been in seminary for the longest, and she is a pastor now," says Dathan. "And in her studies, I remember her calling me in when I didn't have anything to do: 'Eric, come here. You fittin' to study, too.' So I know about the Bible."

Dathan says his mother was constantly promoting Christianity in the home, both in her actions and in the things her child could and could not do. She had house rules, says Dathan. And they were strictly enforced.

"There was never any WWED, no Hot 105, no liquor in the house at any time," says Dathan. "I mean, holidays come around, I have the uncles that like to drink. They couldn't bring it in my house. They couldn't have it around me. If I went and I stayed with them for the weekend, uh-uh, no. It had to be out the house. If they was going to be drinking, they had to go out and go drinking because she was the kind of person that didn't want them bringing it around me. And for a while, she stopped me from going to their house because they were doing it around me. And, you know, I would say that was the main way that she promoted [Christianity] in the house. And the way that I would say that she introduced me was that she just took it slow. She took me to church. She let me grow up in the church and then, when I got older, it was my decision. I was pretty much growed up in that way and that's the way that I knew. And, you know, people, humans have a tendency to do what they are used to doing, what they know to do. Animals, too. You'll see that a bird don't need to have a clock to tell it when it's gotta eat, when it's time to eat. They know automatically when it's time to eat. They have to have a thermometer to tell them when it's time to fly south for the winter. They automatically know that they have, because they are so used to doing it, it's built in, it's a built-in instinct. And so, you know, that's the way I feel. This was what I knew to do."

But Dathan admits that he hasn't always been steadfast in his belief. Like most anyone, he confesses, he too has had nagging questions about the God he's chosen to serve.

"In everyone's life a little doubt must fall," he says, laughing. "I mean, I'm a strong believer, but sometimes you always gonna pick some doubt. Something is going to happen and you'll be like, 'Oh, how can God let this happen?' Or you don't see how you are going to get out of this. And I think that when a person is saying, 'My goodness, how am I going to get out of this problem?' that's a little doubt stepping in right there because you are not looking to God and saying God is going to fix this problem or God will work it all out. You are saying, 'Oh, my God, how am I going to fix this problem?' That's one thing that we have to get over is this 'I' mentality. Because we can't do it. I mean, there is nothing on this earth that we can do. The Bible says that God made the earth and nothing in earth is made without God."

For all the Scripture recitations and pronouncements about faith, you can't help but wonder about this teenager, about his anxieties over his youth, so much of which has been spent worshiping and studying and traveling with adults. You wonder if Dathan misses the parties, the nights out with the fellas, the joys of being sixteen and Black in urban America.

"Yeah, there are some things that I can and can't do," he says, "but I don't feel like I'm missing out on anything because I'm still having fun. I'm young and I tell people all of the time that I may be a young Christian, but that doesn't mean that I'm not going to have fun, because part of being young is having fun. We have a youth minister in our church who is only twenty-two years old and we hang out together and we go to movies and we spend time together after church. We may go out to lunch and we sit down. We yuck it up. We laugh, we talk, we talk about everything. You know, we talk about relationships—a lot of the things that guys are talking about these days—but we are talking about it in the right way. And I still talk to young ladies, but I talk to them respectably.

"And I'm not for all those sexual encounters, either."

Dathan says he's saving himself, studying to show himself approved. He's cultivating an intimate bond with God, one he worries will be corrupted by succumbing to the temptations of the flesh.

Still, he's not sure what his relationship with Christ will yield. Beyond college, he's not sure what his future holds, what his God will one day demand of him. He just wants to be ready.

"My grandfather was asking me about this the other day because I do youth ministering along with our youth pastor," says Dathan. "And, you know, he was asking me whether I'm thinking about being ordained as a minister. I have always been taught that, when you are called, don't be like Jonah and try to run away because then all that's going to happen is that somehow a whale is going to come swallow you up. Whatever it is that God wanted you to do, you are going to end up doing it anyway, somehow, somewhere. You may have to go through something before you decide that you are going to end up doing it. And so, you know, if God decide he going to call me to do it, I'm going to go ahead and do it, but, let me say it like this: It's not anything that I'm planning on."

With that, Dathan laughs quietly. As clear as the wake of his spiritual journey may be, the future is that much cloudier. But he knows better than to question where he's headed. He was born to be born again. Everything else, he says, is up to the God he serves.

RAKEEM ALLAH, 23: THE BLACKMAN IS GOD

NEW YORK—'Round midnight. Firehouse Recording Studios, Lower Manhattan. The gods are in effect, filtering slowly, in twos and threes, into the two cramped rooms that surround the heavily padded sound room a few stories above a dark back street. Brown faces beam warm smiles and cold stares alike from a variety of frames—

hooded sweatshirts, baseball caps, braids, bandannas—as brothers trade handslaps, fraternal hugs and occasional glances at anyone unfamiliar.

Officially, this is a recording session. Gathered are members, friends and hangers-on of the Wu-Tang Clan, which on this night is still a relatively unknown cabal of MC's. In the months to come, Wu-Tang will explode onto the national rap scene with its gold-bound debut album, *Enter the Wu-Tang*. That uncharted hip-hop Xanadu known rap fans call The Underground knows the Wu well enough already, having been stormed by their hit "Protect Ya Neck," a gritty eight-rapper anthem making noise from New York to Los Angeles and a lot of places in between. The group is smart enough not to rest on its recognition. *Enter* is a work under construction, and since hip-hop doesn't really make much room for second chances or comebacks, the gods're here to make sure they get the album right.

At the helm of the production is Prince Rakeem Allah, the RZA, née Robert Diggs. Like the others, he sits behind the mixing board draped in an oversized sweatshirt and jeans. A bandanna covers his braided hair. Like the other young men pouring into the room, Rakeem believes devoutly that he is God.

He is a member of the Five Percent Nation of Islam, a small Muslim sect whose numbers—estimates place membership at perhaps 200,000—belies the profound impact the religion has had on a generation of young Black men. Through hip-hop—and such famed gods/MC's as Rakim, Big Daddy Kane and Brand Nubian—the Five Percent Nation has found a pulpit, a forum from which its members spread a gospel that, in addition to proclaiming the Black man God, also declares the white man the Devil.

Some have called the religion specious, racist, even. Others have accused it of attracting thugs and drug dealers, of giving them a religious foundation for their reckless hedonism. Whatever. What is certain is that, in Five Percent Nation, young Black men the nation over—the Five Percenters are clustered mostly in New York and New Jersey, though there are members as far west as San Francisco—have found a faith that affirms their identity, their sense of relevance to the world around them. And, as Ntozake Shange says, if young Black men need to call themselves God to feel good about themselves, then so be it.

Besides, how much more unbelievable is the notion of the Black man as God than, say, Immaculate Conception, a woman being born of a man's rib, Moses parting the Red Sea or any of the other fantastic voyages America's traditional religious texts take us on? How much wilder is the notion of the white man being grafted from the Black man than the idea that Jews are God's chosen people?

Officially, this is a recording session. But as the brothers in Wu-Tang gather about Rakeem to listen to him break down the science of the Five Percent faith, the session begins to feel more and more like a revival meeting. Occasionally, his comments are punctuated by a stray "true, indeed" or a contemplative "hmmm." The gods are building, their term for the hours they often spend discussing their various takes on the Five Percent faith. In the background thunders Wu-Tang's "Bring the Ruckus." Meanwhile, Rakeem teaches on, starting where you'd expect a man of faith to start when discussing God.

In the beginning . . .

RA: The Five Percent Nation goes back to 1964, when Clarence 13X Smith, the father, was down with Temple Number Seven, with Malcolm X and all of them. They were teaching a lot of the Muslim belief to the older people, a lot of the drug dealers, in order to try and get them to reform themselves. But there was nobody getting it to the youth. The best way to start to fix something is to start with the beginning. What Clarence 13X Smith did, he took the knowledge, grabbed all of the documents—you could say he stole them or whatever—put them all together and administered to the youth. He taught them. He said, you got the knowledge, the wisdom and the understanding. Knowledge is man; wisdom is woman; understanding is the child. That is the best part 'cause that goes into that man or that woman. He felt that you got to bring it to the youth, and that is why the Five Percent Nation is mainly a youth group because it is directed for us so that we can recognize at an early stage that everything is real.

There is a lesson written by Elijah Muhammad, the Sixteenth Degree, that says the five percent are the poor, righteous teachers who don't believe in the teaching of the ten percent. The Five Percent Nation is any five percent of any group of people that have the knowledge and the focus to know what is going on. Within every group, there is only five percent of that group, and with the government it's five percent that runs the whole country. The father, he recognized that a lot of these doctrines the Nation of Islam was teaching before, it really wasn't expressing them to the youth. And he was a member of the Nation of Islam; he thought that what Elijah Muhammad was teaching was good—but Elijah Muhammad was missing out on one fact and the fact was, Who is God?

The Nation, my idea of it is that it came political, became a profit, making money off it. You got a million Muslims working for you and they're all giving donations, selling your cakes, selling your fish. Elijah Muhammad, he had the biggest import and export of fish in the whole world 'cause he stopped everybody from eating pork, so now they got to lean more to the fish. He sells the fish. It was more of a money-making thing. With the father, he was like, cut all the spirituality and give it to the world. In the sixties we couldn't really catch on. If somebody walked up to you and told you that you're a god, you're the Black man, you made all of this, you ain't going to catch that. But if you take it to another way . . . Elijah Muhammad, he took it to the religious form. Changed the name to Allah. What the father did, he said, "Jehovah, Allah—all that is you. You're going to make it all happen yourself."

Elijah Muhammad wasn't deceiving people; it's just that he knew the times. Elijah was one of the wisest men in America. Definitely the greatest Black man born in America. You got to feed them baby food first. The father was saying that it's getting too late to give them baby food. You got to hit them with the raw beef right now. So Elijah did what was right for his times. He did it from 1934 to 1964. In 1964, the father came with his idea and that's lasted to this day. Both nations of Islam prosper and manifest the same type of knowledge. It's just that, in the Five Percent Nation, you have more freedom. If you're a member of the Nation of Islam and you speak about what you're not really supposed to be knowing at your level, then you are going to be punished for that. For instance, when Malcolm X started speaking, he got silenced. It was going through a religious ministry. When you're dealing with Freedom of Speech and dealing with a street level and allow them to memorize as much as they want, that's freedom. That's what the father gave us.

Let me explain something. First, God, the word *God* is "wisdom, strength and beauty," according to the Greek language. Also, God is a supreme being, and to be a supreme being you must be supreme to other beings. Man is supreme of animals 'cause he got the power to do this shit. Now, the Black man is a superior man. This is not a racial remark. He is supreme amongst all other beings. He is the supreme being of the planet Earth, and that is what God is. It is his nature to be God. You go according to your nature, and if he's doing what he is supposed to do, he is going to receive those Godly divinities naturally. Just like Jesus. He couldn't have dealt with sex or nothing 'cause in those times you didn't deal with sex without getting married, so he didn't deal with sex. He carried himself in a righteous manner and studied. The same ability is in every individual. You have to manifest it up. When I say I'm God, I am God by nature. It is my nature to be God. I am going according to my nature. The universe is your own universe. We are dealing with this on a mystery level. You know for an actual fact that the whole universe is a cup of water and all you are is one drop of that water. But you still belong to that cup, you are just a small amount, that same divinity. We recognize that all of us control everything. Individualistically, you have control of your own destiny. There is no mystery spirit that's going to be telling you what to do. That is what the father taught. He said you can pray five times a day—Muslims pray five times a day. You can do this all day, doing salat. They get all stimulated. You do martial arts all day, you are going to feel stimulated. The father said we are from the street. We don't know when it's time to pray five times a day.

I do feel obligated to use what I know to elevate the conditions of Black people. I personally feel obligated. I feel like I got a dog to walk. My plan is far-fetched. First thing you got to do is take care of self. Once I take care of myself I am going to take care of the next man. In the Bible, God gave Adam and Eve their chance to enjoy the Garden of Eden. Elijah said we must get land and we can't get land. It's too expensive. If we can't get land, we got to get people, 'cause people stand on land. If you got one thousand people, you got some land, you're covering some ground. You can't feed all those people. You can tell them how to feed themselves. Then, once you got that, it's all looking for the same common cause.

What the white man got, he has society. Society is a group of men that work together for a common cause. We don't have that. We don't come together for a common cause. If you make a million and I make a million and we come together for a common cause, okay. But every Black man ain't conscious. You just can't leave yourself as an open target. Once I receive my little promised gold, I am willing to share mine with whoever needs it. I am not going to give mine to a fool. All he is going to do is use me and move on. I think that is what the Black man's mentality is like. We are acting like bitches. It can't be like that. You have to hold your own. You got yours and I got mine and we come together, then we got something. You don't got nothing; I give you half my shit and then what happens when you use my half up? You are going to ask for the other half, and niggers do that. I've had it done to me a hundred times. The father told all of us the 120 lessons. The 120 lesson is something from the Nation of Islam. It has the one to ten; that is called the student enrollment. First question they say is, What is the original man? It has the one to thirty-six, breaking down on how we was brought over here as slaves, through John Hawkins in Jamestown, Virginia, 1619. The original deed was 1555, but they tell you how the first ship landed and it took sixty-four years to study us and figure us out and [they] had us in those little concentration camps or projects—and it's still a big project. That is the 136. And then you got the one to fourteen, breaking down about Moses and Columbus. How can you discover something that was already here and the Indians . . . ? Told you about Jesus and how he taught justice and equality and he didn't even teach Christianity 'cause they force that on people with a sword, the Teutonic knights. They were chopping off heads to force it. The same thing Muhammad did with Islam, though. He went with a sword. That's why he put a sword in the flag. Then you got the 140. It breaks down how much your planet weighs, what makes rain, hailstorms, earthquakes. A lot of brothers hear rain, hailstorms and earthquakes, and they think a mystery god is causing that. They were thinking that was magic. It also tells you about the history of the Devil.

The questions are answered by Elijah Muhammad, and [he]says that the white man was grafted out of the Black man. Inside the Black man there is this Everyman. You come from darkness to light. Out of the darkness they made the light. When you read the Bible, it says in the beginning there was darkness and God moved upon the many seas. They make it seem like it is all magic, but there is not too much magic inside of it. It is just something that you forgot.

Then after that you got the Plus Lesson. They be breaking down the atom of Islam. It will break down how your eyeball is similar to an atom and similar to the Black man 'cause the pupil is the black spot of your eye. That is the original spot, that is the original man. After that, you got the brown and the streaks of yellow and red and then farthest away from the black you got the white, which is the last man that could be created. It's got stuff that breaks down like that. It will break down how come fingernails grow.

DD: Let's talk about some of the practical applications of this. I believe that if your God isn't doing more for you than he already has, then you would get rid of him anyway. Your religion has to have certain practical applications. It has to be able to affect where you are living and how you live right then and there. Tell me about what you consider to be some of the most practical applications of your religion. It is okay to know how much the earth weighs, but how does that, if I'm hungry, feed me? My people are out here naked; how does that clothe them or how do you use that as a tool?

RA: One of the major principles that we realize is hunger. You can't sit at home and wait for some mystery to bring you food. That is what you do if you're on welfare and you're sitting at home; you are waiting for something to bring you food. We don't advocate . . . some brothers only live up to what they know. Sometimes the condition is stronger than their knowledge. You don't sit and wait for somebody to bring you food, clothing or shelter. You have to go out there and get that for yourself. It can't be classified as a religion, it's a way of life. It's being able to know what time it is. It is knowing that everything is well. It is real. That is the main focus—reality. You got to watch your health. As you build your mind you got to build your body. You stop eating swine. Niggers smoke mad weed and drink beer. We have been eating swine for so many years it is hard to stop doing that. It is hard to stop eating swine. I don't eat beef or none of that. Swine was my first stop. As far as beers and blunts, brothers is into it. They know that shit is causing harm. I smoke blunts, and I won't even sit here and act like I am going to justify it. I like drinking 40's and shit. I like skins and all that shit.

That's a contradiction. This is what I was saying. Everything is real. There is a good side to things and a bad side. In order for the Devil to exist, if God is the one that made everything, He made that. He got us with that shit. You read Ezekiel? He made him walk around. He made him defecate and draw flies and shit and then use that same shit to make a curse on somebody else. That's voodoo, man. This is supposed to be a great God, but why is He always acting on human emotions? The individual had to have the qualities of this. Even if you made man in the image of you, then you had to look like this, too. If you made man in your image, then this is how you must look. If we made the white man, if we was here first, then this must be the exact replica and then you are going to have some other motherfuckers like apes and all that shit.

DD: What is the role of sisters within the Five Percent Nation?

RA: We call our Black women our earths. We used to call them our queens, also. They reproduce us. The earth is the only planet that can give forth light, and the man is considered to be the sun. The women cover themselves. You don't show no man your body; only your man is allowed to see that. Only the man who lives in your garden. We teach our women to know the proper food to cook, stay away from the swine. Sometimes women nowadays is bad. I try to teach home economics. I'm walking the dogs in the house. You got a lot of women who want to be out there in the world and you can't really be doing both 'cause I can't do both. I can't try to be a home-starter and a working man. We stress our wisdoms—we call them wisdoms also—we tell them, "You got to cook, keep the house clean, keep me happy and I'm keeping you happy, and keep yourself refined at all times and learn the lessons for your benefit so you can know and you can tell other sisters." Not for the benefit of knowing and trying to use it against me—'cause you know how women like to get their shit together, too, and shit. The key to a strong nation is through the woman. My woman, I deal with equality with her so that keeps us equal. I am not making this a male chauvinistic statement, but we know that women have some limitations or whatever that she can't reach up to, just like we got some limitation that we can't do that they can do. As far as the physical world, man is more physical. Woman is more emotional. What I stress is to reflect my life properly.

DD: I figure when you are at war that you make full use of all the soldiers that you have at your disposal, and I am just questioning whether if making yourself the center of everything and everybody else revolving around you, you may be somehow repressing and constricting the potential that women have by making them secondary to you in the struggle that black folks have. Do you think that might be the case?

RA: That could be the case in some homes. Not my home. Right now I teach my wisdom like this: If I'm not around, do something. The first thing you do is what's going to maintain our kingdom. That is only like three hours a day. Second thing you do, I don't care what it is, read books, do something. Reflect me. Don't wait for me to bring you food. She's got a choice.

DD: That's three hours a day and she can do whatever else. Isn't that still defining somebody's role?

RA: I am not going to deny the fact that there is going to be a limitation placed on what my woman is doing nowadays, 'cause right now I am at a stage of war. The only way to keep your nation strong is through your women 'cause they got to teach the kids. If the woman is bad, the kids are bad. We don't see the kids that much. I might see my daughter thirty minutes a day. As a woman she may get four hours a day.

Equality is down the scale. You can't just have it. I am not with that shit. I don't want my woman out there. I want her right here. I got problems at home. We got problems at home. That is our main fucking problem is that there are no families. At my age group you don't get too many brothers with your girl and their baby. The woman don't feel she can be contained. Women is water. Water can take the shape of any container it is in. But sometimes it is hard to be contained. You got to squash that shit. Even if it is going to hurt her for a second. Women got to start their role and recognize there is a reason for that shit. We'll go through history. We will see. Let's take the simple thing: shelter. Who got the most potential and the most physical ability to build shelter? Man. You got some women, but man is the first candidate for that. For hunting and getting food. Women produce babies. I can go plant seeds. Women out-number man. I can plant nine seeds, but she can only have one baby at a time. I can make nine. It is war now. I can produce nine. That is nine months that she can't do shit, and after she had it she's got to go through a healing process and every two years she's got to go through that. She can't go through all that, even though they feel that they could. When it is time for being a woman, you can't handle it.

DD: How'd you become attracted to the Five Percent Nation?

RA: I became attracted in 1980. My cousin, the Genius, he was telling me about it. He was breaking down different things in the Bible. I used to go to church a lot. I used to live down South, in North

Carolina, for three to four years. I was going every Sunday to church. I was already faithful to religion. I would read the Bible and then Genius started breaking it down to me in a simpler form and then I started taking it on myself to learn. I was like eleven years old. Next thing I was full-fledged. In seven months, I learned all 120. I was just into it. I started going around building. When I first got the knowledge, it felt like, "This is the shit that we got to know! This is real!" It was reality.

Prior to that, as far as education goes, I always had my 12.9 reading level since sixth grade. I was always in the top classes. Always one of the top students, with a bad attitude. That's how come it was easy for me to learn 'cause I already knew the words anyway. The mathematics of the Five Percenters helped me through high school because there are words in there and science in there, and I got awards for science and shit. The main thing was that the shit was reality and the shit had me open like a fallopian tube. I just felt like this is real. I was a believer in shit, but I was always confused and shit. I would look at the picture of a white Jesus. I couldn't see him looking that soft. He looked pretty soft in that picture. When I got the chance to hear some more brothers come with the real shit, I went home and told my grandmother and shit. She was like, "You buggin'."

In 1980, the Five Percent Nation was a deadly gang. I went back to my old neighborhood in Brownsville and I told one of my boys; he was eleven, I was twelve. I said, "I'm a Five Percenter," and he ran. He thought I was going to jump him because they was fucking niggas up back in those days. My grandmother thought I was down with a gang and shit. I remember when I was eight years old, some Five Percenters beat the shit out of me. I even had a little fear. Once I started seeing what was going on, though, I said you can recognize that. In anything you do, you are going to have brothers on that bullshit. They are going to make a bigger name than the brothers who are going to write the shit. The bad niggas always get exploited. Television going to exploit the bad. My mother flipped a little bit, but she realized that "this nigger is doing all right." I'm not fucking up. I'm proud to be out here now. My mother definitely

supported it because it's me, my brother Divine, all of us, the top
five boys is all righteous and shit and she really supported. She held
her weight and shit. There is eleven of us with no Pops around no
more than about three or four years of the whole stretch. My Moms
was getting welfare checks and whatever. Your father don't become
your father, the white man becomes your father. Now she is sitting
home and playing the numbers and hope to God this and all that
shit. I used to tell her all that God shit and she'd scream at me. She
walked her dogs, though. Even through all that, Islam and the
knowledge I had, it kept me above it. I knew that this is all shit
happening. It is happening to me.

My mother was playing both parts and I know we missed out on
something. Me personally, I made up for it by being around other
guys and being in the streets and shit. My little brothers, I can see
their lack. They're more emotional. When you got no father
around, you start getting all soft. They are more emotional. I'm
more rugged 'cause I got the streets in me. My Moms did an excel-
lent job and at the same time you can't forget that the welfare
checks was my motherfucking nigga. The food stamps, that is my
man. That limits you right there. She couldn't go to work. She let
the white man be our father and shit. He is only giving you such-
and-such amount. It's a struggle. That is the whole point I am
making. Even though she is walking her dogs, the struggle is deep.
The result of any benefits is none.

DD: Let's talk about white folks for a minute. Let's talk about how,
as a Five Percenter, you conceptualize white people and their role.

RA: First thing I say, for the fifty-thousandth time, is that white man
is the Devil. When I say that, I'm not trying to be kicking no dirt on
nobody or nothing. Now, you got good and you got bad. You got a
good God and you got a bad God. White man, might as well say he
is God. He is the God of his own wicked world. It is my duty to be
the God of the righteous world. Make the shit right. These devils
always fucking with something. You turn on the TV, they're fucking
with the whales, with the insects. Black people have been here, and
we're up on that shit. They're new on this planet. If you study

mathematics they say the white man has been here six thousand years. If you read the Bible, Moses, 4000 B.C.—that's about six thousand years. That's no time. The planet Earth, scientists say, is sixty-six trillion years old. They found Black remains dating back millions of years. So these niggas is new on this planet and they're fucking with it. They've fucked up the ozone. Everything was lovely about forty years ago. They did this shit in no time. They're getting ready to leave this shit, so they are willing to fuck it up before they leave. Ever watch that movie *They Live?* It's a movie by John Carpenter. It stars Roddy Piper. They take the glasses and put them on and then they can see the aliens. The glasses don't represent nothing but the third eye, the dark shades, the dark side, the reality, the black side of things. You start seeing the light, and he saw money. The white man said, "This is your God"—and so that is their God.

These are dead niggas on this money. The death of George Washington and Abraham Lincoln is money for them. It is valuable for them. Those are dead presidents, and you can't even live this fucking life without dead presidents. They got the shit backwards, screwed. They can't help it, though; they think they're doing some shit. They are just fucking shit up. They're making some new AIDS. Trillions of years, and AIDS comes twenty years ago? How all of a sudden it just popped out of nowhere? They are fucking with shit. They are fucking with the laws of nature. If you fuck with nature you are going to get a bad, bad offspring. It's like when they took the killer bees, they start fucking around with certain bees, making hybrids and breeding and making mutants of shit. These devils are just fucking shit up.

RAS BARAKA, 24: SLAYING GOD ON THE ALTAR OF POLITICAL CONSCIOUSNESS

NEWARK, NEW JERSEY—Putting in time on the streets of Newark, Ras, like plenty of young brothers around him, fell under the sway of the Five Percent Nation. He had sought God elsewhere, but just didn't seem to be able to find Him. He had never bought into the notion of a divine trinity, so Christianity was out. As a child, he'd seen his parents, poets/activists Amiri and Amina Baraka, frequently practice African religions, but the beliefs seemed too esoteric for their son's tastes. Besides, even they'd begun moving away from God as he grew older, drawn more toward scientific socialism and, thus, an increasing disbelief in any supreme being. Ras grew frustrated with his search and finally turned to the Five Percenters, who, in turn, taught him to find God in himself, to believe that the Black man was himself God incarnate.

But in time, he began to find fault with this, too. It just couldn't contain him, couldn't satisfy his developing Black consciousness. It left him with too many unanswered questions, too many nagging doubts. As he had with other faiths, Ras left the Five Percenters. When he did, though, his search for God ended—and his lifelong commitment to the Black liberation struggle began. It was then, Ras decided, that God, the God he'd spent much of his teens hunting for, was not to be found.

That God didn't even exist.

"When I was younger, I was confused about spirituality," he says, "because religion is definitely involved in our society—Black people, the Baptist church. All my friends, my mother and father: church, church, church. We never went to church when I was younger. My mother and father were into traditional African religions and stuff like that. Things of that nature. When we got older they were socialist communists. They don't believe in God.

"I was in the Five Percent Nation. I believed that the Black man was God. In the community, brothers in the Five Percent Nation used to come around, and I'd listen to them talk. I thought they were doing something positive and they were together all of the time. I liked what they were saying, so I said, 'I'm going to check it out.' I went to college and I was still doing it. My father and mother didn't really know. I wasn't like one of those guys that was really out with it. My younger brother is in the Five Percent Nation now, and my mother and father know about that because he is really out about it. But I used to think that the Black man was God and the

Black woman was earth. As my ideas changed I started to read more to understand more things. My relationship to that is different. Some of the things I couldn't prove no more. When I can't prove it no more I start not to believe in it. When it starts not to have any relationship to anything, then I start to think, like, This is a little silly. That is how I started moving away from that. People say the Black man is God, the father of the universe, the Asiatic Black man. I used to say a lot of stuff but I didn't really understand that. Now when I look at it, I say, 'What does that have to do with the fact that I live in Newark, I'm a schoolteacher, I'm trying to make ends meet and most people can't survive?' And you're telling this man that he's God. He wishes he was God, he'd get the hell out of the situation he is in. People would say you have to have knowledge of self, and if you had knowledge of self and you had God, you would be all right. I started to see that wasn't true. Some people had knowledge of self and still didn't have nothing. They felt good but so what? They felt good a little while but you can't feel good if you can't feed your family."

Ras says the lure of the Five Percenters was the unity the group seemed to promise, the sense of belonging it engendered in Black men all too used to existing as outsiders.

"It's appealing to them. It's something strong, almost like a gang," he says. "But the religious aspect of it makes you feel good about yourself, gives you some self-esteem and self-respect, and that is what you are looking for and that is what it is good for. That's what they need. They're not really into [the spiritual aspect] as much. They haven't come into a different level of consciousness, is what it is. They haven't read different books or been around different people or seen different things or things haven't been explained as blatantly as things had been explained to me."

As indirectly as directly, Ras says, the influences of his parents, of their roles in the shaping of the Black consciousness movement, molded their son and kindled his spiritual curiosity.

"Even when I was younger," he explains, "I was always peculiar about the concept of God. I wondered why God was benevolent to some people and wasn't to others. I watched this movie *Frances*, about this white actress who they thought was a communist. They harassed her and they gave her a lobotomy in the end. At the beginning, she gave a speech about why she thought God was dead. She said she used to pray to God every night to help her and she used to pray to God when she lost things. She lost a hat and she prayed to God and sometimes she would find it but then she would wonder why God would help her find her hat personally and would let other little children lose their parents or other people to starve. It just caused a questioning and a dichotomy. Some of the explanations that you get for the reason why never sat tight with me when I was younger. I would think, I wonder why God don't like us, then. What it is that we did? We must have done something wrong."

For a while, the Five Percent Nation gave Ras the answers he sought so earnestly.

"What it explains to you on that level is that the Black man is God and that the white man must be the Devil and he is using his powers to put us in the situation that we are in," he says. "We can overcome this when we find out that we are God and we teach the babies and make them realize that we are God and we raise everybody else to be righteous human beings and righteous gods on earth and one day we will slay the Devil. We'll slay the Devil mentally, the mental ideas of white supremacy. That was an explanation about God for me then. It was something that I could relate to."

By the time he turned eighteen, though, Ras was on his way out of the group.

"Some of it I still like, but a lot of it I don't agree with because my ideas change," he says. "That's what God was for me then. I always had a relationship to things spiritual. Spirits and stuff like that. Being able to feel stuff. Unexplainable."

Attending Howard University started him thinking about new ways of exploring God, though Ras admits he still held on to some of the beliefs he'd brought with him to college from the Newark streets.

"The relationship that you have with other people, what they were doing, they change you," he says. "I learned more things about other religions; I started to look into that. There were still some things in the Nation I agreed with. I still thought the Black man was God and I was battling between whether I was a Five Percenter or whether I should be in the Nation of Islam. I was introduced to the Nation of Islam in college. That affected my idea about that. A lot of sisters were into more traditional African religions. They practiced those things, and all that stuff interested me. I would become confused and I wanted to inquire more and more about the relationship between all of this.

"Sometimes some of the brothers would pray. Some of them don't believe in praying 'cause they think you are praying to a mystery God. I definitely don't believe there is nobody up there up in the sky. I always believed that hell was on earth or that if there was hell, it couldn't get no worse than this. I might believe that your spirit stays here. Your feelings, your memory, your ideas live while you are gone 'cause you are matter and matter can't be created and destroyed. You exist without the physical. I don't believe in reincarnation. If the white man ain't the Devil he is sure doing a good job impersonating him, and if he wasn't the Devil, what could the Devil do to us that ain't already been done? That is what we used to say. If there is a hell, what can we possibly go through in hell that we ain't going through now?"

Still, Ras's faith was slipping, giving way to an approach he says is based far more on reason, on his ability to divine for himself the results of his material conditions. In time, he drifted away from the Five Percent Nation altogether. I ask him whether he believes now in any god at all.

"I don't," he says. "I think that the supreme being is a collective mind of the people. The collective consciousness of human beings on the planet. I think that is the supreme being. The intelligence. In the Five Percent Nation, they say the mind is the supreme being, the Black mind. What makes you, that is what exists. It is the collective of you that makes you God in the beginning. The beginning wasn't you 'cause you weren't there physically. Your mind was there 'cause it can't be created or destroyed. You were there beginning in the essence, when things were being created per se. Things were coming into existence. That is the essence. I believe in the collective consciousness of everybody on the planet. That's what keeps the world and everyone in it moving and dying at the same time."

But Ras isn't doctrinaire about his atheism. He understands that to carry out the work he has chosen, to labor diligently and effectively among his people, the activist must accept that God is real to many, and he's bound to respect others' faith.

"People can do what they want to do," he says. "I don't believe in McCarthyism—as long as they don't try to impose it on you. It don't bother me at all."

Still, Ras can't help but be a bit disdainful of what he sees as blind and unfounded faith in a being no one sees, hears or touches.

"Sometimes [religion] affects what people think and their ability to progress in a lot of ways because they are caught up," he says. "It's like the quest for fire. Early man couldn't understand how to acquire fire. They needed it for warmth and to cook things, and finally when they got it they didn't know where it came from. My father told me a story like in the movie *Quest for Fire*. They ran through the water and the water would put the fire out and they wouldn't know why the water put out the fire. They would make up reasons why the fire would go out—like maybe we're cursed or maybe the fire is evil and we are too good for the fire—until they figured out that the water was putting out the fire. Then they moved on to another level. They had to find out what that was about. That was wild because that is like men. When we come up against things that we can't overcome at this point, because we haven't acquired the proper tools and elements to overcome these things, we make it so spooky and unreal that even little children won't understand that.

"Most kids go, 'That's crazy. That ain't helping us. You're going to church every Sunday. You pray and that ain't helping us one bit.' That is how you look at it: 'I still live on the same block in the same city. That ain't helped us. This same dude on the corner keep whipping my ass every day.' You still make the same amount of money since you first went to church. 'It ain't helped us none,' to little kids. 'And the preachers, they're stealing money.' That is how you look at it. That's how I used to think about it when I was younger. These people buy the dream and whatever."

Ras says this type of spiritual cynicism is running rampant among young Black men.

"There is nothing there to explain the world to young men otherwise," he says. "Society hasn't progressed. We can't even protect ourselves from the elements. We're in a very barbaric state. We think we're advanced because we have a lot of bourgeois technology. Society hasn't developed past the steam engine yet. There hasn't been anything as great as the wheel or penicillin, even. From the poorest of the poor to the richest, all can benefit from penicillin. A VCR is useless for people's lives—only for luxury. That's what I mean. If a strong wind comes, we are defenseless. Like when the water floods in the Mississippi River. It's a catastrophe. That effects us because the people see this stuff going on and they are like, 'We don't even have enough information to protect ourselves, and we pray to somebody who won't even and can't even protect us. The only person that is protecting me is my boys around me, and I'm making money 'cause I'm doing whatever I'm doing.'

"They don't attribute that to anybody upstairs. The good die young. Why should they die young? Seems to me they should live long. People got explanations for that, that this is the Devil's world and all types of stuff that people don't buy into. The reason why I'm saying that young people don't challenge spirituality is because the people who have the information don't know how to challenge it. They are not looking to challenge it. The other young people don't know how to challenge it. These people reinforce it. They want you to believe that. Put your money in the plate. Pie in the sky after you die, work hard."

Ras says the cynicism has also led to a widening generation gap between young Blacks and their parents. No longer are we content to accept their cosmology, certainly not so long as our lives are inundated with violence and squalor—material conditions that persist despite our people's centuries-long supplication for manna from heaven.

"The advancement of capitalism is so harsh," he says. "Over

fifty percent of Black children grow up in poverty. It is so harsh or hard a lot of the time, and they don't see their parents making any way out for them. They feel like they got to make a way out for themselves. The drugs, the violence and killing is becoming more tense and concentrated because of television and video. We can now show violence all over the world to everyone. Show the whole world that this is the Black community killing one another. It gets like that. Plus, we are in a backwards state. The state has organized its forces against us. We feel there is no movement in our community. When there is revolutionary action going on, the families are closer together. The unit in the community is closer together, the ideas are more positive.

"Say there was a cultural revolution going on. We wouldn't be talking about 'I beat my bitch with a bat' or this thing. It would be something different. When there is a movement, the culture is tied into the movement. Society and your social behavior is tied into the movement because the songs are different. Say it out loud, 'I'm Black and I'm proud.' Even different singers. The art is different. Marvin Gaye, Roberta Flack used to have songs that were very conscious-oriented. Writers and stuff. That affects society and what is happening socially. What parents and people are thinking. They are thinking about moving forward and defeating something as opposed to a hopeless type of attitude where people are just beating on us. When that happens, the ideas from the larger society seep through our community. A lot of it is unconscious and some of it is orchestrated. Luke Skywalker did a video with Fidel Castro in it. I was like, What the hell does he know about Fidel Castro? First, I thought he was just some nut. I saw that Castro video and I said, Wait a minute, there might be something else to this because that to me is like, one instance you're talking about facedown-ass-up and then you got some stuff about Fidel Castro! That has a lot to do with the behavior and the ideas and what's going on in our community. Parents think the kids are hopeless because society says they are hopeless. They think the kids are the problem 'cause society says the kids are the problem. Children don't vote or pay taxes or control the Board of Education: They have no say in what is happening in society. They are not fighting the people who are doing the things to them. They are looking to the adults to do that."

This, says Ras, is why he cannot afford to believe in God. This, he says, is why he believes in the power of struggle over prayer, in the power of the masses over piety. Prayer equals activism for Ras Baraka. And God equals the will of the people.

"I just believe in the collective consciousness of the people," he says, "that collectively the people can bring into existence and put out of existence anything that they will based on the consciousness and the collective mind, the collective spirit. You definitely have to believe in energy or you are not scientific. Energy and matter can never be destroyed. In that sense, I believe that his spirit will live on or that I can feel what you're thinking. I used to think stuff like that was silly, but now I see it as scientific. Everything can be explained scientifically. It's just that some things haven't been yet 'cause we haven't progressed to the level that we should be."

JAMAL D., 23: GOD AS QUANTUM PHYSICS

MIAMI—Jamal didn't intend to go looking for God—and certainly not at eleven, twelve years old. But look he did, pulled along by a mother desperate to drive away the personal demons that had haunted so much of her life.

She looked wherever her soul could, delving into faith after faith, only to be disappointed and compelled to move on. As a result, Jamal bounced from temple to church to altar like other children change schools. He practiced Yoruba for a while. He was a Jehovah's Witness, a Seventh-Day Adventist, a Baptist. But these did nothing to draw him any closer to an understanding of some higher power. Rather, the sojourn his mother had taken her unwilling child on only drove Jamal farther from any faith in God. By the time he was thirteen, he says, he was so confused that he decided it better to simply not believe in anything.

"I was going through a big doubt session. I was like, 'There is no

God. There can't be any God,' " he says, sitting on the edge of his futon in an apartment on the outskirts of downtown Miami. "I was chilling in the bed one evening, right around the same time I was contemplating suicide. I was like, 'There definitely is not a God.' I was crying my eyes out, saying, 'All this is wrong; all that is wrong. I don't know how I am going to get through all this.' "

Somehow, though, he managed. And in time, he came to understand his mother's religious dabblings as a cry for help—help she got when she was admitted to a mental hospital when he was about fourteen. The treks through various beliefs ended then. Jamal was free to search out God on his own, free to believe or not believe. He chose to keep building on the foundation, however shaky, he'd been given coming up.

"With all of these constructs that were thrown into play, whether it was the Yoruba, the Christianity and going to church, I always felt that I had some connection with something," he says. "I won't even say higher, just something.

"If you ask me today if I'm very religious, I'd say I am very much against institutionalized religion. I'm not a very religious person. I will go to church every once in a while. I don't feel that church is all that. If you feel that church is good, I will push you toward it. Whatever you think is good is what you need to be pushed at. For me, I couldn't care too much less. I am at the point where I simply believe in the things that are. I believe in this. I can touch you. I believe of what is in here because it works. I believe that we are here governed in this universe by the universe. I don't think there is one particular creator.

"The word *God* comes from the Greek and Roman word, which comes from the ancient Egyptian word *neter*. *Neter* is a better word because it means 'principles.' A 'god' is a European extraction. They took it from that word *neter* and tried to bring it up to be some type of thing much like you and I, a human, egotistical being, when in actuality the *metu neter* were principles that were idealized because they were so great. The principles hold so much truth that we can take them and say this is what we need to understand. That is why affirmations are so good. You have an affirmation and it's true and you throw it on the wall and it changes things. It throws your spirituality into key because that is reality and you should adore that. If you are depressed and you think you are not worth anything, you should have a big poster of you sitting right on the wall 'cause that will change you. That will make you say, 'I am worth something.' It will make you become what you are supposed to be. Egypt was about that; they presented the whole perspective. The word *neter* comes from Egypt and that whole reality. That is what we need to get back to.

"I believe in God, Jehovah, Allah, It, the Pantheon. I believe we are all here as God. We are God incarnate. It is in us, it is us. What we are coming to understand as a society, technologically, is the truth.

"I think of it as quantum mechanics, because it's a new science that is revolutionizing the mind. It says something like this: You take a piece of paper and put two slits in and shine some light through it. The light goes through. If you saw the waves of the light, it goes through in patterns. If you do one slit it acts a certain way, it bounces off the opposing wall. If you do both slits it is like a wave. The light goes through and bounces off each other. Light beams are particles and not waves. Newtonian mechanics is what this society is based on. It is an observable phenomenon. If I observe light as a particle, we know it acts like particles. If you analyze it, we know it's a particle. By Newtonian mechanics, it can't possibly be a wave as well 'cause a wave is a wave and a particle is a particle. When you see them through the slits, the particles themselves are acting like waves. That is impossible in terms of Newtonian mechanics. Quantum physics is saying that if you observe this that way, it will be that way. If you observe it this way, it will be that way.

"It's a long digression, but you got to follow me. With that understanding, in terms of us as a universal thing, it is all interconnected. Einstein played with it. With Einstein's theory of relativity, he was doubting the very thing that he was proving, because the theory of relativity not only suggests that things are relative, it suggests that everything is relative. That is our reality. We are now scientifically proving that everything is connected.

"[Psychologist and author Na'im] Akbar says this. If you picture our understanding as a vast tapestry, picture it with amazing complexity where every strand is interwoven, and each strand is woven such that you cannot possibly separate one strand from the other. If you were to successfully get one out, you would unravel the whole tapestry. That is the whole understanding that quantum physics pushes. It says that we are all one juicy thing. We are all interrelated. It makes no sense for us to fight each other. Sexism and racism is what tears this society apart.

"Anyway, once we understand that these forces are what shape our reality, we just sort of be. There is a reasonable sense of morality then. What we do is we look at morality in terms of what we're taught. Oriental philosophy has never done that. You find those monks being some of the most peaceful people in the world. Some of the people that practice the martial arts, you find them as being some of the most peaceful and understanding people. All of that comes from where? Egypt. All of the martial arts. We need to understand this. Once we understand that we are the creators of all that is, there is no stopping us.

"Why should there be an egotistical of what 'God,' per se, is? God is some personified being when we have no idea what God looks like. Why should it be male? Why should it be Black or white? Why human?"

Hard to Earn:

8

On Work and Wealth

PROLOGUE: FOR THE LOVE OF MONEY

Somewhere along my road to adulthood, opium, to invert Marxist metaphor, became the religion of the people. Crack, to be precise, was the new gospel obsessing us Black boys. Selling, using, cooking it up—all exploded as the new abiding fascinations of a generation that grew so versed in the dope game that we would eventually rewrite the rule book.

I certainly wasn't above that fascination, enamored as I was with the thought that sixteen- and seventeen-year-old dropouts could earn thousands in hours without ever leaving the comfort of their own street corners. I stared enviously at the shiny Ford Broncos and Volvos that, exorbitant sound systems thundering, careened continually up and down our blocks. I marveled at how the girls flocked to the dealers when they walked into the clubs and skating rinks, at how the kleig lights glistened rainbows off their thick necklaces. I was amazed at how, seemingly overnight, niggas I'd been chucking dodgeballs at on the elementary-school playground only nine years earlier now heard their names spoken in awed whispers. Meanwhile, here I was, Mr. 3.8, without a dime to show for all those A's. Damn, how I ached to be down!

I never was, though. I partied with some of the dopemen, ran the streets with a few, but I never could bring myself to join The Game.

Not that I was noble or opting instead for some moral high ground. In fact, I used to harbor a bizarre sort of shame in my refusal to sell drugs, because my reason was simple and obvious: I was afraid. Afraid of getting caught. Afraid of going to jail. And— once closer scrutiny of the rule book made us realize that murder was standard operating procedure in drug dealing—afraid of dying.

This isn't to say I didn't get into trouble. I did dirt, sure. I was a stickup kid off and on in high school, squandering many a late night throwing the barrel of my friend's .38 to people's heads to speed them out of their Adidas Top Tens, leather coats and Starter jackets. My sporadic little crime sprees were prompted by the usual suspects —petty greed, a desire to earn props, boredom, mischief. Yet stickups always seemed, to common thinking around the way, second-tier crime, at best. You robbed people on impulse, generally, just because you saw them with some fresh shit you didn't have. If they had money on them, that was a plus, but really, you were in it for the gear. Jack moves were cheaper and faster than going to the mall. Just whip out the pistol and growl: "Yo, nigga, don't turn around. Just check all that shit in. Move wrong, motherfucker, and I'm poppin' ya." As clean and quick as it was stupid, when you think about it.

But slingin' them boulders, now that was where the real fame and fortune lay. Armed robberies were juvenile by comparison. And growing up, I saw us learn early to treat drug dealing as the business adults had always known it to be. I saw teenagers cobble together cartels out of ragtag crews of childhood playmates. I saw them set up elaborate distribution networks, calculating just how many crack houses one block could support before becoming oversaturated. I learned the mechanics of Triple Beam scales in a way no science teacher had ever taught, got a firm grasp on supply-and-demand laws that had seemed like so much boring gibberish in sixth-period econ class. It was the 1980s, and greed was the greatest good.

And never had young Africans on these shores been more American. The Game for us gave truth to all those wonderful lies American schoolkids are fed about all the joyful opportunities America holds out for them. "Just go to school, get a good job and make good money" was our directive, and we were drilled on it incessantly by our parents, teachers, heroes and role models. None of us wanted to believe our squalor was of other men's making. None of us wanted to bear the weight of knowing that our station was meant to imprison us, not be a launchpad to better lives. None wanted to accept that wealth and power had been intentionally placed beyond our grasps. Nope, not while there was milk and honey to be had.

Moreover, being the hyper-Americans that Black folks can be, we took a shortcut. Education—and not just school, but the totality of learning to interpret and then control the world around us—was the middleman who got axed. After all, if the point of education was, as we'd been tricked into believing, to get money, then why waste time with Algebra 3 if flipping a few kilos would sweep you into a world of champagne wishes and caviar dreams?

The Game was about Black kids mimicking power brokers, about Black youth showing just how right-wing George Bush and Richard Darman and William Bennett and their ilk could make us. It was about rugged individualism ("I gotta get mine"), about megabucks ("Make money, money, make money, money, monaaaay"), about eschewing the welfare of the collective in favor of hoarding wealth for a few ("Don't ask me for shit!"). "It's business," Nino Brown explained, "never personal."

Many of us started rolling not because every dope man was a millionaire, but because, for the first time in our young lives, that kind of wealth was even possible. To be sure, most Black kids on the street didn't make the sort of money that your local Newsbeat team would have you believe. Most of the friends I saw scurrying around the neigborhood in their fancy cars were worth far less than the rides they'd leveraged themselves to the hilt to buy would tell. Most worked for what toward the ends of the tragic arc that was many of their lives, they would come to understand was chump change. Most realized that even in The Game—or perhaps especially in The Game—the rules are stacked against them.

That is because, quite simply, white folks in America control wealth, who acquires it and how. Just like white folks in America control crime and drugs and guns and all the other growth industries they use us to front for. What we didn't know was that America, for all its pretensions about egalitarianism and equal opportunity, is an oligarchy with great PR.

Read, man, they'll tell you that themselves. They'll tell you, as the Federal Reserve did when it told you that "by 1989, the top 1 percent (834,000 households with about $5.7 trillion net worth) was worth more than the bottom 90 percent [94 million households with about $4.8 trillion net worth]." They'll tell you that that 1 percent saw a 70 percent gain in family income during the late seventies and eighties, the largest increase of all income groups. They'll tell you that the vast majority of this nation's corporations are concentrated in the clammy hands of a small number of white people. They'll tell you that the rich get richer and the poor get straight fucked.

But we don't challenge the economic despair-ities in our lives. We don't object to America's continued blatant mislabeling of the contents of its capitalist dogma. We don't think to ask how a people forced into slavery for two hundred years can allow anyone to sug-

gest they're lazy. We don't think to question how we can be expected to "go out and get a job" when companies move by the
hundreds not only out of our neighborhoods but the entire country.
We don't talk of white politicians' "cycle of dependency" when it
comes to their salaries; of the inconsistencies that come with attacking "welfare as we know it" as some sort of drain on the public
coffers even as the banking system that allowed for a $500 billion
S&L debacle remains intact. We don't ask ourselves why our mothers have to stand for hours on welfare lines, why being laid off is as
much a part of our fathers' jobs as lunch breaks, why we cannot
shape our infrastructure, economic system, form of government or
much of anything else that so quietly but effectively dictates the
poor quality of most Black lives.

Instead, we continue the charade that allows prominence and
ostentation to pass for power and wealth. We foolishly call ourselves
survivors because we'll do anything we have to to eat and stay alive,
but we refuse to commit ourselves to the social struggles necessary
for those lives to flourish. We watch passively as generation after
generation lines itself up in front of the slot machines of American
"opportunity," mindlessly plunking down our lives in hopes that
something, anything, good happens. And even when a few of us hit
—a comedian here, a power-forward there—we never stop to ask
who owns the casino where we're pissing away our futures.

I'm still afraid of The Game, less now for what it might do to
me than for what it is doing to so many of the brothers I used to
play dodgeball with. Add to that the unspeakable agony that crack
addiction has brought to millions of individuals and families in this
nation. Add to that the frustrating understanding that you can't
believe much of what America promises, even when those promises
are made on the hush-hush in the underground economy. Some of
us see this now, too. Where we thought we were just getting paid in
full, we were being bought off. And now we're paying—in the
mounting body counts of Black children, in the pell-mell rush to
build more prisons for a youth population that, while designated
"out of control," is very much under someone's sway, in the nineties' nihilism that has arisen from the ashes of eighties' hedonism.

Crack still runs rampant, but its glamor has dulled somewhat. We know now that the streets can kill. We know, too, that wealth without the institutions of power—without judicial appointees who'll pardon us, without congressmen who'll fashion bills for us— is as fleeting as it is dangerous. Sadly, too many of us don't care. We still play The Game, as it is the only one we've ever felt we had even a modicum of control over. That money is still our faith, those successive generations of disfranchised Black children our proselytes. America's hedonism has become something of a secular faith for us. Upon crack rocks, a vital chunk of our generation—a swath of our warrior class—has built its church.

But when it's done with us, America'll be more than happy to send it all up in smoke.

CHRIS WALLACE AKA THE NOTORIOUS B.I.G., 20: STRESS, THE STREETS AND STARDOM

NEW YORK—The outside of the apartment building off Fulton Avenue hums with the quotidian activity of Black male life. Teenagers zip by on bicycles. Others range the block in small cliques, laughing and shouting at passersby and friends hanging out windows. One group in particular swarms like electrons around the apartment stoop, joking and passing a blunt and recounting life back in the days.

At the nucleus stands Big, the six foot, 240-plus-pound griot of the crew. He is at once this block's favored homeboy, its latest hope and, by his own admission, formerly its most ambitious hustler. A one-time crack dealer, Big now stands at the threshold of hip-hop stardom, having parlayed a lilting, rakish tenor and that ineffable ghetto stylishness called flavor into what should be one of rap's most formidable debut albums, *Ready to Die*. His are street stories, to be sure, grim yarns of gunplay, beat downs and dope deals. And while Big's lyrics carry the requisite amount of nihilism and attitude, these are but obvious themes in rhymes whose emotional reach extends with equal poignance to warmth, humor and the wariness of a young brother ready to die yet equally capable of savoring life.

By the time you read this, the Notorious Big ought to be a bona fide hip-hop star. But celebrity is something that artists must adjust to, particularly when they've spent much of their lives in obscurity. Big is handling the adjustment well, but the changes have nonetheless brought to his life stresses far different from those he faced selling drugs. Perhaps they aren't as life-threatening, these matters of checks and contracts, but they're formidable enough to evoke in Big fond remembrances of when his money came differently, when the dough flowed in knots rather than royalty payments, and when the only type of taxes he saw were appended at the end of a restaurant receipt.

Stardom, he says, hasn't dulled his pangs for street life. He claims he's tempted sometimes to give all this rap shit up for a return to the drug scene. He won't, though. He knows he'd be trading in one set of concerns for another. Besides, Big is living an opportunity that many Black boys in urban and suburban America can only dream about nightly. He's rocking mics on stages across the country. He's gearing up for videos. He's rolling with some of the biggest names in Black music. Yeah, Big's paid 'nuff dues to get into the rap game; he's not going to chuck it now, not with fame so close. So instead, Big endures the headaches, the stress of rap-music celebrity. He endures and he adjusts, though he has learned that not even dreams-come-true look the same in reality as they do in your head . . .

"I got a five-year, five-albums contract. This shit is a headache now. And my album isn't out yet, so you can imagine like what shit, when shit is pumping! I'm going to be more stressed. After five albums, I'm going to wipe my ass clean of that shit.

"But I ain't stressing whether my shit will sell. Niggas like my shit. Niggas that have most of my shit, they know what time it is.

They see a million in me. I feel a million in me. I used to only feel like seven hundred thousand. I know I'm going to go gold. Now I feel a million 'cause I've been writing some shit.

"But, yeah, this rap shit is stressing too, Holmes. This shit is just as stressing as the game. I ain't going to lie to you. This shit give a nigga headaches because of deadlines on raps and shit. This ain't no shit that I was used to doing. When I was hustling, I'd just make up rhymes as I go along, 'cause it was about crack. But now, now I got to write songs.

"It wasn't no real, like, I always wanted to be a rapper. I was into the game, man. I mean, I always liked the music itself, singing. I used to sing more than anything, before rapping and shit. I used to come up with little limericks and shit. But when I was fourteen years old, I got introduced to crack. That was my full-time job. It's all I was into was drugs. Drugs. I wanted to be the largest drug dealer in the world. Then when I knew I had little rapping skills, I was like, 'Shit, I could rap, too?'

"But I never was deciding to leave the drugs alone. That wasn't nothing that I really said I was going to do even when I got in; when I got my contract, I was still hustling. I was out of town making negotiations while I was hustling. That shit didn't really hit me that it was something that I had to give up until I really started getting into this hip-hop shit. Now I'm seeing what kind of future I could really have just strictly off the rap shit.

"I ain't going to lie to you, though. To this day, I still feel that the drugs is the thing for me to do 'cause that's all we got. If a nigga can't play no ball or if a nigga ain't no comedian, a nigga got to work somewhere, straight up. Either a nigga got a motherfucking jump shot or they got a crack spot. So I figure I got both. If I got a little MC'ing skills and I can knock off a key in a month, I'm all right. To this day, if I was to get some money, man, I feel like I might get me a key, man. Fuck that. Double my shit. [Bad Boy Records CEO Sean 'Puffy' Combs] is the one that's stopping me. I really thought that I could get my loot, buy a key. But I see I can't do that. Puff start talking about, 'You know that shit going to come back at you, man. God don't like that shit.' But that shit don't phase me 'cause I know where I'm going. I'm like, 'God? I rather you say you was going to smoke me.'

"On the illegit side, my man Chico was the first one to put me down, he was around then. He was booming since he was like thirteen and shit. He was our age and shit. We used to always see him coming through with the dip Fila shit. He leased shit. He used to be like, 'Come fuck with me and I'll put you all on.' We was like, 'Fuck that crack shit.' I was robbing niggas, know what I'm saying? I was robbing niggas, getting my money. Fuck that crack shit. But I seen that shit was type easy 'cause that nigga was getting it. That nigga was hitting Ma Dukes off for like fifteen hundred, sixteen hundred dollars, buying her living room sets and shit. That's shit that I wanted to do. That's pimping. That is straight up pimping. Fifteen years old, you're stepping in the crib, 'Here goes seventeen hundred dollars. Go get you a little living room set or something.'

"Some of us just do it for self. As far as me, her, it was just me and my Moms, anyway; so as long as I had money, she was going to be all right. Even though I knew she wasn't going to agree with it, but my Moms is the type of person where if she knows I'm doing something wrong and she keeps telling me not to do and I keep doing it, she knows there's nothing she can do. She's not going to stress herself out. She's old and shit. She doesn't need to be stressing her brain. She'll hope for the best, that I'll just learn my lesson and not fuck with it. Even that ain't work, 'cause I was getting locked up and I was still in jail like, 'I got a half [ounce] home; when I got out of jail I'll bag my half up and I'm going to get back.' There wasn't nothing really to stop me. The only thing that could have stopped me to get out of the game back then was to get killed and that was it. There was nothing niggas could do to me, stick me up, threaten me.

"I wasn't fucking with school. School was pretty boring, to tell you the honest truth. It's like I didn't see the school system teaching me shit, you know what I'm saying? I don't really remember nothing that I can really sit back and be like, 'Well, that's one thing from school I remember, this and this and this.' All my wisdom I learned from out here, man. All my . . . this is street knowledge.

Fuck that. I mean, of course you're going to want your child to go to school and shit, but at the same time I'm going to teach my child the game, Holmes. Little bit of everything.

"The only reason I went to school was for the bitches. I ain't going to lie. I had one class when I was in high school that I got high grades in. I had a ninety seven in Law. I was dealing with shit that I wanted to know about. I can't see me thirty-one years old no matter what and somebody asking me about *xy* squared to the second power. Nobody's going to expect from me no stupid shit like that. That's something that's not going to pertain to me, know what I'm saying? Law is something that I felt I had to learn about because these crackers ain't shit, and they'll flip shit around on you. So I want to at least be informed and aware of the shit. That's the only reason why I passed that shit.

"Only thing about math that it was good for was adding up that paper, getting that money. 'Cause, see, money is important like a motherfucker because that's power. Money is power like a motherfucker. You can show me a nigga, the most intelligent nigga in the world, he could be dead-ass broke, niggas ain't trying to hear what the fuck he got to say. But you could show me a stupid-ass nigga with an Acura Legend Coupe and he'll sit there and tell you about something that you know he wrong, but I'll bet you about four niggas in the vicinity will think he right just because he have a Legend. And I see it on a regular.

"So I was into the money. But I was also into music. I was always into hip-hop. I don't remember the first hip-hop record I bought, but you know what song I used to like, though, when I was little? The cowboy shit, the Rappin' Duke. 'Dah-ha-ha-ha.' I just always used to do my own rhyme to that shit, knew I could make it fly. I was making up little bullshit in my head and shit. But that was when I was in the crib by myself taking decks of cards and shit trying to make houses and shit. I was so motherfucking bored for self. I was in the crib trying to build up shit.

"But it seemed like every time I wrote a rhyme, it was doper than the one before it, to me at least. Maybe other motherfuckers may not feel that way. But every time I sat down and wrote something, it was always better than what it was in the beginning. I mean, I remember when my name was MC Chrissy D, went to motherfucking MC Dynamic to MC Quest. I was doing a little bit of everything until finally it just came to Biggie Smalls. We was watching this little gangster film up in crib, one of them Richard Pryor/Sidney Poitier pieces, and one of them gangster niggas name was Biggie Smalls. Niggas was all ready calling me Big, so Biggie Smalls just, the shit fit. Gangster-ass nigga. Shoe fit.

"So now I'm into this shit. But like I said, it's hard. I ain't used to writing raps on a deadline. I ain't used to waiting on checks and shit. I'm used to going out and getting my money on the street. Sometimes, I feel like I just been slipping, man. Feel like I just been sitting down collecting paper, I ain't got no strength no more.

"But fuck it. I'm going to get mine."

EDDIE L. BURNSIDE, 24: BLACK COP

JACKSON, MISSISSIPPI—There aren't many jobs that ignite passionate debate among young Black men. Generally, most brothers are willing to accept that, in an age where unemployment among young people can soar as high as 40 percent, you often have to take what you can.

But if any one job is likely to cause a stir, it'd definitely be police work. It's no secret that, long before the name Rodney King became synonymous with rampant police brutality and racism, the cops were regarded as the enemy, or at best, discomforting allies, by large swaths of Black America. Still, even big-city police forces have, as a result of aggressive struggles by Black politicians, unions and civil-rights activists, seen an integration of Black faces into many of their spaces over the past thirty years. Of course, white men still run most departments and still predominate the ranks of street-level cops. But the numbers of Black men and women donning blues, batons and badges are growing.

To the vast majority of young men in the communities they now patrol, however, race consciousness seems lost among cops. Ask Black boys how they feel about Black cops and they're liable to tell you that they can be worse than their white counterparts. They'll tell you that Black cops don't bring any special understanding to policing Black communities; that the question at hand isn't merely a matter of how many African-Americans you can fit into the uniforms, but what impact their presence will make in curbing the brutality, flagrant disrespect, corruption and apathy that cops have always brought to the browner quarters of their precincts. They'll then answer that question by telling you that they've only further entrenched those woes, that Black cops are blue first, Black somewhere farther down the line—maybe. They'll say that Black cops not only imitate their racist white coworkers but defend their bigoted practices. They'll tell you how Black cops are Uncle Toms who, to prove their loyalty to the badge, will kick your ass worse than some of the white boys. They'll tell you that Black cops would rather swear allegiance to cops' unwritten code of silence than promote justice for Black folks within the department and on the street.

Hence the refrain that has become near-anthem on city streets from coast to coast: "Fuck tha police."

The presence of Blacks in police work has compelled many in our communities to reassess the idea that someone can simply carry out his duties without being held to a standard that promotes the best interests of the collective. Even drug dealers are many times allowed off the hook, allowed to exist as men merely "doing what I gotta to survive," more than Black officers. With policemen, we are forced to challenge the job description and thus are forced to deal with the notion of labor not merely as a source of income, but as an activity meant to elevate and preserve our people. Yes, the same should be demanded of our computer programmers and chefs and electricians, but it's not. They're doing what they have to. They're doing their jobs.

Not so young Black men such as Officer Eddie Lee Burnside.

Nonetheless, Eddie welcomes the scrutiny, he says. He's secure in his standing in the community, about his role in maintaining it.

He insists that he's Black first and foremost, that he'll sell his soul to no one, not the force, not his friends, not some code of silence. He's a cop who cares, he says. He cares about his job, sure. But he cares also about the communities he patrols, about the people whose lives he feels responsible for, even about the Black men and women he's often forced to put behind bars. He's no Tom, no dupe for his white bosses.

At a small restaurant in the slow-beating heart of downtown Jackson, he explains that he got into this job to help, not to hurt; to benefit, not to brutalize. Still, they're not lost on him, the contradictions of being Black and a police officer. He knows that he shares office space with men who without question have beaten, even murdered, their share of Black people. He knows he is in the employ of a department whose history is awash with the blood of innocent African-Americans. Even as we met, investigators and attorneys were looking into a rash of unexplained hangings in Jackson jails. The cops call them suicides. Given white Mississippi's infamous hankering for strange fruit, the Black community isn't quite rushing out to buy these excuses.

But Eddie Burnside presses on in the employ of the JPD. Part of a new class of cops to sweep into the department, the three-year veteran says he represents change. And no matter what the challenges posed by the past, change must continue on toward a better future.

"I feel that as a Black person, there are not many ways you can help your people," he says. "I can by being a cop.

"It takes a person from the environment to know this. A person from Beverly Hills couldn't go to some of these low-income areas. Or even someone from north Jackson cannot come to southwest Jackson and help people 'cause they don't know what it is like to be poor. They don't know what it is like not to have. You have to be from that environment in order to help that environment. Like jail has counselors. I don't think a counselor who hasn't been in that environment can come and help rehabilitate that person, because you have to be there. You can read and you can research, but you got to be there.

"Nobody can tell me what it takes to be a cop. No one can tell me the feeling that I feel when I wake up in the morning and I'm getting dressed and I look in the mirror and I ask myself, 'Am I coming home today?' Most people don't face that every day. 'Am I going to make it?' You have to be from an environment and help it.

"Most white cops certainly can't help. You have some, an elite group, that probably can. You have white poor people. You have some that try hard enough and sometimes succeed. Then you have some that just don't give a damn. Some of them think the answer to Black people's problems is to lock them up like slaves. A Black person goes to a call that is dealing with Black people and handles it differently than white people. A Black officer can go to a call and feel the pain and know how Black people feel in the situation because either they have been in the situation or know something about the situation."

Eddie says it is this gap in understanding, this distance between Black realities and white ones, that has led to much of the animosity he has watched white officers exhibit. They just don't know us, he says. And as a result, too many of them think we're animals. Like the rest of Black America, Eddie says he is still shaken by the most highly publicized example of that animus.

"Everybody is talking about Rodney King. If Rodney King had been white—I am not crazy—and if four Black officers had beat him up, they would not have been acquitted.

"I have mixed emotions about the way some Black officers supported those guys. I wasn't there. I don't know what happened. From the part I saw, if a man is on the ground and he has been beaten like those guys were beating him, he wouldn't fight back. Did you see Rodney King swing, pull a gun? Rodney King was on the ground. If they had stopped beating on him, he would not have got up. I've been in fights before myself. One too many. He's not going to try and retaliate. Through that whole film, Rodney King didn't throw a punch. I would feel bad. I really don't want to be associated with nothing like that. Even though I put this vest on, I am still a human being. You are human, too."

Still, ever the policeman, ever the protector of property and (perhaps) people, Eddie is quick to criticize the rebellions that were the response of Blacks and Latinos and some whites to what was so clearly a miscarriage of justice. "People don't have the right to take stuff and lose their damn mind," he says.

He says his concerns over the injustices done King nonetheless weigh as heavy to him, but I find it hard to be moved. The Rodney King trial is a no-brainer for most young brothers, even a substantial number of white Americans. I ask him about matters closer to home, about the hangings in Jackson jails. The police department has deemed them suicides. But many, particularly African-Americans here in Jackson, fret that the deaths harken suspiciously back to the days when lynch law terrorized Black Mississippi.

Burnside registers little emotional reaction to such a chilling proposition. He seems inclined to accept the police's story, though he confesses that he cannot escape the nagging implications of the hangings.

"I have no knowledge of the hangings," he says. "They just say that guy hung himself. I don't know. I have slight doubts. Where I come from, back in the slave days, Black people went through hell. Black people like living. Did you ever hear of a Black person who wanted to commit suicide? Never. It's always a white person. No matter how bad it gets, Black people always find a way to stay alive. I don't know too many people that would hang themselves. Black people don't like pain. They've been through a lot of pain. That's torture, hanging yourself. If a Black person is going to kill himself . . . just think of it. Have you ever read a paper that said a Black man committed suicide? Never. Black people are superior to white people. Black people been through so much hell that no matter what, you keep on striving and fighting. People have their way of keeping us down, but we always manage."

Eddie says he hopes the controversy around the hangings passes, that justice is served. Meanwhile, he tries not to take sides too openly. But only because he wants to be fair. He makes clear that he doesn't condone cops protecting officers who've committed crimes. He denies widespread accusations of a code of honor among cops that forbids policemen to expose their corrupt colleagues.

"I've never heard anything like that," he says. "There is no such thing in this department. There is no such thing as a code of honor. You are enforcing the law to the best of your ability and that means treat everybody fairly."

Flashes of that eighty-one-second videotape blot my brain. Rodney on his knees, hand stretched out in desperate supplication for mercy. White boys whaling on him still with the batons. White boy with his foot on Rodney's neck. Tasers. Blows. Stomps. A no-brainer, right? Right?

There's no code of honor, Eddie tells me, but he's not so sure he'd turn in a fellow cop turned crook.

"Sometimes some people just lay back and eventually they will get caught," he says obliquely. "You can get away with a lot of things, but eventually it will come back on you. You get caught eventually if you continue to do something wrong."

But would you turn him in? Would you "snitch," as a code of silence might define it? Would you "squeal"?

"Squealing, I always keep the concept of cover your own ass," says Eddie. "If ever somebody makes an allegation that I did something, I will always tell the truth. As long as I can go to bed and sleep at night with a straight conscience, then I will do it. In the same sense, I am not going to go out there and volunteer. I just don't get involved. I always take care of Ed."

I say: But you're sworn to uphold the law, right? That doesn't mean being blinded by blue . . . does it? Okay, example: There's this cop you know, right? And he's doing something wrong, brutalizing a brother, shoot an old woman in the back, robbing and/or shaking down drug dealers. You pick the crime. Anyway, your job is to uphold the law and this person is violating the law, why wouldn't you get involved?

"Sometimes, it depends on the situation or what he is doing. You don't want to be labeled as a squealer, and then again you don't want to be associated with bad cops. Disobedient cops. You don't want to be associated with it. If it is going to affect your career, but if it is not affecting your career, if you're still doing what is right, I don't get involved. I don't agree with it, but I don't get involved. It bothers me, it's on my mind. But they'll get caught."

You hope.

"They always do."

Yeah, right.

Eddie reminds me that he tries to stay clean, to do right. It could be on a T-shirt, his philosophy: LAW SEE NO COLOR.

"If you break the law you can be yellow, green, blue, Black. I am going to take you to jail," he says. "That's what I get paid to do. I don't get paid to take white people to jail or Black people to jail. I get paid to take people to jail who break the law. Black or white, I will take you to jail.

"I catch more flack from Black people than I do white people. Black people say, 'You're an Uncle Tom. You're going to sell out.' I say, 'No, you broke the law.' If I get a white person, sometimes the white person will be so kind. 'Okay, I was wrong.' You have some that go off. They will say, 'I know such-and-such. I am going to have your badge; you don't have to do that.' This man has broken the law, I have to take him to jail."

But that's not why so many Black Americans live in fear of the police, I think aloud. That's not why grandmothers and schoolboys and rap producers and sportswriters fear the police. Not because cops lock them up for crimes. Not because Black folks don't want to be protected and served.

Rodney. A no-brainer, right?

Eddie says he cannot be blamed for the misdeeds of his colleagues, says that Black cops do indeed try to avoid the pitfalls of their racist counterparts. He doesn't bully kids outside nightclubs or pull over shiny German cars bearing Black boys.

"There is no law against driving a Mercedes or BMW," he says. "If I look in there and he don't have a tag, I am going to pull him over and say, 'Why don't you have a tag?' If I look in there and I see four guys, bandannas, homeboy look, I will be kind of suspicious, but that doesn't give you a right to pull them over unless they break the law. There's no law against driving a BMW. There is a thing called probable cause. I have to have probable cause to stop that vehicle. I have to have some reason in my mind that those guys have done something wrong. If I can't come up with a probable cause, why pull them over?"

So why the anger, the loathing, the sound and fury? Why the dirty looks from the twelve-year-olds on the corner? Why "Fuck Tha Police" and "FTP" and "One Time's Got No Case" and "Illegal Search" and "Black Cop" and "Crooked Officer" and . . .

"They probably had a run-in with a law enforcement agency somewhere, and they had been mistreated. I was reading the news: Tupac shot two off-duty cops. I guess his next album is going to be *I Shot Two Cops*. I wasn't there, but maybe these young guys had been in a situation with an officer and feel they have been mis-treated. They just expressed it on the record. I don't agree with 'Cop Killer' or 'Crooked Officer.' I don't agree with that because I'm not a crooked officer. That doesn't affect me. I go to work every day for eight hours and enforce the law and I come home knowing that I did everything I could do to help society. If you are an angel, you have to live by certain rules. No matter what, he has to keep his composure. I feel like an angel; I have to go out there every day and try to make peace. Keep peace.

"Yeah. It hurts me sometimes to see this [drug dealer] making a thousand dollars a day, and I am making a little over a thousand dollars a month. But I can go somewhere and I don't have to watch my back. I can go home and sleep at night knowing I made that honestly.

"It's possible some young Black men get harassed by cops for no reason. I can understand some white people may get mad 'cause this Black guy is legit. A white cop sees a Black guy that's legit and he will think he's selling dope because other guys you run into who are selling dope have the same things that people who are making it legit have. Cars and homes. As a Black person, I don't get mad. I get mad when I see drug dealers making money. Drug dealers don't realize they're getting ahead, but look at your people."

So Eddie's not bothered by your assessments of the police. Far more people pose far greater threats in the course of their work than him and his colleagues. Sure, he watches his own ass. Sure, he's less than convinced about claims of rampant police brutality in Black communities. And, no, it may not be wise to depend on him to testify against that white narc who tore your car apart in the course of a "routine search," only to find lint and a few tarnished nickels between your seats. But Eddie insists that he's doing what he can to help.

Plenty of others, though, would question who exactly he purports to save.

JOHN COPELAND, 24: GIVING BACK

MIAMI—was the flames that drove John Copeland out of the house in 1984, the acrid smell of Black rage burning in Liberty City. He was a teenager when the so-called "riots" came, when the acquittal of a police officer accused of gunning down a Black man sent his community into rebellious fury. He didn't go to join in the looting and burning. He wanted to end it all somehow. He wanted to be a salve to the wounded spirit of a downtrodden Black Miami. Instead, he could only watch as the city burned.

Six years later, Black fury again scented the Miami air when the city's fathers snubbed Nelson Mandela during his visit. In a move that further polarized Blacks and the city's Cuban community—the latter comprised significantly of the reactionary, anti-democratic and Eurocentric middle-class whose privileges Castro had revoked when his progressive revolutionary government swept into power— Miami's Cuban-American mayor Xavier Suarez became the only U.S. official to refuse to greet Mandela, a supporter of Cuba's liberation government, when the South African leader visited to attend a convention of the American Federation of State and Municipal Employees. But the resulting Black anger wasn't combustible this time. This time, it lashed out where it would do the most good: It hit Miami's pocketbook. Blacks organized a three-year boycott of the convention cottage industry, driving hotels and caterers and convention centers into economic straits by refusing to patronize them. There was nothing blind or unorganized about it. It lasted for three years. And it hurt.

With the city coffers thinner and with white businesses craving resolution, John at last got his chance to be the soothing presence he had longed to be. He agreed to step into the breach, to work to broker a new, more progressive relationship between white industries and the Black consumers they had neglected so. Respect, economic reciprocity—they were long overdue John's community. John figured he could help deliver at last. So now, he serves as the director of Miami Partnership for Progress, a nonprofit group devoted to building strong, two-way bridges between the community and the tourism industry.

He left a cushy job with McKinsey & Co. to come home again. Miami had produced him, had helped make him the scholar, athlete, Harvard grad and executive that he rose out of Liberty City to become. He felt he owed the community something. By all appearances a political moderate, John wasn't trying to strike revolutionary poses or set himself up as a spokesman for all the people all the time. He just felt that it was his turn to give something back.

"I'm here and I'm getting paid but, and I'll start with that, when I look at this, it is me being able to make a contribution," he says. "As far as my career, this isn't going to get me too much farther down the line. I'm doing this because I want to, these are the things that are important to me; the issues that we're dealing with are things I think can have an impact on the community that I grew up in. Miami isn't necessarily considered the best place for African-Americans most of the time. Atlanta would be a place, D.C. would be a place, New York, maybe L.A. But Miami wouldn't be the first one on the list and that's something we want to change. The bottom line is, we want to make this to be and to be perceived to be a place where African-Americans can be successful in employment in general. If we can look back on Miami in fifteen years from now and say that is the case, I will feel good that we started something that led to a whole change of what Miami is."

While not necessarily rare, neither is such talk about mass progress a common theme among young Black professionals. Too often,
the college-educated men and women of our communities measure
their success by the amount of distance they put between themselves and the neighborhoods that reared them. Which isn't to say
they aren't loved. Black communities often cherish their success
stories, root for them passionately—only to be sorely disappointed
when those successes feel little compunction to return to their
roots. We've seen many an athlete and accountant and author and
academician ascend to the pinnacles of their profession, then forget
about the homes and hoods left behind. Consequently, we're cautious, even skeptical, about our middle and upper classes, sometimes to the point of disdain. Our history has made it their responsibility to return to where they made it, to look back and give back.
We often don't expect them to shoulder that obligation, preoccupied as they often are with taking the loot and running.

John has returned, though. He's paying back debts long overdue.
He's only twenty-four, still climbing the ladder to corporate success
himself. But he's determined to take as many Black folks as he can
up with him. And in the process, he hopes to ensure that the flames
that charred Miami twice in his childhood, in '80 and '84, never
return.

"Our mission is to level the playing field for black Americans
here," says John, seated in a conference room thirty stories above
downtown Miami. "We want to get Blacks more involved in all
levels in the tourism industry. That's management. That's owner-
ship. And it's also the entry-level jobs, banquet waiters and that
kind of stuff. We want to make sure that when you go to one of
these places, you see people like us. In addition to, we're spreading
to other industries as well. We are looking for expansion opportunities for Black businesses. We are looking to sponsor trade missions
to the Caribbean and Africa. We are going to provide scholarships
for students in hospitality management. We have created an internship program. We have established a program for high school se-
niors who are going to college and find summer internships for
them for their years during school. Hopefully, that would lead to a

job offer. We are working to create the largest and only African-American-owned convention-level hotel in the country. There are twenty goals along those lines that we are addressing, and again, all of them are lined up at leveling the playing field for African-Americans here.

"My job in particular is to make all that work. So it's task-force management. We have for each one of our goals twenty volunteer task forces that are out there working. I also am our chief public relations person, so I have to go out and make the speeches and issue the press releases. Fund-raising I haven't had to worry about much. Most businesses involved are completely behind the initiative, so the money has been pretty straightforward."

John says philanthropists big and small donated about $200,000 in 1993, the partnership's first year. Other businesses have helped by donating office space, personnel and equipment. While John is canny enough an office politician to show appropriate gratitude for the donations, he's frank enough to admit that, in many cases, support for the Black community has been long overdue. Noting this, he recalls how the partnership evolved, how it rose from the quiet, determined collective action of the community that raised him up, as well as with aid from powerful allies in labor and women's groups.

The snub of Mandela by the mayor and his cronies "was sort of the spark," says John. "The other issues were the underlying economic disparity in this community. I grew up here, so I can tell you that I have seen the riots and everything else, and Blacks really are disenfranchised. And so that [indignation] was all built up. The biggest issue was the Cuban population here did not issue the protocol. Mandela sort of was snubbed. The problem was that he had at some point supported Fidel Castro because Castro had supported him when he was in prison. That is a point of contention for the Cuban population here. Government officials, like the mayor of Miami, didn't hand out the key to the city like he got in other places and were unwilling to issue an apology. For me, I took it as personally as anybody else would. I respect him a lot, and I hoped that they would have respected all that he had done. That's where I drew the line. They, on the other hand, were acting to the relationship with Castro—but I still maintain that you ought to at least respect what he stood for and where he came from and then the reasons behind what was going on. Instead of rioting this time, it was more of a quiet riot, if you will. They decided to boycott.

"It wasn't just Blacks, either. For example, the American Bar Association didn't hold their conference here. The National Organization for Women didn't hold their conference here. I think the AFL-CIO was supposed to have something here, and they didn't do that. It was more of an across-the-board appeal for the issues that were on the table. The issue was Blacks aren't fairly represented in industries, particularly tourism, and so that was communicated to folks. It wasn't just the Blacks not going. It was actually them telling people not to come here for a convention, them telling people not to come here as tourists.

"So they negotiated for a year and a half with pretty high-level people in the business community and they came up with the organization of Miami Partnership for Progress. I had been living in Atlanta. I was doing management consulting up there with McKinsey & Co. Basically, the clientele there is Fortune 500 companies and they are sort of corporate doctors: they come and fix things. I was practicing that profession in Atlanta and actually had a chance to work on a project down here in Miami. This was my hometown, as I mentioned, and I wanted to come back and see if I could contribute and work with the CEO's and big hitters. I had a chance to come back and do that. Having grown up here, I already knew the Black community pretty well and the people who were involved in the boycott. When it came time to pick somebody to run this show and stand in the middle, my relationship with both of them had caused them to look to me.

"I had inklings of what was going on for the past year. The project that I mentioned that I did with McKinsey and Co. was from March of 1992 through August of 1992. This was in the middle of negotiations that they were undergoing. They would come and go, 'Oh, what do you think about this?' So I sort of got tapped in. In March we started talking about it. They pulled me down here a couple times to feel me out and see if I would be able to steer the ship, relatively speaking. I guess I'm pretty young for somebody who is serving in this capacity, so they had to get comfortable with me being able to handle it. The second thing was, I had to get comfortable with what I was being asked to handle. There was a need to get mutually comfortable. I had to get comfortable with the idea of coming down here and the capacity that I was going to be in. I wanted to be comfortable that this was a job that wouldn't be too much of a stretch.

"It is too important to me and my community for me to get in over my head. I got comfortable with the level of support that I would get; that the business community was really committed to doing this, at least the folks that were involved; that the Black community was going to try to get over some of the things that we tend to have and need to get over in order to make this work and so it was . . . I felt pretty good about it. So everybody got comfortable and I got brought down. It also was symbolic, me coming back from Atlanta down here.

"Hopefully, my coming is setting a tone for other students. There seems to be a pretty big problem with brain drain down here, as they term it. A lot of the folks don't recognize the opportunity in Miami and perceive there are greater opportunities elsewhere and so don't look to Miami as that's where they want to work. So my coming down here was supposed to be symbolic of us working to address that issue and get others to."

So far, John says, he's satisfied with the interest and involvement of the participants, though he wishes more businesses would join the effort. Many, however, maintain a disturbing distance from the Black community, keeping opportunity at a remove as well.

"There are two levels of resistances we've received," says John. "There's passive resistance, which says, 'I don't have a problem with Blacks, but I have my list of things to take care of; I am not going to be proactive about hiring and recruiting. You go find Black employees and they go through my process and they make it, fine, but I am not going to be making an extra effort. I am not going to do the extra things.' I think that is probably mostly what is going on. It's not so much that people are actively resistant to including the Black community—although there is some there. I wouldn't tell you that there isn't. But it's more of a passive . . . either a lack of acknowledgment that race is a major issue or they just aren't willing to expend the energy to do it. Efforts like this one heighten the awareness and get out and do the legwork and help people through the process."

The moderate surfaces again as John details what he believes is the African-American community's role in maintaining the historical divide between Blacks and big business. He won't fault white supremacy alone, or even give it the majority of the blame. He believes fundamentally in "the process," in the ideal that integration does work in the workplace and so, by extension, does the America he dreams. Some may regard John's notion of evenhandedness with suspicion, as blaming the victim in an effort not to incur the wrath of the business interests that back him. This, of course, wouldn't be a first in assessing that strain of Black activist leadership that hitches itself to corporate America. But John's willingness to criticize his community is more than about being fair, he says. It's about devising methods for ensuring the health and welfare of the Black community through frank critique. He doesn't believe merely in the process, but in the capacity of Black Americans to make it serve their interests. But for that capacity to pay dividends, John says, some collective reflection—indeed, straight talk—is in order.

"It's been hard dealing with some of the Black community," he says. "I grew up here and I knew the community pretty well. We tend to sometimes shoot ourselves in the foot on some things. We are sometimes overly critical. A lot of these things have some historical basis. It's not coming totally out of the blue, the level of mistrust and stuff for past wrongs. But I think at some point we need to get over that and start moving forward.

"There are things that are probably more particular to Miami, and I am not sure they are the same in other cities. For example, there is definitely a resentment in Miami's Black communities of anybody that comes from someplace else. Like you're from Detroit. If you came down here and did what I am doing now, there would have been public outrage at the fact that they brought in somebody who was from outside the community trying to do something like I am doing. By the same token, because I had been gone for about six years, some of them were looking at me, trying to sniff me out, but luckily I passed the sniff test so far and we're moving forward.

"We want to be included in the mainstream, but then on the other hand there are sections that would scream pretty loudly for development of our own areas—and it is pretty hard to have both ways. I think we need to worry about our own communities. I don't know if you saw the town meeting in D.C. at the Congressional Black Caucus, but Maxine Waters and Louis Farrakhan and Jesse Jackson and Ben Chavis were all on the panel and were discussing what we need to do and where we need to be headed. They raised a lot of good points. My feeling is that it's not any one way to go about doing it. It's a pretty comprehensive approach. The folks that are screaming that we just need to be assimilated, I don't necessarily buy that. I think there are parts to that which are true. The folks that are screaming that we need to totally disengage and focus on our community, there are some truths there—but the real answer is somewhere in between. Again, I try to look at things pretty practically and systematically and come up with something that is workable and is going to give us the best results. Frankly, I think it is a combination of the two, but our community seems to be polarized a lot of the times. To say a combination of the two, you can't get away with that. That is why I say we sometimes shoot ourselves in the foot. You can't be over here screaming for this because there are a lot of things that need to be done in our community. By the same token you can't be talking about solely looking at our own community because there are a lot of folks who don't live in the Black community that are Black. It is going to be a give-and-take type of thing."

Certainly, some of his ideas are enough to make the nationalist quarters of Black America—many of those folk John says are screaming for internal community development and Black self-determination—bristle with indignation and annoyance. But he's trying, he says, to be honest, to be realistic. He, too, is disturbed by his analyses, but for different reasons. John envisions a protracted struggle for economic improvement in the community, one, he says, that is hampered only by what he describes as an often frustrating level of financial unsophistication among, in particular, young Black men.

"It is pretty depressing sometimes. There are individuals who are very set about business and economics, and there are other folks that are equally smart but just haven't either had the exposure or refused to let it soak in. I was talking to another brother about my age a couple weeks ago about this. He is trying to start his own business, and the sacrifices he's making in doing it are causing him not to drive the fanciest car and he doesn't have the gold chains and all that kind of stuff. Other folks that are in the same age group tend to ostracize him for that. The things that they are interested in are not necessarily the things that are going to get you where you need to be when you're thirty and you are driving that car legitimately. It is a little frustrating. Like I said before, there are some individuals out there who have been pretty smart about all this. There are some others who are intelligent but just aren't applying themselves.

"Part of it is exposure. Some white individuals, their grandparents give them stocks in companies. They are taught to invest in the bonds and it is important. If you look at the national stats as far as where white people put their money versus where Black people put their money, Black people put it in the car, put it in the car." John pauses for a quick laugh of collective self-deprecation, then resumes. "White people invest in stocks and bonds and real estate. It is just a different mentality, as far as what you are going to do with your dollars. Part of that can be attributed to the fact that Black incomes are less, so if you only have thirty thousand dollars and you have to buy a car, then that is going to be a big percentage of where you spend your money. But we need to start being smarter, even if you are making less money, about what we are doing. You can invest a little and get something back as opposed to putting it in a car. You are going to continue to have that lower level of income. That is something that we have to deal with. Trying to come up with ways to get people thinking about being an entrepreneur and, when they are, be sophisticated about it. A lot of money is being spent in this community and others to do that. We have to feel our way around. It is something that is important and it is something that is being addressed."

John isn't casting stone sanctimoniously, he explains. He's only addressing the pervasiveness of oppression in our communities, only noting the myriad levels on which racism and exclusion operate. He cites himself as a good example. He was his class valedictorian. Busted a 1,500 on his SAT's. Got accepted to Harvard. Still, he says, growing up in the heart of Liberty City, he had so many ideas, so much information hidden from him. It just didn't trickle down, this financial know-how he saw his peers strutting up at Cambridge. Black America isn't taught to make its money for it, but rather trained to work for its money.

"Even though I was making A's and doing all those types of things in school," he says. "I didn't know about stocks or bonds or any of that type of stuff growing up. It is not like your grandparents give you a savings bond. If they had money they would, but that is just not something that comes naturally so it definitely is an issue of exposure. I don't think that our folks are any less able to be sophisticated. It is just a matter of access. So I like the things that the NAACP is doing with NationsBank, building these community centers where they teach about this financial stuff. That plus a whole bunch of other things are the first steps of what I like to call a thousand-mile journey. We are definitely in for an uphill battle. You got to start somewhere."

DERON THOMPKINS, 22: JACK OF ALL TRADES, MASTER OF CEREMONY

MIAMI—The world is Deron's classroom, his daily experiences his tests and textbooks—and equally as much what he terms his "real job." He learns and earns through living, he tells me proudly, not as a consequence of regurgitating something he picked up from a teacher in some college. He'll never go to college, he says, though the hundreds of books that clutter his room mark him as an avid reader. College isn't for him. Too many lies being told. Too much about institutions he doesn't trust.

He prefers to think of himself as "a life student."

"Yeah, I'm learning," says Deron. "I read every day. That's what I tell people: I'm a life student. At the college bookstores, they still give me student discounts," he adds with a chuckle, " 'cause they like that. I tote a book in my pocket all the time. If I could read all day I would do it, but I can't. I got to work."

Work takes many forms for Deron. He's picked up a number of skills in his twenty-two years, very few of them from a chalkboard, he emphasizes. He's an accomplished airbrush artist, having been drawing steadily since elementary school. He is in heavy demand as a neighborhood barber. He works as a janitor. He fixes small appliances and works on cars. He cuts grass. He DJs parties. He writes songs.

Above all, though, Deron is a dreamer, a man whose visions' boundlessness can often seem matched only by their incongruity. He dreams of cutting a rap record someday. He dreams, too, of owning his own airbrush factory, of seeing his art hanging in museums and galleries. He dreams occasionally of wealth, but more about comfort, about caring for his family through the work that he, not society at large, has deemed valuable. He has determined that he will lay his own path, that he will make his way through this world along a path of his own design.

For now, though, he pushes mops at various sites for a custodial company.

"Mopping has got to be the toughest part of my job," he says. "It's brutality on your hands. Mopping, sweeping. Sometimes, I think them Cubans I work for are punishing me. I guess I got one of their cousins' positions. I was mopping, raking. It was one thing after another. I have been there almost a year now. I have never done a job over a year. The reason why I stayed there, it is at night and I used to stay up at home that late. I can knock it off in two hours. Sometimes I rest, I do some push-ups, stay in shape. I read the Qur'ān. I write some lyrics. I got to stay. I got to do it, but if I make my record and get me a nice place, I will just read and write for humanity."

And it'll happen, too, insists Deron. He'll be a rap star one day. If not, he'll be a world-class artist. He won't be held by a nine-to-five forever. He's got dreams. He doesn't worry much about whether they'll work out. He's invested a lot in making them real.

He's competed in subpar local talent shows to prove his prowess as a rapper. When he was fifteen, he even stole some DJ equipment. For his painting's sake, he spends a lot of his money on his airbrush equipment, and endures hot days in crowded hangouts around Miami hawking his airbrush skills to any T-shirt or jean jacket or pair of Levi's that strolls by. He cuts hair at all times of the day and night, taking customers whenever they decide to fall by. He does it all while pushing that mop and still manages to find time to continue with his "life's studies." He knows how this plays to some minds. He knows some, even friends and family, think he may be squandering his life by chasing dreams that follow so many disparate tangents. Deron, though, disagrees.

"People think I'm unrealistic sometimes," he says. "But I am superrealistic. Effort plus ability gets results. I am inspiring myself to go on. I am working hard. It is more effort than the average man wants to put in, but a man who wants to accomplish much, he got to sacrifice much. Much time, much money, much practice. Me having so many friends, they tend to pull me away, and I try to tell them. I tell them, What are you, the Devil, you trying to distract me. I don't know. Like, I pinch to read. In the morning I read by the hour. Friends be calling. They be wanting to hang for no reason, waste five hours. I can't do that. I try to read and then I got the night job. Being a custodian, that's the bottom of the line, so I can't go nowhere but up."

He'll get there somehow. By the mic, by his hands, by the sketch pad. Somehow. He doesn't see any need to resolve what you might see as incongruencies in the tapestry of his hopes. "I used to play football, and I used to be late to practice all the time. I used to draw, and after football practice my wrists used to be so sore. My dad was like, 'I don't want you to be playing football, you might break your wrists and can't draw no more.' He wanted me to just draw, but I could do a lot of things. It's hard to choose. I'm going to try to do all of them. If one of them makes it, it will back the other."

His father encourages him to take those book smarts, those life's lessons, and apply them where he thinks they'll do Deron the most good. Go back to school, son, he urges. Get that sheepskin. Get that j-o-b.

Deron smiles when he thinks about his father's advice. He understands it springs from the well of his pop's love. But he can't accept it.

"I learn more things in life than in school that really help me out," says Deron. "Now, yeah, I need money. A lot of people say go to school, earn your degree, you will get more money. But you still got to work for somebody and draw what they want you to draw. Money is so hard to come across, yet it is so easy. Most brothers ain't doing nothing. The few that do, stand out. Me knowing that, I can make money easy. But I'm not really interested in being rich. If I got rich, I'd take care of my mother, buy her a house in Gainesville, which is where my family is from. But instead of being rich, I'd rather be noble and smart. So right now, I'm just trying to make a lot of intelligent moves.

"I observe. When I went to this recruit, this audition for college, I saw a lot of them brothers that was still going to this art school I used to attend as a kid. I had drew some pictures at home and brought them with me. Brothers there were still using the same pictures they had in tenth grade. I thought they was getting all the knowledge 'cause they were going to the New World School of Art. But I was the one really working. They were just out there with the name: New World. The name don't really mean nothing."

Deron says he's thinking of taking a nighttime art class, but that's about it. And he's only considering that to gain better mastery of the equipment that he's accumulated in his room.

He chooses to place his faith in himself, in his innate ability to pick up tasks from those around him, in his unshakable confidence in the assorted talents he's gleaned from his father and his mother, herself an artist. He doesn't see the need for formal training. Besides, life is the real work here. What colleges offer courses on that?

"If I practice, I will get better at whatever I do," says Deron. "That's all I need. I want to get like those Chinese masters who approach things like walking. You had to learn how to walk. I want to just build. Life is a building process. I think with education, they teach a lot of people, but they save the knowledge. They teach you all this bull. I want the knowledge. I know how to master things. Master of your world—not the whole wide world. For that, all you really need is the basics 'cause you can build from there."

TODD STEWART, 17: SCHOOLWORK AND SPORTS

WASHINGTON, D.C.—Todd acknowledges the odds. He recognizes that the chances of him finding a place in the National Football League are, at best, slim. At worst, of course, they're nil. He's surveyed the terrain of his dreams and has seen the pitfalls: injury, eligibility, simply not being good enough.

He has chosen to brave the potholes, the hidden land mines, nonetheless. He has decided that his basket is sturdy enough for all of his eggs, his balance steady enough to keep them from spilling. He wants to be a football player. That's all he's ever wanted.

So now, in his senior year at Anacostia High, he's laying the foundation for that dream. He's starring as a defensive back. He's also trying to figure out which college he'll attend. He's being heavily recruited by several major schools, he tells me, from Iowa to Wake Forest. Coaches write him. They call. They sweet-talk his dad, who also happens to be Todd's head coach.

"A number of schools are recruiting me: Oklahoma State, Kentucky, Tennessee, Clemson, Maryland, Wake Forest," says Todd. "The coach from Iowa, I'm on his mailing list. They send me letters, but they haven't called me. Until I hear from one of the coaches, I don't count them as a school that is recruiting.

HARD TO EARN: ON WORK AND WEALTH

"I was really interested in Oklahoma State 'cause a guy from out here signed this year, and my father has some old players that played for Oklahoma State. A recruiter calls once a week and talks to me for like fifteen minutes and then talks to my father for almost an hour. He's trying to sell me through my father. I told my father they are going to get the short end of the stick because when it comes down to it, they aren't recruiting my father. I'm the one that has to go to school there. He understood what I was saying. He explained to the coach how I was feeling, so the coach talks to me more and tells me about the school."

Todd is flattered by the attention. But he's also worried. His grades aren't that good, he confesses. He blew the SAT, scoring ninety points below the seven hundred minimum. He did well on the ACT, well enough to be eligible, anyway. But this matter of grade-point averages and entrance exams still bothers him. Proposition 48—the rule that requires student athletes to maintain a grade-point average of 2.0 or better to be eligible for play—casts a long shadow over his dreams. He thinks the NCAA is out to wreck young men like him, out to derail their dreams of pro contracts, with all these academic requirements and eligibility rules.

He explains these fears to me as we sit in the school's gym. Todd speaks quietly, his light drawl fighting to be heard above the din of several students gathered on the bleachers. Brown-skinned, lean, he wears a T-shirt, blue jeans, a small Afro. His 'fro sways a bit as he shakes his head in disgust at what he considers an NCAA plot to stem the tide of Black athletes flowing into the nation's universities.

"I heard John Thompson speaking at a Nike convention at Howard University," he says. "What he was saying was that, really, the NCAA is trying to keep a lot of Black people from going to college. They are trying to cut us out. They make it harder. I can't understand why they want to do that. I remember the time my father told me all he had to do was take the SAT to get into college and they gave you a minimum of seven hundred and now it's going up to nine hundred. And you have to have a 2.0. If you have a 2.0, then lower the SAT requirement, that is what John Thompson was saying. I feel what he was saying was true: They are trying to keep the Black people out of college."

Compounding his irritation is the fact that Blacks have turned college athletics into a boom industry. This isn't lost on any Black kid who hopes to muscle his way into pro sports. They study the numbers crunching of Division I sports as much as they do the internal logic of the games they play. They see the million-dollar deals Reebok and Nike cut with athletic departments. They see the shoe endorsements college coaches get. And since kids like Todd are the engines that make these programs go, is it really unreasonable for them to expect to be oiled just as thoroughly?

Knowing that he'll be a cog in one of those engines one day soon, Todd is befuddled by the skewed mathematics of this industry.

"After every Michigan game, they sell Chris Webber's jersey and he can't get any of that money," says Todd. "It goes to the college or the coach. I think that is wrong. If a player is from Detroit and he's at UCLA and doesn't know anyone at UCLA, your family life is hard and you don't have any money. So some way you are going to have to get some money. When it comes back to the NCAA, they want to punish you. But they're making all that money on football and basketball games. At least give the players something. Financial aid helps, but it's not going to get you through four years of school."

If Todd seems a bit more preoccupied with athletics than academics, it's because he is. He gives lip service, of course, to the value of education. He'll tell you that he wants to get a college degree because "if I get hurt or anything, I'm going to need the education to keep me going." He'll express vague dreams of enrolling in a criminal justice program, of being an FBI agent one day. But these dreams seem to sit on the periphery of his ambitions, on the far side of his hopes.

There is a nearer side that contradicts this, a side that has little use for teachers who stress classroom achievement, for those who think jocks slide by, for anyone who calls him lazy for applying himself more on the football field than in class. It is this side that looks for the quick way out; that sought out the ACT, when Todd floundered on the SAT, because he thought it was easier to pass; that aims for little else than the minimum on tests and report cards.

This, of course, is the side of young jocks that many recruiters and coaches prey upon. This is the side they court, the side that enables boosters and alumni and unscrupulous athletic directors to turn 100-to-1 longshots into cornerstones of our children's hopes. This is the side teachers egg on when they pass students along because they have wicked jump shots, the side that reaps for coaches million-dollar shoe contracts, book deals and lucrative lecture honoraria.

This, for young men like Todd, is also a blind side.

"A teacher told me one day that the athletes have it too easy," says Todd. "I really didn't pay too much attention, but the way she said it kind of made me mad. An athlete only needs seven hundred to get in college, but a person on academic scholarship has to get one thousand or more. Academics, after school, they go home and study. You don't go home and practice or play on a Saturday. She doesn't see it that way. She found the news that I passed my ACT disturbing. Instead of congratulating me, she was asking why couldn't I get thirty. I said I tried but didn't get it. I'm happy with my score. I don't know what her problem is.

"I'm not the best student. I do enough just to get by, C's and B's. My brother is an hour society student. I look at his report cards, and I just do my own thing. I just get grades to get by. My oldest brother, I remember the first time he got a C and how upset he was. He plays football and everything, but it was the dedication in the class he had. I would rather hang out with my friends instead of study. He's twenty, and we grew up in different times. The friends he hung out with were more into school. My friends don't have too much hope. They didn't pull me down, but you don't want to outdo your friends.

"I remember I was in junior high and my friends and I had the same classes. I could see that teachers passed them 'cause they played basketball real good, and they would go on. I saw what they couldn't do so I didn't do as well as I could. I didn't try to hurt their feelings.

"In a way, teachers have passed me on because I play football well. The main thing was that teachers here want to see the students go on and do things. If you fail a student, it might take away from his chance to go to college or take away their self-esteem. The student might just give up. I don't think they passed me just because of my football skills—but they passed me because they saw that I had a chance."

A chance. It's often rare and elusive for the young Black men who populate D C.'s working-class enclaves. Todd knows this. He's seen the awful price friends and relatives have paid for even the most normal missteps, the most quotidian indiscretions of youth. His cousin was gunned a couple of years back. Just a week before our interview, Albert La Shon Preston, another star member of Todd's football team, was shot to death in a neighborhood dispute. Preston was the third member of the Anacostia football team killed since that summer. On the day we sat in the gym, TV cameras whirred in the hallways and on the school steps, recording the melancholy that had settled over the school as students too accustomed to death once again mourned a lost friend.

A chance. This is why athletes like Todd throw themselves so vigorously into their goals, driven not merely by dreams of glory and celebrity, but as much by fear. Todd wants out of striking distance, away from the drive-bys and bloodshed and the latest news that so-and-so took a bullet to the head the other day. He's burnt out on death. Maybe football can put some ground between him and those mean streets, between him and that creeping sense of mortality that sneaks up on him each time tragedy touches his young life.

And everybody—d-backs, recruiters, teachers, everybody—knows sports is the fastest way out.

"The main thing I'm looking for in a school is location," says Todd. "I want to be somewhere quiet, away from what's going on out here. I can be myself, and I can play.

"At least I'd have the opportunity to see if I could make the pros."

An unspoken desperation tinges his voice, one that seems to obscure for him the irony in his remarks. He doesn't just want college. He needs it. And he's not willing to let this matter of grades and standardized tests get in his way. I ask, point-blank, what's more important to him: the grades or the gridiron. His answer is just as point-blank.

"Until I get to college, education is secondary."

ANTHONY "COUNTRY" MEYERS, 19: JOBLESSNESS

LONG BEACH, CALIFORNIA—"Basically, for a brother around here in the nineties, it's kind of hard," says Country. "They get frustrated not having money. I'm not the type of person to rob so I figure the easiest and the fastest way on the streets for making money is selling dope. Don't get me wrong. I don't want to do it. I don't even like it, to be honest. But I figure that's the fastest way I can make money. I'm not down with all that robbing and stealing and killing. I might as well just go ahead do this, make as much as I can, save as much as I can. It's hard to survive right now."

Country sits forward in the chair of a friend's home and, unprompted, repeats himself: "I don't want to do this. I want a job, is what I really want."

Jobs haven't proven that easy for the brother to come by. Country has lost more jobs than some people have held. Not because of a poor work ethic or an inability to get along with anyone. No, rather, his jobs have simply up and vanished. A pharmacy he worked at laid him off. A concession stand where he slaved dried up. Five months ago, a construction company he toiled for moved away. He's devoted at least three hours to job hunting every day since.

You tell him not to sell drugs. He'll say, Okay, what then? You say get a job. He'll say, Fine, where? He wants, needs, answers.

Country doesn't live in that bullshit fantasy world from whence political rhetoric flows. He doesn't see the robust America where jobs are plentiful and work, no matter how hard, is good. Opportunity hasn't come close enough his way for him to even say it's passed him by.

The America he knows sees hundreds of thousands of unemployment applications each month. The America he knows saw GM and IBM lay off thousands. The America he knows saw Boeing and Firestone and hundreds of other major corporations pull out of Black communities, from south-central L.A. to the east side of Detroit. He was a child when the manufacturing sector began to let Black folks know it hardly needed them anymore. He's a man now, and the message is finally starting to hit home.

And for a young man who's kept a job since he started high school, the message has been a harsh one indeed.

"A lot of the good jobs are far out," he says, "and I don't have any transportation to get there. When I was doing construction, we was doing a certain amount of work in different places. We would do five- or six-month jobs and go on to other ones. But then after one job, they told me they was relocating to Irvine. But with my lack of transportation, I wasn't able to be hired—so they had to lay me off. I have been laid off ever since and looking for work. I thought I could find work by now. It hasn't been that easy, though."

He tells me he also receives some unemployment benefits, but they don't take him very far.

Country says he's kept a positive attitude and has searched vigorously for new work. He's applied everywhere from the few fast-food restaurants that dot his neighborhood to any of the number of potential construction jobs he sees posted in the unemployment office. "I don't want to take just any type of job," he says. "I want a job that's good for me, something that will enable me to eat and take care of myself. Sometimes, I feel like I'll take anything, but I can't even find that."

But he keeps doling out résumés.

"I get frustrated, but I never stop 'cause I'm not a quitter," says Country. "I feel I can do anything within my will. I always had work.

I never been out of work, except for lately. I have experience doing a lot of things. I worked in the medical records office for a pharmacist for like eight months, filing, answering phones, etc. I did all the medical paperwork. I was laid off there 'cause somebody took over the company and temps had to be laid off. I have my construction experience, all-around food-service experience. I worked in concession stands serving food. There was always something to keep myself going while I was in school."

School was no easy matter, either. Yet one more Black boy suffering under the burden of miseducation, Country dropped out of school for a while, frustrated with lesson plans he didn't see as holding much value. He worked instead; it seemed to make more sense. Eventually, though, family and friends convinced him that education—not the low-wage gigs he was holding down when he left—was the best route to prosperity. To hell with the textbook lies, they said, go back. He did.

"I graduated from Long Beach School for Adults on Thirty-second and Orange," he boasts. "I went there and got my diploma on February 2, 1993."

His voice drops briefly as he toys with the irony of his circumstances: "Now, I graduated and I'm out of school—and am looking for work." But he's not disillusioned about school. School was good for him, no matter his employment status. A man needs to be educated if only just because. Country wants to attend college, too, a junior college first, then a historically Black university, probably somewhere in his native Texas.

Says Country: "You can learn at all colleges, but a Black college to me seems like it has more to offer. I want to go to a Black college that can teach me more of my roots and teach me my trade as well. I need to learn. I don't want to go out here in California 'cause there's so much brainwashing going on in school. I went through that. I'm planning on going to school in January to start my class. I'm taking a Human Services course. I can get a job in the probation department. School is another thing: Financial aid has been hard to get. So I'm trying to get my money stashed for anything such as school and all. I want to be dependent on myself."

If he can just find him a job, he says, get off the streets, he'll be able to put some of his plans in motion. If someone would just give him a chance, he'll straighten out everything that his economic straits have crimped. He's hopeful that opportunity, elusive as its been, will wander somewhere near him soon. Meanwhile, he stays on the lookout.

"People say they are pleased with my work experience when I go look for a job, but I don't know, obviously I haven't been called back, so I don't know what to say on that issue," he says. "I've been doing pretty good so far. I just keep up the good work and don't never give up 'cause there's always something out there. I look every day. I get my résumés typed up and go out on job hunts every day, me and my friends. Go out in the morning, come back about two or three o'clock. That's what we do every day. You just got to have patience to wait and look.

"I don't like being on unemployment. It comes, but it's not enough to survive. It's just a third of what you were making, even though it is something. I'm happy for that, but it's not enough money to live off of. Now, I have enough money to do what I want to do, but I want to do it legally. There are no jobs, so I have to do what I can until I find one."

We go 'round and 'round about the crack thing. The author insists that drugs aren't the way, that they only ultimately kill the folks he'll need most. He agrees, agrees that he's poisoning minds and souls as much as respiratory systems. He agrees that he's wrong. "I already know it's killing of our race," he mutters somberly. But he knows, too, that he's alive and housed and fed. The author condemns nonetheless, but understands far more.

As though it may be some sort of consolation, Country explains that he resists the drug dealer stereotype. He's not out here riding around in fancy, loud cars or flashing gold or serving as a walking billboard for Fila or Guess? In fact, he says, he's broke often, even with the few rocks he slings from Long Beach street corners. "Most of these brothers ain't making a lot of money," he says. "They're just trying to get by, too." And when he does make money, he says, it goes straight 'neath the mattress.

"I buy things I need for survival," says Country. "Clothing, food. I put some money to the side for transportation. I help my family. I used to live with my sister and she's got kids and doesn't need a grown man just sponging off her. So I moved and now I live with my homey and his son. I had my own apartment, but rent was too high for me to keep it by myself. So I try to help out with rent. I got to have enough money to buy dope when I start back over again, too. That's it.

"I save all my money 'cause if you're already doing something illegal, you might as well use it to the best of your knowledge. You might as well preserve it if you are going to need it. It wouldn't make sense to go out there, blow it and get caught. It is too easy to splurge money, so I put it aside or I just give it to my sister and she'll keep it for me.

"Before, I had a bank account. It's too easy to get involved in checks and all that. I just give it to my sister or I keep it. I had experienced a little thing before where I had a checking account and I was getting my checks. I am not good with a checkbook. I don't deal with easy money. I just stay away from the banks. When I get older and get a job and stuff like that, I will get one, but right now there's too much money [to be made] to be putting in the bank. I don't need no scene. I just keep it within the family so I don't have to worry about the cops."

Country has enough worries. Unemployment depresses him. So does selling dope, seeing the fiends he's helping destroy, seeing the families his product rends. "Psychologically, it's hard." If he could work, he would. You think he wants be out here, dodging squad cars, fretting the any number of knuckleheads who'd like nothing more than to move in on a dealer who works solo? You think he wasn't happier welding beams and pouring concrete?

"I'm scared," admits Country. "That's the thing about doing work legally. You don't have to be scared of anything."

Except, perhaps, of losing your job.

TIMOTHY WASHINGTON, 23: DO FOR SELF

LOS ANGELES—For much of his academic life, Tim had danced to the tune of the mantra of the upwardly mobile: Get a degree, get a job, get paid. He majored in business at Morehouse University expressly for these reasons. He wore the right clothes, met the right people, made the right moves. In 1992, he got his degree. Shortly afterward, he got his job.

Tim landed a salesman spot at Kraft General Foods, in the marine sector, where he sold macaroni and cheese and spaghetti and other items to cruise lines. While not exactly getting paid as he hoped, Tim was earning in the mid-$30,000 range, an impressive start for a twenty-two-year-old who'd studied his way out of the concrete killing fields of south-central.

"I was in pursuit of the corporate structure," he says, nursing a soda at a corner restaurant booth inside the Crenshaw Mall. "That's the way I was brought up. And it's my experience that that's the way a lot of us young Black men are being brought up—to go out and get a degree and get a good job with a big company paying benefits, so to speak. And then you're set. You work all your life practically, then you retire."

But his benefits didn't cover peace of mind, which, Tim says, eluded him throughout his career at Kraft. He was dogged incessantly by worries over how far he could go in the company, in any company where his only stake was as a workaday drudge. His concerns sprang in part from the general anxieties Black company men often suffer when working around all whites, in part from stories of the calamity and frustration of the working Black men in his own life: His father was snubbed at a company he'd worked for for more than two decades, passed over repeatedly for promotions in favor of younger, whiter men, his twenty-year loyalty seemingly lost on the men whose business he'd helped build. Tim believes fervently that his father's professional woes were the source of much of the pain and bitterness, of the alcoholism and emotional pain that wracked his personal life. Even as a kid listening to his father's stories, he couldn't help but wonder where, along his own fast track to management, lay the glass ceiling that would check his broad ambitions.

"My father's experience had turned me off a lot to the corporate structure," he says. "He never really recovered. That led him to drink heavily. He always did drink, but after that, it just went up a notch. That had me thinking about how you spend your life at a company, promoting it, building it, only for something like being passed over to happen. So I was like, 'That'll never be me.' "

It seemed the fears had little foundation at first, as Tim trundled steadily along the fast track at Kraft. After starting as an intern in a program designed to offer minority students inroads into big business, Tim was promoted three times within eight months of landing the full-time slot, each job demanding more of him than the last. It was exhausting but fulfilling, Tim says. He was learning, and he was liked, both of which made the long hours worthwhile. Both of which soon vanished upon his third promotion.

Suddenly, Tim found himself confronted by an older boss with little appreciation for the younger pitchman, whom he saw as a threat. In an ironic twist on his father's corporate battles, Tim was now the new man in, the fledgling worker dispatched to be groomed for a top spot by the loyal vet. But where his father trained his workers despite knowing the young white turks would likely replace him soon, Tim's boss only lashed out.

"I was a young Black man," says Tim, "and he was an older white guy, probably about fifty-nine, sixty. So in a couple of years, he would be out the door. He had brought an important segment of the business to Kraft General Foods, and there was no one else who knew the work, knew the jargon and knew the contacts. We were doing about $6.5 million a year and I was to be his successor so . . . So they brought me in fresh, to learn under him for two or three years and take over. He just had a serious problem with that. It was just crazy because he was just trying to do everything in his power to force me out of there.

"There were problems from day one. Like, the first day I got there, he changed my start from eight A.M. to seven A.M. After that, things just started happening. I was working on weekends. I was having stuff shipped to my house, at home. I was delivering stuff on weekends, I was working from seven in the morning till seven or eight at night. And the more I looked at it, it wasn't really worth it. I mean, they were probably paying him eighty thousand a year. I'm making mid-thirties and I was basically like the gopher. You know, I was running around doing everything that he didn't want to do or didn't have time to do—and I was working thirty-five miles away from the job one way. So, to work, I'm up at five in the morning to get there at seven. I'm leaving at seven or eight o'clock at night and then got to drive home through L.A. traffic. By the time I get home, it's time for me to go to sleep so I can get up and do it all over again.

"Plus, he was putting the blame on me for different things that would occur, like people not receiving products or just things being screwed up. They were his mistakes, due to miscommunication, because he didn't feel he had to tell me anything. He never really kept me informed of what was going on. There was no training for the position. They just put me on, like, 'Here you go.' They just threw me out in the water and said, 'Go ahead and swim,' basically. A lot of that came back to haunt me. And it was really their fault. If you put someone in a new position without giving them the proper training, then you have to make allotment for mistakes. This guy didn't understand that, and he was making it seem like I was responsible for everything that went wrong. I just started getting fed up with it.

"And I was doing it all for somebody else's gain! So I said, Let me just step back for a second, take a look at what I'm doing. Is it really worth it? Do I really want to do this for the rest of my life? The answer to that was, simply, no."

Months later, he took the biggest step of his life. After a childhood filled with visions of corporate luxury, after a college career spent jockeying for just the right connections to just the right people, after five-and-a-half years of toiling at the food giant as intern and full-time employee, Tim packed up his desk and quit to develop a business of his own.

"After hearing about my father, I always thought about the need to do the entrepreneur thing, but when some of these things started going down at Kraft, that just forced me out there," says Tim.

In the months since leaving Kraft, Tim hasn't exploded as an overnight success. His decision has, at present, yielded as many economic costs as psychological gains. He still longs for a salary, the benefits. He's postponed plans to get his own place. He's had to accept unemployment at times. His dreams are in transit, as is his life.

But Tim accepts the inconveniences, the downsides and disadvantages. He's part of a generation that has seen what the entrepreneurial spirit can achieve, that realizes that with the risks of going business alone come also the prospect of huge payoffs. It's a generation that saw Black boys like Billy Joe Chambers and Rayful Edmund build million-dollar empires from ten-dollar crack rocks, that saw Karl Kani and Carl Jones bumrush retail stores with their own clothing lines, that saw Eazy-E and Russell Simmons fashion record fiefdoms from scratch. In a larger sense, this realization also reflects a growing mood in Black America that the community—its social and business institutions—must indeed be the primary source of its own sustenance. And with business pages reporting deeper job cuts in corporate America each week, many more young Black men are seeking ways to go it for themselves, without having to rely on the scant work rationed to us by car companies and fast-food restaurants and low-end mom-and-pop shops.

"I can't lie and say that I don't miss the loot, but that's all part of the sacrifice I decided to make when I took that step," Tim says. "I knew that I wouldn't have any money coming in. I'm collecting unemployment right now, which is probably about a third, every two weeks, of what I would normally bring home. It's caused some significant change in my lifestyle. I can't go out and buy the things that I used to buy, so on and so forth, but that works. If I'm not channeling my efforts toward figuring out what I'm going to do with this money, I'm focusing on something else to get more. So it keeps me on track, so to speak, 'cause I know I need money and I know the type of lifestyle I want to live. So I guess I just redirect that energy into something positive which keeps me going every day. If I don't have money and I know I don't have money, I got to get up and do something to get some money, you know what I'm sayin'? That's the way that works."

But he's free and in full control of his destiny. His hopes are his own to realize. And he's not without numerous prospects. Among his pursuits is Tim's venture with an older Black man to develop a plan to market rapid-transit systems to big cities here and abroad.

"These are trains that use one third recycled products, can be built for one third of the cost of any existing train and there is no major modification to the existing infrastructure," Tim contends excitedly. "It can run alongside elevated or underground existing highways and thoroughfares in any city—using technology that already exists or just hasn't been applied to rapid transit, so the technology is there, it just needs to be implemented."

He joined the venture shortly after leaving Kraft, plunging in fast and head-first to gain ground-level footing with the upstart concern. He wanted to be an owner, a partner, not just another drone hustling to build something he could not control.

"I've known this gentleman who had the idea since I was probably about five or six years old," says Tim. "So, I have been hearing about, you know, the things that he was doing and trying for practically all my life. And when I was to the point where I was ready to step on board, it was really an issue of great timing because he had just put together a team of people to go ahead and form a company and become a legal entity. So I was right in there at the right time. As opposed to working for a major corporation, I was in the process of the formation of a major corporation.

"There's no money right now, so it's just a matter of putting in time based on the rapport that I had with him. But when the project does come into fruition, which it will soon, then that won't be a problem and there will be lots of money to go around. So, I mean, I look at it as a ground-floor opportunity."

He's laying other cornerstones, too. A lifetime in L.A. has sparked in Tim an intense interest in the dynamics of the entertainment industry. Together with a group of friends, he has begun founding an entertainment management company he'd like to model in some ways after superagent Mike Ovitz's powerful Creative Artists Agency. But Tim sees his company more as a "one-stop" shop for actors, singers and the like, a business that takes care of business for those too busy to handle it themselves. He'd like to be a player, a mover and, eventually, a mogul.

"Our group doesn't even have a name yet," he says. "We just call ourselves a business group. We meet regularly, eight brothers and two sisters, lawyers, business people, accountants, so on and so forth. And what we are attempting to do is come up with, basically, a one-stop shop for any talent.

"If you come to our company, it's a one-stop shop for anything you need for being developed as a talent, for being marketed. We're going to write commercials that suit you, to market you to different people that want to use you for endorsing. We are going to launch commercials, give you legal representation, do your financial planning, your accounting. I think that it's high time for a business like that because the entertainment industry is growing and growing and growing. You are getting a lot of independents coming up like Fox, a lot of cats that are coming up like Martin [Lawrence]. And it's like, really, high time for a lot of Black entertainers that are finally getting that chance, and those are the people that we want to get to—the Black people who are starting to blow up. By no means are we limiting ourselves, but we'd like to represent our own.

"Our operational theme is to establish a rapport and, basically, build an extended family and just get some trust in us. You can trust that we are going to do the best for you. Because if we do the best for you, then we are doing the best for ourselves. If we can get you some money for you, then that's more money for us. And that's the way the ball needs to bounce.

"Ovitz isn't necessarily a one-stop shop, but he's powerful and he's feared. I don't know him personally. I don't know his history. I have never even talked to the man. I have only read articles about his company and what he's done. He's got a very good concept that we plan to adopt and add to. So, I mean, he's a mogul. Everything that goes on in the entertainment industry he has a hand in or it comes through him. He's in demand."

It's that "hand" that Tim covets most. More than the money or the prestige, it's the influence that lends the most thrust to his entrepreneurial ambitions, the idea that he, too, can shape lives and shake industries. Tim wants nothing more than to mold the world around him—starting with where he grew up. Raised in Watts, Tim says he'd like to be able to reach back into south-central Los Angeles's Black working-class neighborhoods and build on the promise he sees too often wasting away on street corners and housing projects and in city morgues. He wants to create jobs where corporate America has spirited them away. He wants to build community where there is disharmony. He wants to erect hope amid the rubble of despair and broken dreams.

"I think the whole trend is to move toward brothers that have ideas," says Tim. "We got to go back. We need to talk to the brothers and nurture their ideas. And those of us that do have the experience in any kind of profession, we need to help them modify those ideas, help them, you know, show them what they need to read about and research, to make all that stuff happen. It's a global market. It's time to get out there—and everybody's got ideas. Everything that we see—a salt shaker, a tape—everything was always, at some point in time, somebody's idea. But because they didn't cast it away, and they held on to it and worked at it, it came into fruition. But that's what brothers do, man, they throw away millions of dollars every day, 'cause they got dreams: 'Oh, man, I'd like to make a movie. If I did make a movie, I'd do it like this,' so on and so forth. Brothers got ideas that they just cast away, because that money is there now. It takes brothers to get in and have a heart-to-heart with the brothers and say, 'What is it that you're really trying to do?' It's not about giving them money; it's about their creativity."

But creativity won't always sit still, even when there is no viable channel for its release. Creativity, says Tim, makes its own outlets. In neighborhoods like his, those outlets have often been found in the open-air drug dens that the crack trade has made of so many low-income blocks, in the cartels that so many young brothers have cobbled from acquaintances and childhood friendships. This, confesses Tim, is why he has an admitted soft spot for drug dealers.

"I can't really say that I'm mad at those brothers or totally against those brothers that sell drugs," he says. "I'm against the outcome; the means may not justify the ends because it's perpetuating death in our society among our own people. But there are really those fellas out there who, before they go broke, they gonna do something else. I can't fault them for doing that.

"White people do it all the time, you know. I mean, where's the dope coming from? I mean, we make some of the dope, fine, but all of that dope is coming from somewhere, man. All of the guns, we ain't flying no planes in here with guns. That stuff is all being fed into the community. And if we can see that and take advantage of it to a certain point, until we can parlay that into something legal, that may be what you need to do. I really don't have the answer. Some brothers get stuck because it's so easy to go that route."

But crack dealers aren't the only American men to be tempted by the dollar. Capitalism corrupts thoroughly, across class and race lines, across professional boundaries. Corruption, cashing out on principles, they are very much the American way. Even the best-intentioned brother, even the man who believes his sole focus is his dream of building a business to salvage his community, even he can be swayed by the profit margin. Can by-the-bootstraps moguls remain do-gooders, too?

"I can't say how I'll avoid being consumed by just making money. I can't speak upon that because I haven't walked those grounds yet, but I do know I am deeply rooted in the community, first and foremost, because that's where I come from. There are a lot of brothers from that community who, once they get to where they are going, lose contact, lose touch. And they don't reach back. And I think the thing that will always keep me grounded is that I always maintain with the brothers that I grew up with, the people I have known all the time. You can't really lose touch, unless you really lose touch. You can't really carry somebody with you because they will become dead weight—but what you can do is maintain that open-door policy with the brother. And talk to them and let them know the things that you are involved in.

"I talk to a lot of cats I went to high school with, man. And I tell them some of the things that I'm doing and it kind of blows them away. I talk to them like I'm real: 'This is some shit we doin' that's gonna help cut down on the traffic on freeway.' If you talk to brothers like that and be real, you maintain that relationship, man. And you'll be surprised how much they appreciate it because they learn. Brothers want to learn, but the opportunities aren't really there. In the hood is where it's good, but that shouldn't be all you know.

"The attitude is that the system doesn't work for brothers. I think that there's a real conscious movement going on in our society today, where brothers, even the brothers that are out of the mainstream, so to speak, they are not down with working a job now. They need a light to shine at the end of the tunnel and it's gonna take some redoing of their whole thought process. But for that to happen, you have to be in touch."

You can't be behind bulletproof glass or driving by in your Beamer or handling business through the manager who stays among the natives all day while you wheel-and-deal from the comfort of a plush office. Tim knows these types of entrepreneurs, men and women who pillage the potential as well as the spending power of Black America until the hood is dry. They come in all shades and genders, but none leave as bitter a taste in his mouth as the Black ones.

"There are a lot of brothers that have formed companies, and once they are up and running, they don't use those companies as a venue or an avenue to employ people," he says. "As soon as the company starts thriving, they want to sell it off for the big bucks and live high on the hog. The commitment is not there. That to me is a sellout. A sellout is anything that you do when you sacrifice your manhood, your culture, just to get a buck."

Our conversation returns us to the young hypercapitalists Tim grew up observing in Watts, the crack dealers he saw putting in work along Central Avenue and Imperial Highway and Hoover and Vernon. Are they, too, sellouts, I ask? Or are they merely alternative venture capitalists wildcatting on the prairies of our streets, genuflecting in their own special way at the noble altar of rugged individualism? His response begins direct but becomes evasive, as he is hesitant to place too heavy a moral qualification on what he views as one of the few vents for the entrepreneurial genius he so often sees stifled.

Says Tim: "A drug dealer is a sellout, in a sense that he is doing what he is doing at the expense of his people. That may be a necessary that you need to do because it's all you can do. But you got to cut it off at some point, you know. And I'm not saying that it's good, but I can't blame those brothers that are out there doing that. If your mom's on crack and your little brother's starving, and your little sister's selling her body to get money, and you don't have no skills, no training, you didn't even graduate high school, you need money yesterday. So here's your partner offering you, to start you. What do you do? It's business.

"The thing is, legitimate Black businessmen, we got to raise the consciousness of our brothers. We got to raise their consciousness because once they do [drug deals], I mean, that may be something that they have to do for a time, but you don't always have to do that. Brothers become complacent. It's not all about that, but since the system exists as that, you got to get within the system, use that to get you on your feet and then get with something positive or something real that's going to sustain you."

JAY ADANDE, 22: BURNING THE MIDNIGHT OIL

CHICAGO—Humility initially demands Jay tell you he was lucky, that he was in some of the right places at just the right times. But luck doesn't fully explain how a twenty-two-year-old from middle-class Santa Monica developed into a highly sought-after journalism talent. It doesn't explain the hefty résumé, the internships at the top American broadsheets, the plum job covering Big Ten sports for one of Chicago's two dailies right out of college.

He had help, to be sure: a mother who placed him in good schools early, caring teachers, an upbringing in a community free of much of the violence and despair that often short-circuit Black dreams. But just as poverty cannot always imprison talent, neither do square meals and stable homes guarantee quality students. Press Jay and you begin to see his luck as the residue of burnt midnight oil, of focused ambition and rigorous study. There were sacrifices: Jay opting to edit the high school paper over a tryout for the basketball team that would win a state championship; Jay eschewing frat parties and beer blasts to toil late nights at the Northwestern University paper; Jay doling out résumés at every conference, symposium, panel discussion and networking function he could scrape up the cash to sign up for.

After the sacrifices followed payoffs: honor-roll grades, scholarships, summer jobs at *The Washington Post*, the *Los Angeles Times*. Jay won awards, covered major stories, earned a reputation and, eventually, a high-profile job at the Chicago *Sun-Times*.

But there were drawbacks, too. Being twice as good as many of his peers still often only earned Jay the proverbial half-credit. Racial prejudices still sometimes capped the expectations of the men and women he worked for and with, just as cultural divides occasionally made transcending those misperceptions nigh impossible. Jay jousted constantly with the specter of racial stigmas that deemed Black hires inferior, the undeserving beneficiaries of back-door charity and "reverse discrimination." Even when not faced with stereotypes directly, he never let the possibility of them drift far from his mind. That he is a sportswriter—a job that, save notable exceptions in scattered places, remains very much a citadel of white male dominance—has not exactly smoothed Jay's career track.

But he's talented, a fact that puts the lie to the "affirmative action" albatrosses draped unfairly from the necks of young Black professionals who dare capitalize on the struggles of their predecessors. With that, he figures, he has the nimbleness of mind to dodge most quagmires, the resilience to wade successfully through others. These are, in themselves, jobs, struggles that make the nine-to-five that much more taxing, that much more singular from the work of his white coworkers. Nonetheless, Jay goes on undeterred, calmly amassing experience, all the while hacking away at the poor images that dog Black men from the newsroom to the locker room. He continues to tend vigilantly to his craft, mindful of the stigmas, watchful of the prize, the midnight oil burning ever hotter . . .

JA: To get here, you got to be good and lucky or well connected. With me, it was probably a combination of at least two of those. I think I've been lucky in a lot of ways—in the right place at the right time. But I also believe that I've been good, 'cause if I wasn't good I wouldn't be here. I've been able to make the most of these lucky opportunities. I've had the opportunity to go to one of the best journalism schools and [get] a couple of great internships. A lot of people don't even have that chance. Some people might have the brains and everything else, but the scholarship money doesn't come through, so they don't get it. I've worked hard. This is something that I set my sights on.

I had a great ninth-grade English teacher, Ann Colburn. I wrote an essay for her, and she liked it and she said, Would you like to be in the journalism class and write for the newspaper next year? That was the push that I needed. I originally wanted to get into sports broadcasting, and I figured I'd have to start from newspapers and work my way up. It's what I wanted to do, but I'm not sure I would have had the initiative to go and start it myself. So her help was a real big step. It got me started. I could have played on a state championship basketball team. I would've been twelfth man [he chuckles]—but I could've had a big trophy and a letterman's jacket. But in eleventh grade, I realized that writing was what I was going to do in college and beyond, so I better start taking the steps now. I thought that if I'm applying for a journalism school, they'd be a lot more interested to know that I was the editor of my high school newspaper than I was the twelfth man on a basketball team.

A lot of people ask me, 'How did you get this and that?' It's a lot of hard work for a long time, and I made choices way back then. I would have loved to play on that basketball team, but I think I've been fortunate 'cause I've been able to have foresight. I looked ahead and saw that I needed to take that step to do this goal. And in college it was the same way, working at the school newspaper. I put in a lot of hours and made my life miserable a lot of times. I didn't get the full college experience like a lot of people had. I didn't have the freedom to always go out and party. Wednesday night was a big party night at school and a lot of times I had to work on Wednesday night. I didn't get the opportunity to sit around the dorms. I'd come back and my roommate would say, "Everybody was up here and we talked about this and that." I missed out 'cause I'd be at the paper working till three in the morning.

But I get this internship at *The Washington Post*—and it was paying like six hundred dollars a week—and then all of a sudden the same people saying, "How can you spend all your time at the [Northwestern University] *Daily?*"—these are the people who said, "How did you get this great internship?" They fail to see the connection.

Some people would say, "You're lucky you're Black." People don't say it to my face, but you can tell they think that. My response has always been that I knew that was the situation coming to this job. Here I am four or five months out of school, twenty-one years old, I had a couple good internships, but to the outside, if you hadn't seen my clips and you didn't know my whole background, you got to be thinking, This is an affirmative action. I didn't have any real credentials to a lot of people. My approach to that was that I knew the spotlight was on me. I felt that I had to just come out and kick ass. Don't give them any room for argument. I think I proved myself to the point where I think I can be taken seriously, and I was a legitimate hire. I was fully legitimate.

People might say the same thing about college. My SAT score was seventy points higher than the mean for the average incoming freshman that year. I never, ever want to have something taken away from me because of my race. I do think I've had opportunities because of my race—but that's something I took advantage of. I still got to go to the schools!

I know Harvard wouldn't have sent me an application to please apply to my school if I were white. I knew that, but you have to play the game. And I don't think there is anything unfair about that. Thirty years ago I wouldn't have been able to go to this school. Let's not talk about unfair. I don't feel I have to apologize for anything like that because I've never abused it. I feel I've proven my worth. Maybe I did get this shot 'cause I was Black and they want to hire a Black writer—but it still give us only two Black full-time writers on the staff! It's not like there is some gross injustice being done toward white people out there. I think we are up to four full-time Black people on the staff. There are a lot of good white writers out there, but there are a lot of good Black writers out there not getting a shot. I'm one Black writer who got a shot—because I was Black or not, I don't know. I like to think it was because I was good and Black. I like to be honest. I believe in myself. I'm not saying I'm the best writer, but I do think I can write well and do my job, so it's not a matter of being just Black. It's a matter of being good and Black.

But growing up in a culturally mixed setting—my mother is white, my neighborhood was mixed—I feel advantaged in dealing with America, period. That includes corporate America. I feel I can deal with any situation. I think I was also fortunate to grow up in Santa Monica with a racially tolerant climate. There were a lot of different people of different races around—my friends. We'd sit down there, and we'd start roasting on each other. We could get pretty ugly with ethnic slurs, but at the same time I was kind of proud. I'd look around, and we had a guy of German descent, couple of Jewish people, Korean, me being Black and maybe a couple of other ethnicities. I always felt comfortable no matter what situation I was in. As I started to grow older, sometimes I'd look around and say, "Hey, I'm the only Black person in this room." Most of my friends were pretty tolerant and open-minded people, otherwise I wouldn't be hanging around with them. It's unfortunate that the more you learn, the more aware of color you are; at least, I felt that way. It seems like it should be the other way around. I kind of grew up thinking we were basically all the same, but then the more I was at college, there is a big difference. We are of a different heritage and a completely different situation than what white America has to go through and different backgrounds, in many cases, but there is nothing wrong with being different. It's just that you're different and one shouldn't try to be the other. It doesn't mean that the two can't talk to each other, but you just have to realize where each other is coming from. My whole thing is always respect. All it takes is for people to respect someone else's background and where they are coming from. I always say you don't have to like me, just respect me. I don't care if people don't like me.

That's one reason I don't think [enjoying early professional success] affects how brothers see me. I don't think I'm going to go up to somebody and think I got more money than you. I'm never going to think I'm better than a Black man or anyone else—as long as they are working hard to take steps toward a goal. I'm never going to say anything bad about someone if they are not in a great college. But, hey, if they're working and taking steps toward their goal, trying to make something of themselves, go ahead. I'm proud of them and that's the case where I do feel luckier. They might be great, but maybe they didn't have the opportunity. In that case, the only difference between them and me is that I'm luckier and I had maybe more advantages growing up. But sometimes I drive by some people just sitting on a corner. Or if I see a guy just not making the most of what he could. I know there's a history of racism in this country and it's not set up for Black people to succeed. But I believe anyone can do anything, and it's been proven time and time again.

That doesn't mean I'm seen too much differently than brothers who aren't professionals. I've been disrespected on the job before. Not here in Chicago, but . . . This one internship I had, I remember, my first day there, the guy said, "Why don't you have a seat, we'll have a writer talk to you." He said, "This is a stylebook . . ." Now, I'm a graduate of one of the leading journalism schools, and I'm coming off two or three internships. I know what a stylebook is! I felt really insulted right off the bat. I think I'm kind of naive 'cause I don't know if it's race or what—but I might not think that people do things to me or react to me because of my race. Sometimes, though, it's blatant. It's one of the burdens that you have to live with as a Black man 'cause you never know: Does this person just not like me because of my race or is this person just mean toward everybody? And you never know. Somebody could be rude to you in a store. If you're a white person you'd say that person was rude, but a Black person might leave the store and say that sales clerk was racist.

DD: You talk about working hard. How have you, in the years since that ninth-grade class, approached your craft and your need to carve your own space within it?

JA: I believe the reporter is never bigger than the story. And when I write, hopefully, I try never to get in the way of the story. I write simply. I don't try to be too fancy. That was another piece of advice that my ninth-grade teacher gave me. When I was writing my college essays for my applications, I tried to use all these serious and multisyllable words and sound well-educated. I wrote about the importance of education and gave it to her and she said, I don't see you; you're not in this. I don't see you when I read this, and she gave it back to me. She said, Write about something that you like and write about it in a way that conveys you. I wrote about basketball and the influence it had on my life and how it led me ultimately to my career and my interest in this career. I wrote it much more relaxed. I made it less wordy, and she read it and said, That's you. Ever since then I think I've really written in a style wherein I try to write the way I speak. I don't use "bad" grammar the way I do when I speak sometimes, but I try to stay close to the way I speak.

Sometimes, I'm edited differently because of that. When I'm being edited by white editors and I'm writing things, I'm writing for a Black audience, I think. You don't have a lot of face-to-face contact with your readers, but much of what I do have comes at my barbershop. My barber might say, "You wrote this and that." I try and write for him, for the barbershop. I write for the people on South Side, my neighborhood, my janitor, my neighbors, 'cause they are the ones I'm going to be getting the feedback for . . . One time, I wrote that Jordan was "all that and then some," and my editors changed that. Little things like that make me mad.

I know some things are going to be unpopular, but I have larger obligations. We have a rotating column on Sundays. Anyone on the staff can write one, and sometimes I'll write about things, and maybe I'm not completely convinced, but someone needs to give a Black perspective 'cause it's ridiculous that there's not a Black full-time columnist in this city. In a city with such a large Black population—it's ridiculous. There is not enough Black people interpreting the news. The percentage of Black people writing and reporting, there is no one framing and interpreting to give you an impression. There's not a Black columnist in this city. I realize a lot of times, if I don't write something, nobody is. As a reporter, you want to try not to get too close or too one-sided, but I just feel an obligation almost to give their side of the story fairly. I'll go out of my way before using those clichés and certain references to things like how Blacks are [naturally talented]. "White players think, and Blacks are talented." I try to avoid those stereotypes and try to counter them. I try and play up a Black player's intelligence or his tenacity or his work ethic. I don't think it's an overbalance, and if it is, well, it's just balancing out the way the rest of the white media portray Black athletes. I do feel an affinity, or more of a sympathy, a willingness to look at a word and ask is it fair, to try and think of how that is going to reflect on them.

I always try to have more of a willingness to take the extra step.

SEAN "PUFFY" COMBS, 23: BAD BOYS FINISH FIRST

NEW YORK—When b-boys grow up, they want to be Sean Combs. At twenty-three, the founder and top dog at Bad Boy Records is one of the youngest CEO's around. Puff is successful, having rocketed the likes of Mary J. Blige and Jodeci into the platinum skies of R&B heaven during his tenure as an exec at Uptown Records. Puff remains cutting edge, his fledgling Bad Boy label already home to two of the hottest MC's hip-hop currently has to offer, the Notorious Big and Craig Mack. And, with a multimillion-dollar distribution deal with Arista Records under his belt, Puff is rich.

Above all, though, he is, in many ways, the epitome of the urban, Black youth subculture he markets, a quick-witted hustler with a flair for flavor and an uncommon ability to alchemize the zeitgeist of big-city ghettos into both sound and readily recognizable style. He is as much a star as any of the artists he's produced, styled, directed and discovered over the years, the sound he pushes as much the work of his acts as an extension of himself.

Beneath a wicked July sun, Puff sits perched on the hood of his three-series Beamer, bare arms crossed in a light breeze, riding through Harlem's Morningside Park, recollections flowing. He sports an Atlanta Braves cap spun sideways on his dome, a USA Olympic basketball team jersey, baggy jeans, Timberlands. He speaks in low tones but with an assuredness you expect of a businessman currently setting the pace for his industry.

Of course, it wasn't always this way. He wasn't always getting paid. Back when, Puff was doing most of the paying out himself, in the form of some serious dues . . .

"If somebody were to ask me how I got to where I was at, the best I could explain to them is that it's a process. It's not something that happened overnight. If they are looking at me from afar, just looking at the ride and everything, I probably couldn't get that across. But I worked hard.

"I started out as a dancer, in music videos. I thought I wanted to be an artist. I was known for dancing, and I threw parties. Plus I like to entertain. I didn't see no Black people behind the scenes. But then I saw this video, 'Uptown's Kickin' It.' A man by the name of Andre Harrell was in the video and he was behind a big boardroom table with a room full of artists. And he was there pushing away contracts until he got the right one. I didn't know what he did, but I said, 'That right there is what I want to do.' So I started pursuing Uptown, because it had all my favorite artists on there: Guy, Al B. Sure, Heavy D. I knew Hev from Mt. Vernon, where I partly grew up. I told him to look out for me. I was in college at the time, at Howard, but I told him give me an internship. 'Will work for free.' I would do anything just to learn, especially learn at Uptown.

"It worked out—but the only problem was the time that they

gave me for my internship, Thursdays and Fridays. I was in school, so I had to set it up at school where somebody was taking my notes. I was getting up *every* morning on Thursdays at six A.M. to get on the Amtrak to be to work by ten. But then I would come back to school on Friday nights 'cause I would be promoting parties as a way to make extra money.

"I started looking at things from a big-picture standpoint when I went to college. People were there from all parts of the country. I began to see the world as a place to get money."

In the months that would follow, brother blew up—and made history. He rescued Jodeci and Mary J. Blige from Uptown's dusty backburner, working with the label's promotions machine to turn both acts into award-winning household names in Chocolate Cities everywhere. The dues were often grueling—interminable studio sessions cost him plenty of sleep and many a red eye—but the payoffs, ultimately, were sweet. Gold records. American Music Awards. World tours. Moves were, at last, being made.

But to stay on top, you've got to have a game plan, a philosophy. Puff has one, one that has been years in the making but that has remained fairly simple: Keep it real. Terse as it is, his stratagem has not always been the easiest to adhere to, bogged down as he often is by the demands of the day as well as those of a broader income bracket. But he's mindful of his course and so far has walked it well, carving a path to celebrity that runs right through the New York neighborhoods where he first started . . .

"A lot of times success and money change your lifestyle, your outlook and the way you appreciate different things. Because I'm young and a lot of young people haven't experienced success, I think it's a little bit different for young people, because it's really hard for you to change your lifestyle. The type of friends that you have are still in that environment and the everyday things that you see just looking out your window or when you go for a walk just keep you in that reality, helping you not to change, which helps you not to fall off. That's different from someone who is older and is experiencing success and is moving away from reality.

"But one downside for me is that, instead of becoming heroes to the community, sometimes successful people can become outcasts. Because everybody else is down, the mentality of the community is, 'If you ain't down like me, then I don't think you understand. You're too good for me.' That jealous type of stuff comes into effect.

"Of course, I've definitely felt proud of what I did. It may come off like the big head—even to me. I may say something and I think about it later and am like, 'Damn, that was some arrogant shit you just said.' But that's one thing you have to watch about success. As long as you can see and you watch for that, you won't self destruct. But if not, you will.

"On the other side, it hurts. When you try to be successful and bust your ass, you have people in the community who may not like you because you are a success. You may drive through the streets on your way home and you hear your friends or your boys in the streets saying, 'Yo, you changing.' It just hurts sometimes.

"Where you live doesn't have to change your mindset, even though your lifestyle might change a little bit. My formula for staying on is still doing the things that I normally do, still hanging out in the same places. It's not just seeing it, it's experiencing it. Say I make a million dollars or whatever, I'm still being pulled over by the cops. Yesterday I got pulled over by the cops. They arrested me! Shit like that keeps me in that reality, where I still have that hunger and drive, where a million dollars isn't making me feel comfortable. I'm not falling victim to that modern-day slavery, where somebody is giving me something and I feel I should just be quiet.

"It eats somebody up. A cop working eight-hour shifts who isn't making as much money in a week as I'm making in an hour, when they run it through the computer and see you're totally legal, it eats them up inside. That's the nature of certain people, the mindset of America, really. I've seen a whole lot of the people around me gain hope. The nature of Black people most of the time is to just be

jealous. But what I've experienced and what I've paid more attention to is how [his success] has motivated people to have drive to go
to school and achieve something.

"There's a strong lack of visionaries within our community. Society and the school system discourages us from having visionaries,
really, 'cause all our visionaries were revolutionaries. I pride myself
on being a visionary. My visions help other people have visions
whether it be to open up a store, go to school or get a regular job.
Having a regular job for Blacks is at the low point. With a regular
job, you're not the man as much as you might be being a drug
dealer or an athlete. And that's what society has instilled in you. It's
like Big, one of our artists, says in this line: 'Either you're slinging
crack rock/Or ya got a wicked jump shot.' So you want to be either
the best drug dealer or have a wicked jump shot. For myself and
others, the music industry has proved to be a strong outlet for Black
youth. Before, people wanted to be a rapper or a singer—but now
people want to be an executive, behind the scenes.

"There's this whole mindset young Black men are in; it's like a
nothing-to-lose mindset. It has its negative and positive sides. There
will be situations where you hear about young Black men shooting
up parties; that's the downside of the nothing-to-lose mentality. But
on the other side, as businessmen, we ain't supposed to succeed; we
ain't supposed to be living. So the way I'm going at my shit is, I'm
going for mine all out. I don't have nothing to lose by trying to do
it. I have the hunger to beat the odds.

"I think the world has kind of instilled a way of thinking in, not
just Black people, but people as a whole: In order to survive, you
gotta go out there and get yours. You gotta get money. The only way
you can't be preoccupied with money is after you've made so much
money you can afford not to be. I can't sit here and front like I
don't be preoccupied with making money. I got get out here and
think of a way to eat, to survive.

"The only way you get balance is if you change the next generation that's coming up. The balance of my generation has learned
that it needs to get money. 'Cause we're so fucked up as a community, so everybody right now is on some 'the strong shall survive and

the weak shall perish' type of mentality. But I see more and more people reaching out their hand to bring everybody else up. But they're trying to get themselves there first. As the economic status of the community gets better, that'll balance itself out. Right now, you just have people trying to survive.

"I try to give back. My royalties are structured to give some money to charities. One thing I do is speak a lot at schools. I try to tell kids to have vision, don't get discouraged with what they see around them. I started an organization called Daddy's House, for underprivileged ghetto bastard types here in New York. It's a place where they can come and get love. Once a month, I take a group of kids out and show them a good time. I take them for walks. I talk to them, hear what they have to say, to understand what they are doing. One of the problems in our society is we as Black people have a strong lack of self love. If we don't try to instill the love first, it's hard to tell someone don't shoot this person or don't sell drugs or don't kill the community off. How can you love your neighbor if you don't have love for self?

"And it's also about going back and getting my boys off the streets. I'm trying to show them a new way to get money, on the legal side. And my boys who are coming out of college, who bust their asses for four years and can't hardly even get a job at McDonald's now, I'm trying to help them out as much as I can. I can get them jobs now, too."

Violence

$$\boxed{9}$$

THE TOUCHABLES

. . . Ron, Juan, Gee, 'Rome . . .

The names rattle through my head as would an old locomotive
barreling toward its last whistlestop. The faces explode like fireworks
across the tableau of my memory. Some remind of old friends, others of acquaintances. They used to be alive, these names and faces,
borne by proud, if misguided, young Black men.

Now, they are but signposts of days gone by, the stuff of tear-stained Polaroids and fresh tombstones.

. . . *Steve, 'Man, Robert, Andre* . . .

There're still far too many of us dying, and way too few of us who know what's going on. Our idea of manhood has become warped in this land, misshapen by the maddening impotence of the oppressed, by the indelible stains of racism and poverty and miseducation.

We came into this world amid chaos: Watts '65; Detroit '67; Vietnam; COINTELPRO; Watergate. We were born at the bottom rung of a trickle-down America that refused to extend the plumbing past its middle class. Our fathers and uncles had been shipped off to faraway places with names like Da Nang and Ho Chi Minh City. They left as soldiers, war fodder, actually; many returned as paraplegics, junkies and scapegoats with bad cases of post-traumatic stress disorder. They went ignored. The children of these Invisible Men, we, too, went unseen.

Recessions, restructuring and racism drove factories out of our communities. And as the heavy industries so many of our parents had locked themselves into began their slide into the pages of American history, scores of Black dreams of prosperity ebbed with them. Once our breadwinners, many Black parents suddenly found themselves cut back, laid off and beaten down.

Despite this, hedonism in America held its ground and before long, it'd been gussied up and renamed something called the Reagan Revolution. The eighties had arrived, America's long history of lies and gunboat diplomacy in tow.

"Greed is good," went the mantra.

My generation of brothers learned fast. As white men on Wall Street negotiated LBO's and S&L rip-offs, we scrambled to get a piece of any commodity that might allow us a reasonable facsimile of their good lives. Crack and heroin became our stocks and bonds, street corners and abandoned homes our trading pits.

Then we began dying.

. . . *Earl, Dee, James, Terry* . . .

By now, who doesn't know the numbers, or at least comprehend their magnitude? Five hundred seventeen Black boys between ages fifteen and nineteen shot to death in 1985. Another 586 in 1986. In 1987, the number rose to 697. By 1990, 1,441 brothers fifteen to nineteen years old would be gunned down in one year, an actual decline from the year before.

As a teenager, I used to wonder why Black men died so young—even as I prayed I wouldn't be next. I came close enough. Once, a crew of brothers piled out of a brown Nova and leveled 12-gauges at me and a group of my friends, intent on robbing us. They fired, but we'd already begun sprinting for the alleyways and vacant lots. They missed.

Another time, a kid opened up on our football field with a Tec-9 while we were practicing. As I ducked and scampered through the fence surrounding the field, I was both terrified and fascinated by the sparks twinkling with semiautomatic intermittence on the chain links. I just hoped one of them wouldn't lodge itself in my head. When the team finally made it inside, my man Al and I dissolved simultaneously into hysterical, terrified laughter. It was either that or cry like babies, and we'd seen too much gunplay to go out like that.

Outside a dance club one night, a childhood friend walked up and pumped five shots into the back of another brother I knew. I was standing two feet away and was fortunate that my friend didn't consider me among the eyewitnesses he swore he wouldn't leave standing. Still, I helped load the bleeding brother into a car. A week later, I found out he died.

Two weeks before my twenty-fifth birthday, a fistfight between my friends and another crew outside a party erupted in pistol salvos. I watched a brother I'd just shared a spliff with in the party take one in the leg just as he walked in front of me. Judging from where he was shot, I realized that same bullet would've hit me in the groin.

Seven months later, another friend from that group was shot several times in the head.

Like I said, I used to wonder why Black men died so young. Then, one day, I stopped asking. I knew the answer, had known it all along: Black men die because violence is the American Way.

I'm speaking here of both the senseless murder of brothers as well as violence in general. Both are as American as chattel slavery and apple pie.

We are the grandsons of men who survived the lynch mobs. We are the sons of brothers who survived the 'Cong. As infants and adolescents, we were baby-sat by TV's that brought us the Wild West and WWII and Prohibition-era gangland in all their Technicolor glory. We watched a square-jawed John Wayne take out the Indians, and a flinty-eyed Ness trade fire with Nitti and Capone.

When we began sneakin' in the movies, we found ourselves cheering for the likes of Dolemite and Superfly and other ebony figments of white America's socio-sexual neuroses. We watched Bruce Lee hurl fists of fury. And we rooted for Al Pacino to elevate the Corleones and, later, to snuff those stinkin' Diaz brothers.

"The world is yours," went the mantra.

. . . *Darren, Cedric, Greg, Smoke* . . .

As Black America prepares to move into the late nineties, our elders gaze around at the body count, at the subculture that reflects our ambivalence about our mortality, and they shudder. Preachers threaten to steamroll rap albums. Radio stations strike from their playlists songs with references to guns. Civil-rights groups pile onto the firearms-control bandwagon.

Meanwhile, at ground zero, Black children grow more calloused, more desensitized to the bloodletting on our blocks. And the death of Black men continues at such a pace that Black-male murder is now a near-cliché.

Through it all, Black people remain disempowered, and too many of us are working to keep it that way. Too many young Black men have lost faith in their father's ability to protect, in their mother's ability to nurture. Thus, we seek to protect and nurture ourselves.

I suppose this is why—despite all the bloodshed I've witnessed, that my generation has withstood—I don't favor disarming my community. Fundamentally, I don't have problems with young brothers having guns. I have serious problems, though, with the direction in which too many of us choose to aim them.

But again, the art of killing Black men is a relatively new one for Black men, one long since refined by white America. We have learned from the United States that violence can yield power, that subjugation and fear are integral to control. The gun represents influence over life and death, our ability to disrupt the fragile balance of the two. And for a people too long disenfranchised, for a generation too steeped in the violence of American culture, this symbol offers a power too easily abused.

Still, we have nowhere to turn but to ourselves. While we need to lobby for what we are owed, Black America cannot realistically expect a country whose anthem glorifies "bombs bursting in air" to help us stop the killing. We cannot leave our children to the advice and direction of a U.S. that, even as it sanctimoniously mourns shootouts in D.C., maliciously bombs Grenada and Panama and Iraq.

We're on our own. We've got to roll up our own sleeves and wade waist-deep into the morass in which so many young souls have been snared. And not only must we save their lives, we must also make them worth living.

Until then, still other young Black men are destined to be reduced to nothing more than figures and faces, numbers and names, ashes to ashes and dust to dust.

. . . *Jesse, Tim, Ted* . . .

CHRIS ROBINSON, 18: IN THE LINE OF FIRE

JACKSON, MISSISSIPPI—Mere months ago, Chris thought he was invincible. Well, he never *said* he was, but that's how this wiry man-child with the half-cocked grin lived. As though he could do whatever he wanted without consequence. As though he would always be a step ahead of time. That's why he moved so fast: had his first child at fifteen; began dabbling in crime around the same time; bought a gun; joined a gang.

Then, on October 24, 1993, time finally walked Chris down. Indeed, it trampled him . . .

"Well, October 24, 1993, I was at the house, trying to con my dad, my stepfather, into going to this club with me. He didn't want to go with me but I finally conned him into it. So we went out to the club, Wheels; it's out in the country, in Forest, Mississippi. So we was out at the club, dancin' and everything.

"I called myself in a gang, you know, the Disciples. Gangstas. I was at the club throwing up my little gang sign. And these boys—it was about four of them—they kept on watching. I ain't pay no attention to it. I didn't think nothin' of it. Then all of a sudden they just jumped me! We had got to fighting in there.

"The whole time, I was thinking to myself about running out the club. *I'm fittin' to hurt one of these boys.* See, I had a pistol in my car. But they wouldn't let me get outside. They kept on trying to jump me every time I tried to go outside. I told my stepfather to go get my gun. He got it and met me halfway, out in the parking lot. I cocked it and shot it up in the air. Then I started thinking: *No, I don't want to shoot nobody and end up in prison.* So I got down behind a car. I saw another dude comin' toward me. He was shootin' his gun up in the air. He screamed at me, 'Go on, man! We on the same side.' I turned to run to the car.

"Then I got shot.

"I don't know who shot me. All I know, I hit the ground. I thought I had broke my hand or something because it was hurtin' a bit. That's the only thing I could feel was my right hand. I couldn't feel below my back.

"Somebody asked me, 'You all right, man?' I said, 'Naw, I ain't all right! Somebody help me!' And I started coughing up blood. Then I heard somebody say, 'Pick him, and put him in the car.' I couldn't move. Then somebody said, 'If you pick him and put him in the car, he goin' to bleed to death.' Somebody else said, 'Damn all that! Put him in the car.' I had had my eyes closed. I looked up and saw them putting me in a white Nissan. I remember hearing the car tires spin, then I closed my eyes again 'cause my hand was hurting . . .

"They took me to the hospital. I was real cold; I was shaking. They had stuck something down my throat. I was trying to pull it out, but they had strapped me down. They told me they were moving me to a hospital in Jackson. I didn't want to go 'cause my chest had started hurting. We started moving again. They were pulling the ambulance around, and I heard my mama say, 'You gonna be all right.'

"I said, 'All right.'

"I was telling them I didn't want to go to sleep. I thought if I went to sleep, I was going to die. I told them, 'I ain't gonna go to sleep.' But when we were coming in the Jackson ambulance, I had my eyes closed. I heard a nurse ask, 'Is he gone?' That's when my eyes . . . said, 'Naw, I ain't gone.' Well, I didn't *say* it. I shook my head naw. Then she said, 'All right, baby, just every now and then open your eyes. You know, let us know you still here.' It seemed like every five minutes I opened my eyes.

"When I got to Jackson [long pause], I don't too much remember what happened. I know I was in ICU. A friend came up there to visit me. He saw me and passed out. They took me to my room. When I got there, that's when I realized that I got shot in my hand. And then I realized that I was paralyzed."

Chris tells me his injury is classified as T-4. He can't feel anything below his chest.

As a result, he has been forced to relearn even the simplest acts: folding clothes, tying knots, waving. He stutters now, the result of belabored breathing that affects his speech. His wheelchair parked in the middle of his room on the third floor here at Jackson's Methodist Rehabilitation Center, Chris speaks haltingly, our conversation punctuated by light coughs and wheezes as he tries to beat back the phlegm that coagulates in his lungs. When the second bullet smashed into his back, it disrupted the nerve intervention needed to force air through his chest. He can no longer muster the strength to even hock and spit. Now, he has to suck air from a long plastic tube attached to a small wheeled box called an Intermittent Positive Pressure Machine. It breaks up the phlegm for him.

His life was robbed, he says, right down to its minutae. And even as he grapples with the emotional trauma of that loss, he's working hard at putting together a new one.

"The bullet went through my spine. When it happened, I was like, 'Ah, man, this can't happen to me.' I was like, 'Nah!' I kept on trying to move my leg. I just knew I could walk. I just kept on trying to move my leg and just couldn't. Then I just cried.

"You know, I be thinkin' all the time, I'm going to walk again. I be talkin' to the Lord. That's the only person . . . He help me out, though, the Lord. But if I ever get out of this wheelchair, I'll be a changed person. I don't know whether I can change other people. They gotta go through it. You know, like, if the good Lord paralyzes them for a week or so, then that's the only way they will change. They gotta go through this here. 'Cause, you know, I saw people in a wheelchair. I took my legs for granted, you know. Nobody know what it feel like to be in a wheelchair unless they been in it.

"What's the worst part? There are a lot of worst parts about it. The worst part, I guess, is that I can't be there for my kids. I have four, three daughters, one son. And my little brother, I can't be there for him, either. I hope he never ends up like this.

"My day is pretty much the same now. I get up in the mornin', and they gotta help me put on my clothes, put on my shoes, help me get out of the bed. Then I got a lot of pills I got to take, everyday. I got to take some pills to make me use the bathroom. I got to take some pills to help make my pooh-pooh thinner. They gotta help me take my plate to the table. Then I go to occupational therapy. That's like something to teach you how to do everything, with your, just your arms. You gotta learn how to fold clothes over again. They teach you how to put your clothes on, but I ain't been here that long, so, you know, they ain't taught me that yet. They teach you how to do things with your hands. Teach you how to pick up things off the floor. Teach you how to put things up in cabinets and stuff like that. Then I go to physical therapy. And that's like someone showing you how to move around, how to get up on your own, get up out the bed, get in and out your chair. They teach you how to be strong, you know, get your muscle back and stuff.

"I don't usually stutter. I ain't never stutter in my life, but my breath ain't back as much as it should be. And then I maybe have to stutter. 'Cause I can't hardly breathe. Well, I can breathe good, I just can't breathe like I normally should be breathing. And then I gotta get what they call 'a raise' 'cause I be sittin' still on my bottom. With all that pressure, you can get pressure sores. Then you got to be on your stomach for six weeks while these sores heal.

"They rearrange the legs, too. It's like if you have a door and it's oily. You barely touch that door, it'll move a little bit. But if you ain't move that door in, say, a year, and you barely touch it, it'll be all crampy. It won't wanna move. Just like your leg. Your leg gotta be moved, all your joints.

"So that's my day. I just go through this and hope it helps. I'm a Christian now. I'm reading the Bible a lot. I don't gang bang no more. I'm believing in God. He's the only one who can help me now. The doctors don't tell you your chances of walking, but my doctor told me he don't think I'll ever walk again. I think that God can help me. If God wants me to walk again, I will. I'd like to. But if I don't, you know, I'm just going to take care of my kids and do what I'm supposed to. If I don't, I'll just have to learn to live with that."

ANDRE S., 18: THE DRIVE-BY

"I'm about to fuck up the program/Shootin'
out the window of a drop-top Brougham . . ."

—ICE CUBE

OMAHA, NEBRASKA—Black America is well-acquainted with what goes on during a drive-by shooting, what with the staccato sounds of automatic-weapon fire and the cries of young people shot in the night filling the south-central L.A.'s of our world evening in and evening out. And all of this nation has, courtesy your *Eyewitness News* team, become numbingly familiar with the sickening aftermath of a drive-by: the chalk outlines, the fatherless children, the soul-rending shrieks of bereaved Black mothers.

But Andre knows something else about drive-bys: He knows what goes on before the peel of the tires down the block, before there are shots for the police band to report being fired, before the news trucks and on-lookers and EMS wagons arrive. He knows the calm before the carnage, the surreal teamwork and vicious stealth that a drive-by can inspire. You may recognize the shootings from the periphery—from the safe distance of your living room TV or, perhaps, from the not-so-secure perch of a bedroom window—but Andre knows drive-bys from the inside.

By his own admission, he helped pull about seven drive-by shootings—the first when he was sixteen—before he was sentenced to the Omaha Correctional Center in 1993 for burglary. Not as many as some other gang bangers, he says, but enough to whet his appetite for destruction. Sometimes he drove the car. Sometimes he sat in the driver's seat. But he always came when called on to set up one, always planned them through to the end. And when that end neared, Andre almost always pulled a trigger.

"My first one was the most fun. That's when I held the gun for the first time in a drive-by. When you get the gun in your hand, it makes you feel powerful. Like you can do anything. You just go around and start trouble just 'cause you got a gun. You feel powerful.

"The first time, me and some of my homeboys went and shot at somebody who'd shot at us. Earlier that day a couple of my homeboys was driving. My friend had just got this car three days earlier. We drove up to this high school with a whole bunch of dudes. We was all beaned up, in our gear, all red. We went up there, and my homeboy cut in front of some Crip, cut him off. They got out and just started shooting at the car and took off!

"So it was like, 'yeah, Okay.' We knew who they was. So we started planning . . .

"First you got to go get a load to do it in. You don't want to do it in your own car because it would bring too much heat. You get a stolen car or something. The best you can get is a four-door Blazer because it has a lot of room. You get somebody to drive and you have everybody else set up. People think you always have to be high, but not all the time. If you want to you can. Not all the time. What you do do is you got to get ragged up, too, throw on your colors. That's something we always do.

"This time, though, we were high and we were drinking. We drove past where we knew he'd be. First we just passed, turned off the lights. If you see him, you pass the house, come back, roll down the window, stop the car. Sometimes you get out and just shoot, sometimes you shoot from the car. We saw him sitting down, so we just went by and leaned out and . . .

"We pulled off fast after that. There wasn't any regret or anything like that. You don't even think that you just tried to kill another young Black man. You ain't thinking about anything like that. We were like, 'Yeah, got that nigga.' I didn't shoot him, I missed. But pulling a drive-by makes you proud anyway. You feel high, like you just accomplished something.

"It's no fun on the other side of it—and I've been there, too. A couple times I came close to getting killed. One time I was up in north O. I was walking by myself. I was just coming from my homeboy's and two dudes with just this girl—and they was all duded up in blue and I was all duded up in red—they looked at me, 'What up? I'm going to kill you.' I took off running before they could shoot, so they had to chase me around. I ran between some houses and up on a porch. 'Knock, knock, knock.' Nobody answered the door or looked out. Then they pulled up and said, 'We could have. We could have, nigga.' I was crying. They started laughing and said, 'Yeah, your punk ass better cry.' They took off.

"I got home and called my homeboys to get those motherfuckers. Later on, we did a drive-by on them . . ."

TODD STEWART, 17: INNOCENT BYSTANDER

WASHINGTON, D.C.—Todd was supposed to be there. The plan was the same as it'd been all that summer. He was supposed to be out of the house by afternoon, heading from his family's home in northeast D.C. to the Greenway complex in southeast, where his best friends lived. There, as he did each day that summer, he was to meet Andre, Vincent and Gary.

They didn't do much when they hooked up—"We would just sit on the steps of their building or just hang around," says Todd—but that wasn't the point. They were children, milking their summer vacation for all the indolence they could get. Yes, there had been some trouble in the neighborhood, but the four boys generally avoided it. The dealers didn't have beef with them. They were mere children. For them, the boys figured, those streets were as safe as any.

"There were two sides of the street," says Todd, hunched over a long Formica table near a wall in the gym of Anacostia High School. "The guys that sell drugs are on one side of the street, and we hung out on the other side of the street. They don't let us come on that side of the street 'cause they understand that we are young. They left us alone."

And so like clockwork, Todd usually arrived by the afternoon and stayed until late evening.

On this day, however, he couldn't make the appointment. His parents had left early that day, assigning Todd the responsibility for caring for his younger brother. He stayed home. Hours later, someone called to tell him that all three of his friends, none of them older than fifteen, had been shot that day, sitting, as they always did, near their apartment steps.

One of them, Andre, had died.

"There was like beefing," says Todd, still struggling to decipher the "whys" of the shooting. "Two neighborhood dealers didn't like each other for some reason, and so one came, stole a car with ski masks on and had an automatic gun. When the car came around, they didn't shoot onto the other side. They shot little kids—and one of my buddies died.

"Gary got shot seventeen times but he didn't die. I remember going to the hospital. I asked him what happened, and he told me he didn't know. He was sitting on a car and heard a car come to a squeaking halt and start shooting so he started running. He said he felt his legs hurt. He couldn't run, and he fell down. The only thing he remembers is a Black guy standing over the top of him and just spraying. All he could do was cover his eyes with his arms. He got shot all over, the chest, legs, arms. He wasn't sure about my buddy Andre dying, so he was asking me a lot of questions.

"His mother asked me to tell him 'cause she didn't know how to tell him, so I told him that Andre had died. He took it okay. That was the first time one of my friends got killed. That was the summer of my eighth-grade year. From then on it has just been constant. Almost every weekend now I hear about a friend of mine getting killed or shot."

The remark comes with such matter-of-fact off-handedness that you can easily overlook the scope of the tragedy it delimits, calloused as America is to the staggering rates of Black male death. Almost every weekend. For the past four years. Rain, sun, snow or gloom. Almost every weekend. A classmate, a friend, a cousin, a people.

Throughout the nation's capital, as well as all over the country, young Black men like Todd must cope with the psychic scars that the bloodshed has left on their fragile sense of mortality. Most don't fit on any clear side of the victim-victimizer equation, but rather dance along the periphery of the circle of blood tightening like a noose around many working-class Black communities. Like most young brothers, Todd has never been shot. Like most young brothers, he's never shot anyone. He wants merely to get out of the madness intact.

But can you truly be whole having lost friends almost every weekend since eighth-grade? Don't you, somewhere along the way, lose something, at the cemetery or the funeral home or the murder site? Innocence, compassion, even a sliver of humanity?

Todd would like not to dwell on the circumference of that bloody circle. He'd rather think about his future. About football and college and a life away from the melancholy phone calls and hospital visits and wakes. He'd rather do this. But whenever he does, reality always seems to intrude. Gunshots ring. Or is it the telephone? Either way, bad news is holding on line one . . .

"One of our teammates, Shawn Preston, was killed this year," says Todd. "When we lost Shawn, he was the third person on our team to get killed, the fourth person to get shot. There are a lot of rumors going around. Some people are saying he was killed over drugs. I guess he sold drugs for a while, but he saw things happen. He was waking up. One day he came to me and said, 'I saw this dude get killed.' He saw a lot of his friends get killed. His closest friend got killed two weeks before Shawn got killed. Guys on the football team used to mess with him and say, 'You're no athlete,' 'cause you are three things: you're an athlete, a nerd or a drug dealer. Those are the only three things here you can be. So we used to mess with him. But he started getting it together. He went to summer school and got his grades together, stopped hanging around this old neighborhood. He came to practice every day.

"The other night, he was out on his porch. His mother said that she heard some guys out front arguing so she went to the window and she called him in the house. As he turned his back to walk toward the house, some guy shot him in the back. I knew he wasn't hustling because when you play football you practice from three o'clock till it's dark, and it takes a lot out of you. All you want to do is go home and go to sleep or take a rest and get something to eat. I knew he wasn't doing that 'cause it just took too much time. He was getting his life together. That was my finest memory of him, telling me that he was going to change and that he wasn't hanging out with the same dudes. Friday morning everybody was waiting for him to come to the bus 'cause you meet an hour before you leave to load all the equipment and everything. We were waiting, so finally my father, he is the coach, said, 'We can't wait any longer; he must not be coming.' So everybody started boarding the bus. I remember seeing the principal coming out, but she came and pulled him to the side and I saw him put his head down and shake his head, so I thought it might be anything. I didn't think too much of it. But then I heard it first: 'Shawn got killed last night.' The whole time I was thinking, It can't be true, it can't be true. I'm hoping they had the facts mixed up. About five minutes before the game, they told us that he had got killed, that they had pronounced him dead at the scene."

The killing hurt him, as it always does. Years of losing friends still haven't taught Todd how not to care. They've just trained him to manage the grief. But the memories that inspire his pain, they are forever.

"Two days before Shawn got killed a friend was saying to me that things like that only happen to the good guys," he says, "that none of the bad guys get shot. You wouldn't wish a shooting upon anybody, but people you would think it would happen to, it never happens to. The ones that do the dirt never get dirt done to them. It's always the good guys. If Shawn was still out there, doing the same things, I could understand how trouble could have happened. But it is just hard to live with sometimes. I'm just waiting to go to college. I'm so anxious, so I can leave D.C. Maybe I'll go to North Carolina. That's a lot slower than D.C. I know I'll miss it 'cause my family is here, but I just need to get away. I'm tired of hearing about my friends getting killed."

And of course, there is the inevitable fear that, even out here on the periphery of the circle, even for a young soul determined to keep a safe distance between him and the bloodshed, far away may not be far enough. That Todd has never killed is at once a testament to the strength of his parents and community, an admirable show of personal cool and foresight and a continuing stroke of good fortune. That he has never been killed is, to Todd, nothing short of a blessing from God. For, as the circle contracts, so do its edges, so are the lives on the outside brought that much closer to the perils on the inside . . .

"I'm scared for myself," Todd confesses. "Everybody feels that you can take care of yourself if it comes down to it, but you never can tell what things can happen.

"I remember when I was about fifteen. One day I was hanging out with my friends, and they'd gotten into an argument with some guys earlier. I didn't know about it. They got into a near fight, some words were exchanged and they told him you better watch it. People tell you that and you better watch it 'cause it can come true. We were standing outside, and a van rolled down the street. Where I live it's a [cul-de-sac]. You come in one way, you have to go out the same way, so I didn't pay too much attention. We were just sitting on the curb, and we were talking. He came back up, and I really didn't look at it or pay too much attention. As the car got closer and closer, we saw the door swing open. I was right on the curb, and I saw the guy raise up the gun before he shot. My friends started running. He caught me by surprise 'cause something like that never had happened to me before. One of my buddies tapped me and said, 'Run!' By that time he had came back down and started firing. We hang out in row houses, so for every four houses there is a little cut. We ran down through these people's yards, and after it happened we heard rapid gunfire. I was running, you could hear bullets hit the cars and hear windows break.

"We got away, but that made me think about a lot of things. I thought about my friends and what they're going to be doing down the road. You can't sell drugs when you're fifty. Later, I talked to my friend who sells drugs. He said, 'You have to stop hanging around here.' He wasn't saying that I shouldn't come around, but saying that the things they do aren't meant for me 'cause I have a future. He supported me in a lot of things. He surprised me the way he was talking to me. As far as hanging out he said, 'You can't do that 'cause you can just get caught up in something you don't know a thing about. It ain't worth it.' "

VICTOR BROWNFIELD, 22: DO OR DIE

OMAHA, NEBRASKA—Gun-metal-colored clouds gather angrily in the sky stretching above the guard tower at the Omaha Correctional Center, casting an appropriate pall over the sprawling brick prison. A nasty autumn breeze, herald to yet another bitter winter, rides hard out of the distant eastern Nebraska headlands and whips the two flags that rise alongside the guard tower. Inside the courtyard, inmates desperate for a bit of R&R defy the gray skies and winds and cluster in small groups to shoot both hoop and the shit.

Beneath the clouds, through the breeze, Victor Brownfield—inmate No. 43649, to OCC brass—bounds indoors into a small administration building a few hundred yards behind the razor-wire-topped fence that stands between him and freedom. An escorting security officer walks a few paces behind.

A lanky five-nine, Brownfield lopes into one of the building's many cramped offices and greets me with rugged confidence, his gaze steady, his handshake firm and sure. His 'fro is an ebony nimbus surrounding an oval head. His eyes are hard, dark, yet not unfriendly. Crooked teeth overcrowd his smile. His gear is standard prison issue: quilted brown jacket; untucked white T-shirt; beige khakis falling over scarred black brogans.

He talks with his hands as much as with his mouth, clenched fist whacking open palm for emphasis. His tone is thickened with the cool drawl mastered by Midwestern and West Coast badmen, his words deliberate.

No. 43649 has been flowing through the Nebraska penal system for more than a year now: first, Douglas County Jail; then Lincoln Correctional Center; these days, OCC. For the past few months, Brownfield has made his home in the J3 unit of this minimum- to medium-security prison that sits a few miles from the Nebraska-Iowa border.

He tells me he's serving one to three years for a botched marijuana deal in nearby south Sioux City, Nebraska. In the fall of 1992, he says, he'd caught a cab from his home in Sioux City, Iowa, into

Nebraska to peddle three ounces of pungent sinsemilla to a white girl he'd met at a bar shortly before. When he stepped out of the woman's home to catch a cab back to Sioux City, he tells me, a gaggle of cops were waiting.

His official prison record contradicts his story, however, claiming that he's doing time for theft. "He's one of these guys who just want to make themselves seem bigger than they are," says one prison official when I ask her about the discrepancy between Brownfield's story and the official document. She won't detail the theft conviction.

For his part, Brownfield says he doesn't have to pump up his record. His exploits are well known, he says. He's OG, an original gangsta, a staunch veteran of Minneapolis's Worldwide Gangsta Bloods.

He came to Iowa three years ago after his mother moved to escape the chaos of Minneapolis's rugged ghettos. Dreaming of greener pastures and more peaceful streets, Brownfield tagged along.

Thing is, he never left the streets behind. Instead, Brownfield packed his hustle right along with his toothbrush and clothes, exporting his dope game dead into the plains of Iowa. After all, he's Worldwide, nigga. Blood for life. Such is the power of crew, says Brownfield, that you don't deny your affiliation no matter where you go or who you encounter. Without his set, he's nothing, he explains. You can take a gangsta outta the hood, but . . .

"I was a good kid, average, till I was about thirteen. Then I started hanging out with the older kids. I wanted to impress the girls. I wanted to make some money, too. I had this uncle; he was a pimp. I remember he was one of the first people who influenced me. He used to come around all the time. He had a nice car, a lot of money. His hair was whipped all the time. That's when I'd say I really started admiring him.

"Before I was in a gang, I remember I used to get jumped all the time. Like, I'd be walking downtown by myself and get jumped, or niggas would look at me and be like, 'Whassup, cuz?' I got tired of getting jumped. I had been kicking it with the older kids, so I just decided to get down.

"I joined when I was about fifteen years old. I got jumped in. That's when they beat you down. I remember it was the whole set that jumped me in, about fifty niggas. It last about two minutes. Man, they beat my ass. They cut me up under my eye, broke my jaw, busted the back of my head. I remember just going down and niggas just kicking me. But I was going for mine.

"If you can't get up, they help you up. I couldn't get up. So they picked me up and [hugs the air] had love for a nigga. We was like family. I knew I'd do anything for my homeboys. Then we went to one of my homeboys' house and got high, smoked weed, got drunk.

"Then we did a drive-by.

"Me and my homeboys had been sitting around, and they were like, 'Let's get these fools.' I was like, 'It's on, then.' I was ready to put in some work. So we got this van and drove over to St. Paul. We came around a corner, saw a bunch of Crabs just hanging. We started blasting. I had a .357. Some of my boys had shotguns, gauges. One of them had an Uzi.

"I don't know if I killed anybody. I think I hit somebody; I think I saw some people drop.

"After that, we came back to the hood. I smoked some more weed. When I went home, my father asked me what happened. I didn't tell him. I just said I got into a fight. So he took me to the hospital. They stitched up the back of my head [presses a forefinger into a spot at the back of his Afro], wired my jaw. I left the hospital the next day, and when I got out, I went back to the hood to kick it with my homeboys.

"After that, I was just kicking it, you know, selling a little weed, a little cocaine, trying to come up. Then my mother moved to Sioux City. I moved with her. I found me some new homeboys there, but they weren't like my boys back in Minneapolis. They were slow. They weren't into gang banging. I wasn't gang banging, but I was still down for my set. I'm gon' always be down for my set.

"[After being convicted in Nebraska,] I went up to Lincoln, LCC, for sixteen months. That's the Lincoln Correctional Center. I just got down here like a month and a half ago. It was wild up there at LCC. Like, I got up there, you know, and right as soon as I got up there, a whole bunch of Crabs and shit—a whole bunch of Crips— was like 150-deep up there. And it was like a hundred-deep Bloods. And I don't know nobody, knowwhatI'msayin'? I get over there, and I walk through the door, go to my housing unit, put my shit away and I come back out. I'm walking, right? A whole bunch of niggas come up to me, and they say, 'What set you claimin'?'

"So I say, 'This is Blood for life,' youknowwhatI'm sayin'?" [He bends the tip of his forefinger into the tip of his thumb, forming a lower-case *b*, a gang signifier.]

"They say, 'Well, this is cuz.'

"I'm like, 'Well, whassup, then?'

"So I got that bang on. I lost thirty days good time and got twenty-one days room restriction. I come back out. So it's all these motherfuckers out, and they like, 'You a Blood?' I told 'em yeah. They said, 'What set you claimin'?' I said Worldwide, and they said, 'Ah'ight, cool. It's on.'

"We just kicked it from there on.

"I could have said I don't bang, but they disrespected me. Once you in it, you in it to win it. The Crips disrespected me. They said, 'Fuck them Bloods, them slob-ass niggas.' I ain't going out that way.

"I'm gon' die for mine."

DIMMIE WILKINS, 17: DETERRED

LONG BEACH, CALIFORNIA—At twelve, Dimmie flirted with the idea of joining a gang. His older brothers were long since a part of some set or another and, to Dimmie, who'd never really thought much about joining before, banging seemed as normal a way as any to enter his teens. As with so many young men, he was full of energy and short any viable outlets. And having been shy much of his life, Dimmie longed for camaraderie in the hood.

It took the near-fatal shooting of Dimmie's brother to change his mind.

"I needed a hobby. I didn't really want to get into no trouble. I always seen my older brothers when they was gang banging and I seen the direction they was going in. I didn't want to deal with that rough life, but I still thought it'd be cool. This was sixth, seventh grade. At first, it kind of turned me on. Then my brother got shot in his right side right in front of me.

"He didn't die. He almost did. We were out in the middle of the street, in front of my house. It was me and my other buddy. My brother was with his friends. They were fixin' to go somewhere. It was at nighttime. He out there drinking beers. Then their rivals rode past 'cause he had did something to somebody else. They just shot him. Luckily, I didn't get hit.

"He fell on me. I thought he died 'cause he passed out. He was unconscious. I didn't know what was up. He fell on me. I was like, 'Damn.' I went through a little something right there. I was like, 'That ain't for me.' That's all it took."

EUGENE HARRINGTON, 20: "YOU PULL IT, YOU GOTTA USE IT"

ATLANTA—Eugene has lived a life free of the bloodshed that has touched so many other young Black men. He hasn't lost friends to gunshots or stabbings. He's never been shot himself. He's barely even been in a good fight. In fact, the threat of mindless violence has invaded Eugene's life only once—and that time, it came dressed as a cop.

"Me and my buddies went to Piedmont Park and they had a shootout," says Eugene. "We got out of there. We were going right to the car and this cop came out of nowhere with a gun pulled out on us and told us to stick our hands up in the air. He thought we were involved in the shooting. I didn't know whether he'd shoot us or what. When he showed up, we forgot all about the shootout. I just had my mind on him and that gun. That's what worried me.

"But that's the only time I've even had to deal with a gun or violence that way. Guns, I don't mess with them. I have touched one—I used to go hunting with my uncle—but other than that I don't bother. I look at it like this: I don't want to use a gun. And if you pull it out, you got to use it. That's how it is. If you pull a gun out on somebody and don't shoot or harm them, regardless of whether you do shoot at them or not, they're going to come back looking for you. That's just asking for more trouble when you pull a gun on somebody. So to keep from being involved in trouble, I don't have one."

ROBERT S., 16, & DANTE W., 15: YOUNG GUNZ

CHICAGO—Its seventy-eight buildings sprawling for some seventy acres, Cabrini-Green towers as one of the largest housing projects in the country. More than seven thousand residents, nearly all of them Black, call the project home. Dante and Robert are among them.

They've spent their entire lives in the project, enduring some of the most squalid conditions imaginable. Inside building 502, where we meet, the stench of urine, body odor and crack cocaine swirl into your nostrils upon entering. Nearby, children play in a rickety elevator scarred from decades of graffiti. All but two of the row of lamps that line the hallway are blown, leaving the hall with the eerie feel of a dimly lit carnival ride, a ghetto version of the tunnel of love. Crews of adolescent girls with poor perms range the halls every so often, their laughter echoing through the bleak corridors.

At the back of the dim hallway on the first level of the high-rise unit, Robert and Dante, both of them frail, bright-eyed, tell jokes as they stuff handfuls of tortilla chips into their mouths. Robert wears a black bandanna spotted with tiny drawings of marijuana plants, a black windbreaker, jeans and black Reebok high-tops. Dante, his younger cousin, hunched over in the chair next to Smith, sports a blue Georgetown windbreaker, zipped to his chin even indoors. His powder-blue jeans are soiled and hang so low they web across his crotch.

They might not look it, but they are, they'd like to believe, tough guys, gangstas, enforcers, Robert having joined their Vice Lords gang at about ten years old, Dante at twelve. Since then, they say, they've labored tirelessly for their set, robbing, shooting, selling dope, whatever they've had to to show their allegiance. The CVL on the caps affixed to their belt loops are, the boys say, their badges of proof and honor: They're true Lords, baby.

But, Lord, they're babies.

They're postpubescent infantrymen in a war they neither started nor completely understand, a war without purpose or a foreseeable end. Yet they fight, with all the viciousness and passion they can marshall. They fight because this is what they've been trained to do. On the day we meet, a recently reached peace treaty between gangs in the project has brought at least a temporary halt to their war, making the boys feel aimless, more useless than ever. What happens to boy soldiers when their battles cease?

Still, for all the bravado and heated sentiments their war inspires, the boys are obviously relieved about the respite. They don't want to die; few little Black boys really do. But when death seems inevitable, when death seems to offer the only tangible option to life in a dysfunctional ghetto hell, you learn to face death with a hand on your nuts and a scowl on your grill. You learn to say, "Fuck it."

Robert and Dante have learned these lessons. They've learned far too early of the delicacy of life, of the ease with which that life can be snuffed. Cabrini-Green has given them a harsh upbringing, one that peppers the night with pistol fire and police sirens, one that saw guns placed in both their hands even as they were learning to ride bikes. It's the only life they know, the only one they can really envision, even at fifteen and sixteen.

But even they can't help wondering occasionally whether it will be a short one.

RS: I'm alternative school now because I got locked up when I was in regular school. I was doing all kinds of shit. When I got locked up this time, it was for aggravated battery. I popped somebody. He was a Disciple who was talking shit to me—so I shot him. He didn't die or anything; he just got blasted. I was locked up in juvenile for a little bit, but I got out.

You ask me if it bothered me that he was another Black man, but naw. Look man, you don't live over there so you can't understand how we is. Them niggers killed two of our brothers. Fuck that fighting shit, it doesn't matter anyway. You got to look at this. Them boys deep. They got all that. This is all we got. Them niggas is deep, man, deeper than us. I can't even count how many of them there is, but I know they can get us anytime.

It ain't got me scared, but that's the way it is. They got this treaty on. If people want peace, they should go talk to them. Tell them to quit jumping us, and there won't be no pistol playing then.

DW: That's why we joined, 'cause they kept jumping on us. I used to walk around and they'd pick on me, so I had to figure out a way to get them back. I joined a mob. And when I joined, I got them back. I may not have got the exact guys who jumped me, but I know I got one.

Since the treaty, it's been okay. Some things have changed a lot. We don't shoot as much. Now we associate with each other. We're not friends, but we don't shoot. Before the peace treaty came, there was shooting every day. *Zoop, zoop.* The bullets would come by. I remember one time I was walking across a [freeway overpass] and niggas just started shooting. I didn't know where it was coming from. I just ducked down and got out of there.

Do we get used to it? Hell, naw. You just got to react to it, that's all. If you do, you might get killed. If you don't, you *will* get killed. I've never shot one of them, but I done whooped about twenty of them by now.

RS: Yeah, shit be going on over here, but it's cool. This where I've been all my life. I've heard the stuff people say about over here, but this is where we live. I don't want to move. It's wild a lot of times, but there are good times to go with the bad. I'm not scared out here. For what? All my family's here, my brothers are here. Something might happen, but I can't worry about it.

DAMON FLAGG,* 22: DOMESTIC VIOLENCE

DETROIT—Damon swears he doesn't always intend to hit her. Honestly. Just that sometimes, you know, she gets to running her mouth, talking to him all wrong. She should know by now how he is. She should know by now that he ain't buying that. He's a man, girl. A man. But she don't listen. She's supposed to be his woman, man, but she don't listen. She just keeps talking, keeps arguing, keeps pushing him, pushing him, pushing him . . .

Then he snaps.

"I don't like it, man. But sometimes, I'm so hotheaded, so frustrated, man, my anger overthows me. It don't take much to get me upset, you know. She one of them nagging-ass 'hos. Just keeps nagging and nagging. I just smack her. But I don't condone nobody hitting on her, man. That's wrong for me to do it, and I don't want nobody doing that to their girl."

But that doesn't stop him. It doesn't stop any of the men who beat their wives and girlfriends and sisters. Not the white boys on Wall Street. Not the Black boys on 1-2-5. We don't condone it, we say. But we don't condemn it, either. We rarely talk critically about domestic violence, about the misogynist rages that give rise to the beatings, about the near-conspiratorial, institutional silence that keeps our attentions focused elsewhere—unless, of course, the attack involves Hall of Fame football players and white women in Brentwood.

Even when men do talk, we do it where the feedback won't be so harsh, in those dark spaces where vocal support and silent opposition fuse together to make one sexist seal of approval. "Smack that

* Not his real name.

'ho," we say in the locker room. "You need to kick that bitch's ass," we urge in nightclub bathrooms.

Damon's a little more honest than most about his temper, his abusive behavior. He is, sadly, no less abusive for it. Bottom line: He wants control, complete, utter and unchallenged control. He wants his woman quiet when he deems it necessary. He wants her jubilant when he believes the occasion demands it. When he's drunk, he's not sure what he wants, but she'd best figure it out—fast.

He loves her, he says. She loves him back. That's why she ain't left the apartment they share yet, that and the fact that, if she tries, he'll fight her viciously for custody of their child. But she won't try. Ain't nobody going to love her like him, man, don't you know that? They've got a few problems, okay, but they're working them out. She'll just have to suffer with him (actually, it's more like from him) till they get things together.

"The worst time, shit, I gave her two black eyes. We be buckin', man. Arguin' about some silly shit. We was arguing about some shit she didn't do or her mama, something about her mama or something. That was the first time. Sometimes I tell her I'm sorry. Or sometimes she'll hit me. She hit me, I tell her to stop. She hit me, so I hit her back, you know. She say it hurt. I say, 'You can take it; be tough.' But she hits me back. That's how it'll start sometimes."

It ain't right. He knows that. Or says he knows, anyway. But part of him thinks it's necessary sometimes. Justifiable abuse? Some females, man, they get out of hand. Think their pussies are made of gold or something, think it gives them the right to not handle business like they should. Don't care for their man right, don't raise their kids, talk all kinds of crazy shit to you. Someone has to set 'em straight.

"I feel that some Black women should get disrespected. It depend on how I feel. A bunch of these 'hos deserve to get their asses whooped. 'Cause some of these 'hos are trifling, man. Some 'hos go to your house thinking they family. Don't be respecting your Moms, your crib. Bitches like that, you just jap smack them on GP, you know. Then it's some 'hos that just wanna take a nigger for all he got, then fuck another nigger and shit. 'Hos like that need to get their ass whooped." He laughs hard, the outburst belying his deathly seriousness. Still chuckling, he continues. "I feel like this: I'm making money. I can fuck anybody. Your pussy ain't all that. What can you do for me? That's my thinkin', man. 'Hos get smacked. Being triflin', not takin' care of their family. That's a 'ho to straight up get smacked. You know what I'm sayin'? 'Cause I don't respect no 'ho like that."

I wonder aloud whether Damon is continuing a cycle of abuse. Does he beat his girl because he saw some man pounding on his Moms? I ask about his mother, the sort of resilient working-class Black woman from whom legends are born, the sort who tried to raise her boys as well as love them, the sort who held her family together even when the men all around her were bailing out. Did he ever see anyone lay their hands on her?

"Man, naw! I'd beat their ass if they touched my mother. One time, I heard my mother arguing with the guy she was seeing. He was yelling, cussing and shit. I was like, 'Man, kill that shit.' I got to the point where I didn't want to hear him talking like that to her. Fuck that. Chill with that shit, man. But I was never on the verge of fighting. If I have to go upstairs to get the .38, I will, but I was cool. He could argue with her. They're grown. But I feel, 'If y'all are going to argue, talk at normal level. I understand you have to work out your business, but don't talk to my mom like that.' "

His mother taught him not to hit women. She explained that resorting to brute force with those weaker than him was wrong. But as much growing up as he did 'neath her wing, Damon did at least as much in the streets, where brute force often rules. Run or be ran is the prevailing logic, and the last gun left standing is the winner. They still battle for his spirit, these two ideals, Moms versus crew, street sense versus home training. Ask his woman, and the streets seem to be winning hands-down. No, he says, he's conflicted, struggling.

"My mother did teach me not to hit no woman. And, like, to give them respect. That's about it. Your mother can only do so much. You got to experience life, you know. They could give you advice. But you ain't gonna listen to no advice but your own. The only good advice is your experience."

Experience tells him to keep at it, to keep working on his relationship. Her girlfriends tell her, sometimes, to leave, to let him work out his problems on his own rather than on her face. So for now, she stays. For now, she suffers.

"We'll work it out," Damon says. "We've got a few problems, but we'll work it out."

Or, perhaps, she'll die trying.

DARRELL DAWSEY, twenty-seven, is a former feature writer at *The Detroit News,* and a staff member at the *Los Angeles Times.* A graduate of Wayne State University, he lives in Detroit.